Risk
Management
& Introduction
to **Insurance**

Risk
Management
& Introduction
to Insurance

Joël Wagner
Michel Fuino

EPFL PRESS

General Management: Lucas Giossi
Editorial and Sales Management: Sylvain Collette and May Yang
Communications Manager: Prisca Thür-Bédert
Production Manager: Christophe Borlat
Editorial: Alice Micheau-Thiébaud and Jean Rime
Translation: Simon Kroeger
Graphic design: Kim Nanette
Digital marketing: Gabriel Hussy
Accounting: Philipp Bachmann
Logistics: Emile Razafimanjaka

Cover illustration: Girl climbing on the rock on sunset background,
© Galyna Andrushko | Dreamstime.com

EPFL PRESS

is an imprint owned by the Foundation Presses polytechniques
et universitaires romandes (PPUR), a Swiss academic publishing company
whose main purpose is to publish the teaching and research works of the Ecole
polytechnique fédérale de Lausanne (EPFL), of universities and other institutions
of higher education.
PPUR, EPFL – Rolex Learning Center, CM Station 10, CH-1015 Lausanne,
info@epflpress.org

www.epflpress.org

First edition
ISBN 978-2-88915-556-9 for the print edition
ISBN 978-2-8323-2205-2 for the ebook (PDF) edition, doi.org/10.55430/6710VA01
EPFL PRESS / Presses polytechniques et universitaires romandes, 2024

Printed in Switzerland

Contents

Contents

Contents

Foreword

Risk and risk management are central concerns in modern society. Every individual, organization, company, and public authority must manage their risks in some way. Nevertheless, the exposure to risk and the appropriate response are very different for an individual, an international corporation, and a government.

When risk management is mentioned in the context of a management school, it mainly refers to the risk exposure of businesses—which is the context in which this book should be read. Unexpected events can cause unplanned, "accidental" losses to a company. First, we need to define the terms accurately before evaluating risks. From a business perspective, two questions need to be answered: first, how to control possible risks, and second, how to finance potential losses. By adequately evaluating risks, a company can reduce the dissuasive effect of uncertainty—and the potential losses that result—and explore new profitable activities still managing risk exposure. To this end, we examine various risk measures, such as value-at-risk and expected shortfall. Insurance companies play an essential role in risk financing. An introduction to insurance provides readers with a better understanding of the insurance industry and its products. In the context of life and non-life insurance, an overview of the methods used to calculate insurance premiums illustrates some of the activities of actuaries, specialists in risk pricing.

This book is divided into six chapters. In chapter 1, we introduce the topic and provide an overview of the history of risk management and insurance. Next, in chapter 2, we define the terms used to identify and characterize different types of risk exposure. In chapter 3, we look at the tools needed to evaluate risk, including elements of probability and utility theory. The chapter concludes with some principles of risk assessment. Chapter 4 presents the steps involved in the risk management process and an application of this process to the area of cyber risk. In chapter 5 we discuss the economics of insurance and the insurance market, distinguishing between social and private insurance. In the same chapter, we examine the different branches of private insurance and their products. Finally, in chapter 6, we discuss risk pricing in insurance. We look at various life and non-life insurance products and provide the basics for calculating premiums based on the benefits paid by insurance policies. Throughout the chapters, dark gray boxes highlight definitions of terms and relevant theorems. Light gray boxes provide examples, illustrations, and comments that complement the text and give more insight into the topic.

The course on risk management given by the first author at HEC Lausanne, the Faculty of Business and Economics of the University of Lausanne, led to the creation of this book. The teaching materials developed over many years, as well as the feedback of the approximately 400 students who take this course each year, have contributed significantly to the content of this book. The authors would like to sincerely thank Professors André Dubey and François Dufresne, who taught this course before 2014 and shared their course notes. Several assistants, including Vanessa Carrard, Frédérique Hansen, Eliot Jean, Veronika Kalouguina, and Yves Staudt, as well as questions submitted by students from several cohorts, helped improve successive versions of the course handout that eventually became this book. Finally, the development of this book was supported by the Swiss Insurance Association and is a translation of the French edition published in 2022.

The first author dedicates this book to all his students, assistants, and doctoral students, past, present, and future. He also thanks his dear C. G. and F. for their constant love and presence.

Lausanne, January 2024

Joël Wagner and Michel Fuino

CHAPTER 1

Introduction

Risk—or the possibility that an adverse event will occur—has always been a part of our daily lives. Awareness of risk and its management has enabled mankind to gain a better grasp of the future and, thus, to achieve a measure of serenity in a world full of uncertainty. Throughout history, our conception of risk has significantly evolved. While initially associated with hazards, the concept of risk has become inextricably linked with the business world. The simple and well-known notion of a financial reserve is the most telling example. In this context, insurance companies have taken on the role of experts when it comes to assessing the financial risks incurred by companies or individuals. The purpose of this chapter is to introduce the concept of risk through examples—a formal definition will be provided in chapter 2—, illustrate its global dimension, describe some key issues related to its management, and provide a historical overview.

1.1 Global risks

The World Economic Forum is aware of the risks we face globally and has been publishing a report on the perception of these risks for several years. The 14th such report, published in 2019, summarizes the opinions collected from decision makers in the public and private sectors, academia, and civil society (World Economic Forum, 2019). Figure 1.1 presents 20 of the main risks identified in the fields of environment, technology, society, geopolitics, and economics. The graph illustrates the probability of occurrence and the expected severity of these risks based on survey responses. Respondents were asked to rate the likelihood of occurrence and the impact of each risk over a 10-year period. In this context, the probability of occurrence is the likelihood that an adverse event occurs, on a scale from "very unlikely" (1) to "very likely" (5). Severity refers to the potential consequences linked to the risk, ranging from "minimal" (1) to "catastrophic" (5). The

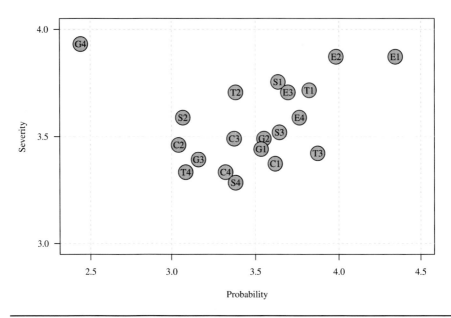

Environment	Technology	Society
E1. Extreme weather events	T1. Cyberattacks	S1. Water crises
E2. Climate change	T2. Cyber dependencies	S2. Infectious diseases
E3. Biodiversity loss	T3. Data fraud or theft	S3. Involuntary migration
E4. Natural disasters	T4. Adverse technological advances	S4. Social instability

Geopolitics	Economics
G1. National governance failure	C1. Asset bubbles
G2. Interstate conflict	C2. Financial failure
G3. Terrorist attacks	C3. Fiscal crisis
G4. Weapons of mass destruction	C4. Structural unemployment

Scales: Probability from very unlikely (1) to very likely (5); severity from minimal (1) to catastrophic (5).

Figure 1.1: Perception of the main risks on a global scale (adapted from World Economic Forum, 2019, figure II).

illustration in figure 1.1 shows the values for the probability of occurrence and severity, averaged across all responses collected.

Environmental risks The survey results show that the most significant risks are related to the environment. First are extreme weather events (E1), such as floods and storms. Severity is measured in terms of damage to property, infrastructure, and the environment, as well as in the resulting loss of human lives. Climate change (E2) is also seen as having a significant impact. This refers to the risk that governments and businesses are unable to adopt or enforce measures intended to mitigate climate change, protect populations, and help vulnerable businesses adapt to the new environment. Then comes the risk of biodiversity loss (E3), which refers to irreversible environmental consequences that result in the depletion of resources for humankind and industrial sectors. Lastly, the report mentions the risk of natural disasters (E4), i.e., geophysical disasters such as earthquakes, volcanic activity, landslides, tsunamis, and geomagnetic storms.

Technological risks Given recent technological developments, the increase in the volume of data and the importance of social networks in modern society, it is not surprising that technological risks are of major concern. Among them, the risks related to large-scale cyberattacks (T1) and cyber dependencies (T2) are thought to have the most severe potential consequences. The risk of a cyberattack refers here to a large-scale hacking or malware attack that could cause significant economic losses, geopolitical tensions, or a general loss of confidence in online services. By comparison, cyber dependencies increase vulnerability to outages occurring in essential information infrastructures (e.g., the internet or satellites) or in other networks, potentially resulting in wide-ranging disruptions. Data fraud and theft (T3) are also among the technological risks identified. They refer to a misuse of private or official data on an unprecedented scale. Located on the lower left-hand side of the graph, the risk of adverse technological advances (T4) relates to the negative consequences—intentional or otherwise—of developments such as artificial intelligence, geoengineering, and synthetic biology, which can harm humans, the environment, and the economy.

Social risks Various significant risks are related to our society. One that is frequently mentioned in the media is the risk of water crises (S1), referring to a major decrease in the quality and quantity of available fresh water, resulting in harm to human health and economic activity. Respondents deemed this to be the most critical social risk. With a lower probability, we see the risk of infectious diseases (S2), i.e., bacteria, viruses, parasites, and fungi causing an uncontrolled spread of infectious diseases (e.g., due to increased resistance to antibiotics, antiviral drugs, and other treatments), resulting in deaths and economic disruptions. This includes diseases causing epidemics and pandemics, such as Covid-19, avian flu, and Ebola. Similarly, food contamination (e.g., salmonella) may cause global crises. With a higher probability but lower severity, there is the risk of involuntary migration (S3), which refers to large-scale migrations caused by conflicts, disasters, or environmental or economic factors. Finally, the risk of social instability (S4) is the last in this category and relates to large-scale demonstrations and social movements, such as riots or social unrest, that may disrupt a country's political and social stability and economic activity.

Geopolitical risks Generally speaking, geopolitical risks refer to administrative or political events or decisions that result in economic, commercial or financial losses for companies or states. The main such risk identified in the report is that of national governance failure (G1), i.e., the inability to govern a geopolitically significant country as a result of weak rule of law, corruption, or political deadlocks. Then, the risk of an interstate conflict (G2) relates to bilateral or multilateral disputes between states that may escalate into conflicts of various kinds: economic (trade or currency wars, nationalization of resources), military, cybernetic, or other. The risk of terrorist attacks (G3) refers to individuals and non-state groups with political or religious goals successfully inflicting large-scale human or property damage. The last risk is the use of weapons of mass destruction (G4), i.e., the deployment of nuclear, chemical, biological, and radiological technologies and materials that can cause international crises and have significant destructive potential.

Economic risks Among the main economic risks, the report mentions the risk of asset bubbles (C1). This term refers to assets (stocks, real estate, goods) in a large economy whose price is excessively and unsustainably high. Another risk is financial failure (C2), i.e., the collapse of a financial institution or the dysfunction of a financial system that may affect the global economy. In the same vein, there is the risk of fiscal crisis (C3), which relates to an excessive debt burden that leads to sovereign debt crises or liquidity crises. Lastly, structural unemployment (C4) refers to a sustained high level of unemployment or an underutilization of the workforce's production capacity.

The results of the World Economic Forum survey outlined above let us provide a broad overview illustrated by selected risks. Still, we would like to add two caveats. First, as with any survey, probability and severity are measured based on the subjective perceptions of the respondents. As we will see later (see chapter 3 on risk assessment and the illustration of figure 3.3), these results are often at odds with objective measures calculated based on observed statistics. Both objective and subjective measures coexist, and either may be relevant in a given situation. Second, the term "severity" covers several types of values that are exposed to losses. It is difficult to quantify and aggregate data that measure human lives, potential financial losses, and consequences on fauna and flora. These are so different that an evaluation of severity by type of value at risk (see section 2.7) will likely lead to diverging conclusions.

1.2 Global natural and man-made disasters

Disasters such as hurricanes, earthquakes, and terrorist attacks get significant media coverage and are often compared to one another in terms of financial losses or casualties. While natural catastrophes are events caused by the forces of nature, man-made disasters are related to human activities. Since 1970, the reinsurance

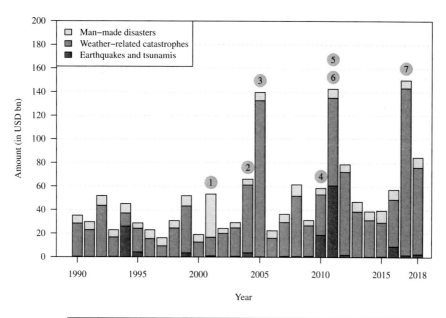

Event	Year	Victims	Amount
1. September 11 terrorist attacks (WTC)	2001	2,996	26
2. Indonesia earthquake	2004	220,000	3
3. Hurricanes Katrina, Rita, Wilma	2005	2,023	112
4. Haiti earthquake	2010	230,000	0.1
5. Thailand flood	2011	815	16
6. Japan earthquakes	2011	15,897	38
7. Hurricanes Harvey, Irma, Maria	2017	3,283	92

Note: The number of victims refers to the death toll listed on Wikipedia (www.wikipedia.org). The amount of losses is given in billions of dollars. The amounts displayed do not include civil liability and life and health insurance.

Figure 1.2: Insured losses for disasters between 1990 and 2018 (adapted from Swiss Re, 2019a, figure 3).

company Swiss Re has published an annual report that evaluates the impact of natural and man-made disasters worldwide. Events are included in the statistics if they exceed a certain threshold in terms of insured losses (claims volume), human casualties (number of dead, missing, injured, or homeless), or economic losses. The three main types of disasters covered are weather-related, earthquakes and tsunamis, and man-made. The graph in figure 1.2, which uses data from Swiss Re (2019a), illustrates the volume of insured losses worldwide between 1990 and 2018. We note a high heterogeneity across the years, with certain periods having a high number of particularly devastating catastrophes. From these global figures, we analyze the concept of risk using a few selected events.

Weather-related catastrophes First, we note that weather-related catastrophes losses occur every year. Their variability and high loss amounts are in line with the high perception of risk associated with weather events mentioned in the World Economic Forum's report (figure 1.1, E1), which places them among the most significant risks of our time. Over the period illustrated, the years 2005, 2011, and 2017 show especially high numbers. In 2005, hurricanes Katrina, Rita, and Wilma hit the Bahamas, Cuba, and the southeastern United States in just three months, from August to October. Statisticians have counted a death toll of 2,023 (see the table in figure 1.2) and insured losses totaling 112 billion dollars. The year 2017 was even more tragic, with hurricanes Harvey, Irma, and Maria occurring in the same season. These caused insured losses totaling around 92 billion dollars and resulted in over 3,200 deaths. Hurricane Maria, which mainly affected Puerto Rico, had the highest death toll, at 3,059, and caused insured losses of 90 billion dollars. We note that these wind-related phenomena often occur in clusters (Katrina, Rita, and Wilma, then Harvey, Irma, and Maria). Similar to the above examples in the Americas, high winds also affect Europe and Switzerland. For instance, storms Lothar and Martin struck Western Europe in late December 1999. Flooding in Thailand in 2011 caused more than 800 deaths and estimated losses of 16 billion dollars. Finally, hurricane Andrew in 1992 was one of the most devastating weather-related catastrophes in the United States. The amount of damage resulted in several reinsurance companies going bankrupt, leading to the emergence of insurance risk securitization operations (see risk financing techniques in section 4.3).

Earthquakes and tsunamis Earthquakes rank among the deadliest events. The earthquakes in Indonesia and Haiti, in 2004 and 2010, respectively, resulted in more than 200,000 deaths each. On March 11, 2011, Japan was struck by a powerful earthquake whose epicenter was in the Pacific Ocean, near the country's east coast. The earthquake was so powerful that it moved Honshu, Japan's largest island, several meters to the east. Tsunami waves tens of meters high hit the coast soon after the earthquake. According to the official figures, the human death toll was around 16,000, and the financial losses were around 38 billion dollars (see also World Health Organization, 2012). Over 90% of these deaths were elderly people who drowned. This natural catastrophe is one of the deadliest and costliest in recent years, and Japan's earthquake-resistant building regulations prevented an even worse outcome. It should be noted that the Fukushima nuclear accident was a consequence of the tsunami caused by this earthquake.

Man-made disasters Lastly, man-made disasters are major losses related to human activity. The report by Swiss Re (2019a) classifies man-made disasters into the following categories: major fires and explosions, aviation and space disasters, shipping disasters, rail disasters, mining accidents, collapse of buildings and bridges, and miscellaneous (including terrorism). For illustration purposes, we will use a historical disaster. During the terrorist attacks of September 11, 2001, four planes were hijacked. Two of them crashed into the World Trade Center (WTC) towers in New York City, resulting in their eventual collapse; the third was flown

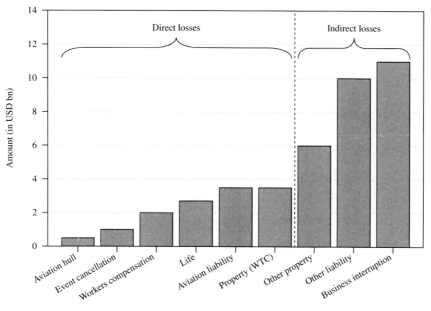

(a) Losses by type of insurance.

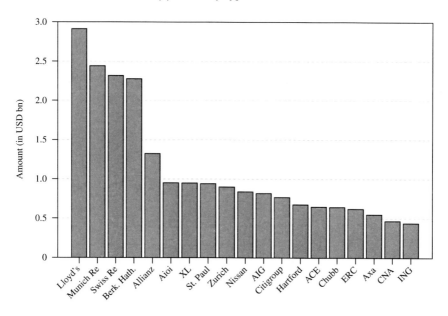

(b) Losses by insurance company.

Figure 1.3: Insured losses for the 2011 World Trade Center attack (adapted from The Geneva Association, 2002).

into the Pentagon near Washington, and the fourth crashed in Pennsylvania (National Commission on Terrorist Attacks Upon the United States, 2004). With a human death toll of about 3,000 at the WTC, these attacks are considered to be among the deadliest of all time. The insured losses amounted to over 26 billion dollars. Some of these amounts are detailed by The Geneva Association (2002) and presented in figure 1.3.

For the WTC attack, we show in figure 1.3(a) the insured losses by type of insurance and by insurance company. Looking at the types of insurance involved, we see that more than 90% of the insured losses were in non-life insurance, meaning that less than 10% were in life insurance. Losses are divided into direct losses, which are related to injuries and property damage directly caused by the event, and indirect losses, which result from direct losses (see section 2.7). In our example, the claims paid for indirect losses are higher than the claims paid for direct losses. Here, direct losses include the destruction of the airplanes, flight cancellations, workers' compensation, life insurance payouts to victims' families, aviation-related civil liability, and damage to the WTC buildings themselves. Indirect losses include other losses, civil liability coverage, and business interruption insurance.

The graph in figure 1.3(b) shows the many insurance companies involved in financing the insured losses. Most of the losses were covered by Lloyd's, Munich Re, Swiss Re, and Berkshire Hathaway, whose primary business is insuring and reinsuring large losses. The remainder, which is still a significant amount, was financed by other companies, including major players such as Allianz and Zurich. Lastly, it is worth noting that beyond the human, property, and economic losses, the event had far-reaching consequences in many other areas, including aviation and security, the economy, the stock market and consumption, as well as politics and military strategy. We are still feeling the impact of some of the attacks today: Islamophobic sentiment, wars in the Middle East, insecurity, and—more visibly—increased security measures at airports (see the risk control techniques studied in section 4.3).

Insured losses by world region   We have seen above that natural catastrophes can cause human and economic losses on a large scale. However, not all regions of the world are affected in the same way; in addition, certain disasters are deadlier, while others cause more significant property damage. For example, Asia is more exposed to the risk of tsunamis than Western Europe. Central America and the coastal regions of the United States are more exposed to hurricanes. These examples illustrate the significant regional differences.

Table 1.1 shows the number of victims as well as the economic losses and insured losses caused by natural and man-made disasters in each region of the world in 2018, according to Swiss Re (2019a). Economic losses include insured and uninsured losses. The highest numbers of victims were recorded in Asia (8,823) and in Africa (2,488). This can be partly explained by the large populations in these regions, but they were also hit by particularly deadly disasters. A more comprehensive analysis must take into account the extent of risk management in each region and the resources devoted to it.

Region	Victims		Economic losses		Insured losses	
	Number	(%)	USD bn	(%)	USD bn	(%)
Asia	8,823	(65.2)	54.7	(33.2)	20.4	(24.0)
Africa	2,488	(18.4)	1.3	(0.8)	0.2	(0.2)
Latin America & Caribbean	959	(7.1)	4.9	(2.9)	1.3	(1.5)
Europe	676	(5.0)	20.7	(12.5)	7.7	(9.1)
North America	329	(2.4)	80.5	(48.8)	52.9	(62.5)
Oceania and Australia	216	(1.6)	2.3	(1.4)	1.6	(1.9)
Seas and Space	32	(0.2)	0.7	(0.4)	0.6	(0.7)
Total	13,523	(100)	165	(100)	85	(100)

Table 1.1: Number of victims and losses by region from natural and man-made disasters in 2018 (adapted from Swiss Re, 2019a, table 2).

Of the 165 billion dollars in total reported economic losses, 155 billion were related to natural catastrophes, while only 10 billion were related to man-made disasters. Looking at the statistics presented in table 1.1, we see that North America ranks first with almost half of the economic losses suffered, i.e., over 80 billion dollars in 2018, followed by Asia and Europe with 54.7 and 20.7 billion dollars, respectively. If we now look at the insured losses, we can see that among the reported economic losses, North America has a total of 53 billion dollars, which is 62.5% of the insured losses worldwide. This means that a large proportion of economic losses are insured in North America. Turning to Asia, we can see that despite having 65.2% of the victims and 33.2% of the economic losses, the insured losses account for only 24.0% of the global amount. This is due to the lower insurance penetration in many Asian countries (see section 5.3). The same observation can be made for Africa and Latin America.

In this context, it is important to keep in mind the significant difference between economic losses and insured losses. Insurance penetration, i.e., the volume of insurance premiums as a percentage of gross domestic product, which measures the development of the insurance sector in a given country, is heterogeneous. While certain catastrophes can cause major economic losses, it is possible that only a small portion of the damaged property is covered by an insurance product. As far as Switzerland is concerned, insurance penetration and density are among the highest in the world. We will discuss the economics of insurance in chapter 5.

Evolution of the number of disasters Natural and man-made disasters are difficult to predict and have catastrophic consequences, making them one of the greatest challenges in risk analysis today. In addition, it is important to consider multiple dimensions, as some catastrophes may cause significant financial losses despite a relatively low number of fatalities. Conversely, other catastrophes may be particularly deadly but cause comparatively little insured loss. Therefore, when

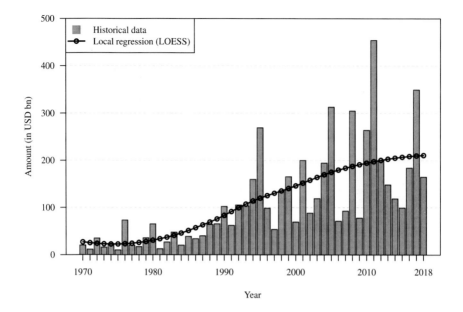

Figure 1.4: Economic losses due to disasters from 1970 to 2018 (adapted from Swiss Re, 2019a, Figure 4).

analyzing a risk, it is important to consider all types of values exposed to the risk, such as human lives and financial amounts, in order to properly assess the potential consequences (see section 2.7).

In the graph on figure 1.4, we show historical data on economic losses, in billions of dollars, caused by disasters since 1970. Year after year, we can see an upward trend in losses, as shown by the overlaid local regression curve. This increase may be related to the increase (e.g., climate change) or emergence (e.g., cyber risks, see section 4.7) of certain risk classes. The high annual amounts, in the hundreds of billions of dollars, pose challenges in terms of financing and insurability. Indeed, as losses have increased, so has the volume of risk exposure, especially as a result of economic and demographic growth. Consequently, insured values are also increasing.

1.3 Examples of risk management in Switzerland

As we will see later in the historical overview presented in section 1.4, Switzerland has a developed insurance market, with a significant amount of mandatory insurance (see also chapter 5). This results in almost the entire population being covered for the main risks they are exposed to. In the public sector, the most important risks are identified, and prevention campaigns are organized. Selected examples are given below, along with the measures taken to manage the risks and provide insurance coverage.

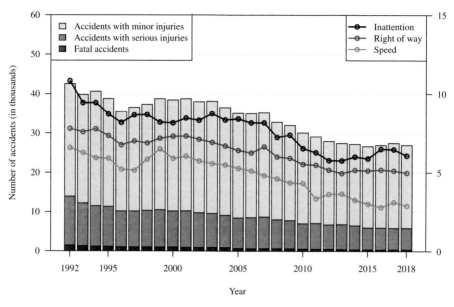

Year	1992	1995	2000	2005	2010	2015	2018	Diff.
Minor injuries	28,634	27,426	28,226	26,678	23,067	20,701	21,126	−26%
Serious injuries	12,403	10,167	9,146	7,777	6,470	5,569	5,464	−56%
Deaths	1,495	1,175	1,050	691	558	409	404	−73%
Total	42,532	38,768	38,422	35,146	30,095	26,679	26,994	−37%
Main suspected causes								
Inattention	10,820	8,713	8,152	8,409	6,531	5,888	6,072	−44%
Right of way	7,789	7,334	7,301	6,403	5,527	5,121	4,975	−36%
Driver error	4,228	4,893	5,959	4,973	4,359	3,926	4,410	+4%
Speed	6,578	5,900	5,894	5,265	4,314	2,999	2,868	−56%
Driver condition	3,821	3,505	3,675	3,311	3,202	2,765	2,822	−26%

Note: The "Diff." column indicates the change from 1992 to 2018.

Figure 1.5: Number of road accidents by severity and main suspected cause from 1992 to 2018 in Switzerland (based on Federal Statistical Office, 2020a).

Road safety Each year, the Swiss Federal Statistical Office (FSO) publishes statistics on traffic accidents, including data on severity and suspected causes (FSO, 2020a). Based on these numbers, we show in figure 1.5 the number of road accidents by severity and by suspected cause (or peril, see section 2.6) since 1992 in Switzerland. Despite the increase in both the country's population and the number of drivers over this period, the data show a decrease in the number of accidents, from 42,532 in 1992 to 26,994 in 2018. In particular, deaths and serious injuries have significantly decreased by 73% and 56%, respectively, over the period studied.

Looking at the main suspected causes of crashes, we note that in 1992, the main perils were driver inattention or distraction, failure to give right of way, and speed. The ranking has evolved somewhat, and in 2018, the main perils were inattention, right-of-way violation, driver error, speed, and driver condition. Although the same perils remain, the number of accidents in each category has decreased over the time period analyzed. For instance, driver inattention or distraction—the peril that caused the most accidents—decreased by 44%, while speed-related accidents decreased by 56%. The decrease in the number of crashes can be explained by several factors. One of these is the improvement of safety equipment in vehicles, such as airbags, drowsiness detection systems, and driver assistance systems. Other factors aimed at reducing the number and severity of accidents include police enforcement of preventive measures such as mandatory seat belt use, the strict measures implemented as part of the federal Via Sicura program, and information and prevention campaigns on the effects of alcohol and distracted driving. We consider these activities to be techniques of risk management by prevention (see section 4.3), with effects on the frequency and severity of accidents (section 3.1).

Fire and natural hazards insurance   ECA Vaud, the public fire and natural hazards insurer in the canton of Vaud, was created by the law of November 17, 1952, on the insurance of real estate and personal property against fire and natural hazards; it provides mandatory mutual insurance against losses caused by fire and natural hazards to real estate and personal property. This public institution is controlled by the state and publishes an annual report that includes the insurance premiums collected and the claims paid for covered losses. The graph in figure 1.6 shows the evolution of the premiums collected and the amounts paid out for damage done to real estate and personal property caused by fires and natural hazards in the canton of Vaud. According to the principle of mutuality followed by ECA Vaud, the insurance premiums for most policyholders are defined as a per mille of the sum insured. This means that properties with the same sum insured will pay the same premium, regardless of the risk exposure resulting from their specific situation. The graph shows us that insurance premiums per unit of insured value are stable over long periods. From 1995 to 2003, the average insurance premium per sum insured was 0.60‰, while from 2004 to 2018, it was 0.68‰ after a revaluation. As for the insured volume, the indexed sums insured have increased from 120 billion Swiss francs in 1985 to 351 billion in 2018. In terms of claims paid, several trends can be observed. First, the amounts paid out for fire are recurring and more or less stable, except in 2001 and 2009. Losses due to fire seem to have decreased in recent years. Second, the claims paid for losses caused by natural hazards are highly variable. The years 1999 (storm Lothar), 2005 (high precipitation), 2009 (hail), 2013 (high precipitation), and 2018 (high precipitation) were marked by significant costs that were difficult to predict, while the costs for other years were very low in comparison.

The premiums collected by ECA Vaud are not intended solely to cover claims paid to policyholders. They also cover operating costs, preventive measures, and the creation of reserves. The latter two are closely related to risk management

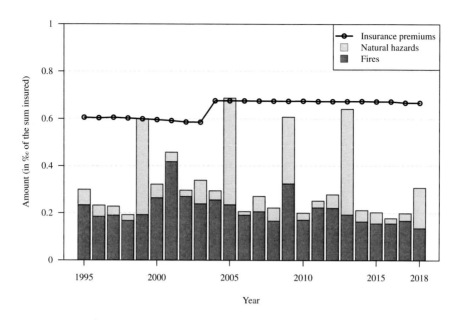

Figure 1.6: Insurance premiums and claims for losses caused by fire and natural hazards for ECA Vaud from 1995 to 2018 (based on Statistique Vaud, 2019).

(see sections 4.3, 6.4, and 6.5). In this context, preventive measures are among the techniques aimed at limiting either the frequency or the severity of risks (see section 3.1). ECA Vaud is particularly active in the field of fire prevention, with structural measures (load-bearing systems, compartmentalization, and fire doors), technical measures (emergency lighting, fire detection, sprinkler systems, and lightning rods), and organizational measures (evacuation procedures). In 2005, regulations made some of these measures mandatory for new construction projects, which can partially explain the decrease in fire claims. Concrete measures to prevent losses caused by natural hazards are more difficult to implement. In most cases, the years in which large amounts of claims are paid are characterized by extremely intense natural catastrophes. In this case, prevention is more likely to take the form of warning the population of an impending event by sending "weather alert" text messages and providing instructions on what to do (e.g., putting away garden furniture and keeping roller shutters up). A list of areas at risk of flooding due to swelling streams and surface runoff in urban areas is compiled in order to raise awareness among the population and to strengthen preventive measures during construction. Maps of natural hazards are available from the cantonal map portal (Guichet cartographique du Canton de Vaud, 2020).

In summary, risk management focuses on three key areas: prevention, rescue, and insurance (see ECA Vaud, 2020). This idea of integrating prevention and insurance is also present in many insurance companies, such as Suva, whose accident insurance is managed by a combination of prevention, insurance, and rehabilitation (see Suva, 2020). Indeed, the physical and social rehabilitation of accident victims requires as much attention as the financial aspects, especially to limit indirect losses.

Enterprise risk management In this book, we will repeatedly refer (see section 2.2) to a company that implements a risk management program. This is because businesses are an environment in which speculative risks (see section 2.4) exist in addition to the pure risks mentioned above. Such risks include strategic, financial, and operational risks that a company takes on a daily basis as part of its business, and that can have both positive and negative consequences. For instance, a business expansion strategy, a financial investment, or an operational change may succeed or fail. In addition, organizations need to consider emerging risks, such as cyber risks (see section 4.7). All of these risks fall under the purview of enterprise risk management, or ERM.

A company's risk management processes (see chapter 4) depend on the specific nature of the company, the competition in its market, and the risk management processes of its competitors. There is no one-size-fits-all approach to managing a company's risks. When risk becomes a priority for executive or non-executive management, even if they do not take specific action, the dynamic between the company and its risks changes. It is also a matter of corporate culture, an issue that requires close attention (see also section 4.5). The mere perception of a better understanding of a company's risks can lead managers to take more or less risks. As a result, risk managers should promote a better distribution of their company's risks and broaden their scope in order to take future possibilities into account in their management activities. In this way, ERM and strategic risk management become complementary processes. Tactical decisions—such as what insurance to buy, what price to set for a particular good, what interest rate risk to hedge, how tight to make digital firewalls, or how much debt to take on—are typically made independently. Tactical risk management using an integrated framework, such as integrated risk management as part of an ERM strategy, adds value by improving the quality of information shared (see risk management functions in section 2.1). In this context, we identify various functions and areas of risk management, including helping to identify risks, implementing programs to prevent and limit losses, training on risk management activities, monitoring regulatory compliance, developing various ways to manage and finance risks, handling claims, and designing products and contracts.

Among all types of risk, financial risks are particularly numerous and difficult to apprehend. Since the beginning of this century, there has been a series of financial crises. In the year 2000, the dot-com bubble burst, leading to the collapse of companies whose business model was based on high-tech stocks (Ofek and Richardson, 2003). Many companies experienced a loss of liquidity after acquiring start-ups following their initial public offerings. This was followed by the housing bubble in the United States, which burst in 2008. A large number of financial institutions incurred significant losses due to the subprime crisis related to high-risk mortgages (Blundell-Wignall, 2008). In Switzerland, many companies suffered losses as a result of the removal of the CHF/EUR exchange rate cap in 2015, which had been set by the Swiss National Bank at 1.20 francs per euro to prevent the value of the franc from skyrocketing against the euro. More recently, the scale of the economic crisis set off by the Covid-19 pandemic is still difficult to quantify. Financial risks have to be strictly controlled, as insurance coverage is often not available.

1.4   A bit of history

Risk management is not just the responsibility of individual entities: the insurance industry was originally founded on the idea of (natural) risk pools. Risk pools still exist in the principle of common defense against risks and the collective assumption of economic risks across a family, a clan, a tribe, or a community. At the same time, the concept of risk sharing has evolved through mergers into cooperatives, laws, or commercial contracts. In order to cover the financial consequences, insurance appeared and saw its role change over time: cooperative groups dedicated to mutual aid in the event of an accident; insurance based on trade, which led to the development of insurance as a promising branch of the economy; insurance at the initiative of the state, which made insurance mandatory in certain areas in order to stabilize infrastructures and maintain social harmony (see the topic of social insurance, which we cover in section 5.2).

In this chapter, we explore the origins of the word "risk," the history of risk management, and the emergence of insurance. We provide the reader with a selection of stories as well as a coherent historical overview illustrated with concrete and documented facts that we consider essential. The references included in the text may provide further insight into the facts discussed.

The origin of the word "risk"   The etymology of the word "risk" remains uncertain (Pradier, 2006). According to one theory, its origin has to do with the transportation of goods by sea. In 1853, the work of German philologist Friedrich Diez—the founder of Romance linguistics—helped to establish the timeline of the word's appearance. According to Diez (1853), the Latin word *resecum* means "something that cuts" or "reef," i.e., an obstacle near the water's surface and a navigational hazard. Later, he associates the word *resecum* with the risk to which cargo is exposed at sea, marking one of the first uses of the word "risk." The use of the term in everyday language began in the 12th century in northern Italy, a region dominated by maritime trade at that time. The terminology then gradually spread throughout Europe. At the same time, the word "risk" soon acquired an economic and legal meaning, appearing in many political, legal, and regulatory documents, where it referred to holding a legal subject liable for a possible financial burden associated with an enterprise—not necessarily a particularly dangerous one—whose outcome is uncertain (Piron, 2004). At the same time, phrases such as "taking a risk" and "putting at risk" were coined. The concept of risk carries with it a certain judgment: we speak of chance in lottery games to represent randomness but of risk when we speak of risky investments to refer to danger.

The concept of risk management First appearing between 1955 and 1964, risk management is a concept that represents an awareness of risk at the enterprise level (Crockford, 1982). One of the earliest books devoted to the subject was published in 1963 and entitled *Risk Management in the Business Enterprise* (Mehr and Hedges, 1963). Risk management has long been associated with the use of market insurance to protect individuals and businesses against various losses caused by accidents or, more generally, by pure risk (see section 2.4). From its inception, the concept of risk management has been related to that of insurance, as it is primarily concerned with covering the financial consequences of risks to which a company is exposed (Harrington and Niehaus, 2003).

Other forms of risk transfer and management as alternatives to market insurance (see section 4.3) only emerged later, as insurance was perceived to be very expensive and to provide inadequate protection against pure risk. The use of derivatives as a risk management tool began during the 1970s, and grew rapidly in the 1980s as companies developed their financial risk management processes. In his 2013 article, Georges Dionne presents a detailed history of risk management and financial regulation (Dionne, 2013). The article also provides an overview of the major theories in finance that have influenced risk management, including Markowitz's 1952 theory and the capital asset pricing model theory developed between 1961 and 1996.

In the 1980s, the focus was on the managerial aspect of risk management. While the first EU regulation on the solvency of non-life insurance companies—a precursor to the Solvency I regulation—was adopted as early as 1973, it was not until 1988 that the concept of risk management was formally extended to banks, with the publication of the Basel I regulation, which was implemented in 1992. Later, new methods of financial hedging, such as derivatives, were created. Meanwhile,

Year	Description
1963	Publication of the first book on risk management (Mehr and Hedges, 1963)
1963	Concepts of moral hazard and adverse selection (Arrow, 1963)
1973	Solvency I regulation on non-life insurance
1979	Solvency I extended to life insurance
1988	Basel I regulation on banks
1980ff.	Use of the concept of value-at-risk
1992	Concept of integrated risk management
2000ff.	Use of the concept of expected shortfall
2004	Solvency I regulation on insurance in the European Union
2004	Basel II regulation on banks
2009	Solvency II regulation on insurance (implemented in 2016)
2010	Basel III regulation on banks

Table 1.2: Key dates in the history of risk management (adapted from Dionne, 2013).

integrated risk management (IRM) emerged in corporations in 1992, and the new position of chief risk officer (CRO) was created in the 2000s.

Financial firms have developed internal risk management models and risk measures such as *value-at-risk* and *expected shortfall*, which have been in use since the late 1980s and 2000s, respectively (see section 3.5). Using these tools, firms can determine the appropriate financial reserves needed to cover the risks to which they are exposed. Regulations have evolved with the publication of Basel II in 2004, Solvency II in 2009, and Basel III in 2010. Table 1.2 provides a summary of some key dates in the history of the industry.

Risk pools and early insurance   The first traces of risk pools or risk sharing date back to around 2000 BCE in Mesopotamia (Molin, 2006; Abdel-Khalik, 2013). The triggering event was the invention of the spoked wheel, which first appeared in present-day Iran and Turkestan (Bakker et al., 1999). With their maneuverability and ease of use, these wheels were used to create lightweight carts and caravans that could be used to transport cargo and valuable goods. As transportation developed, caravanners were increasingly exposed to daily hazards that could damage their cargo, mainly natural hazards such as the desert and quicksand, as well as human hazards (raids). Eventually, the merchants decided to share the cost of their losses. Thus the concept of risk sharing was born.

This pooling of risks had a number of advantages, including compensation from the community in the event of a loss. However, we can also see significant drawbacks related to adverse selection—with high-risk merchants being more likely to join a risk pool—, premiums that were often paid retrospectively—i.e., on arrival, which means those who hadn't lost everything would cover the losses of others who would ultimately not contribute to the pool—, and moral(e) hazard, which encourages risk taking due to mutual insurance. These drawbacks are relatively well studied today, and since the seminal work of Arrow (1963), the concepts of moral hazard (see section 2.6) and adverse selection are systematically taken into account by insurers.

In ancient times, relief organizations were established. For instance, around 1400 BCE, stone masons in Lower Egypt paid monthly contributions to a fund that would compensate them in the event of an accident (Tanzi and D'Argenlieu, 2013). However, the industry that seems to be at the origin of insurance as we know it today is maritime trade (Brulhart, 2010). In Greece and Ancient Rome, there was a form of maritime lending that allowed multiple shipowners to redistribute the risks involved. Plutarch mentions the story of a certain Cato who, in the 2nd century BCE, would lend money to sailors for their expeditions provided they formed an association of at least fifty members. Such a procedure spreads the risk of misfortune over fifty expeditions (Boyer, 2008). It was therefore a secured loan, sometimes called a "bottomry," thanks to which merchants could have the funds necessary to launch their expeditions and lenders could earn very high interest, between 30% and 50% of the capital lent (Brulhart, 2017). Furthermore, Roman law was based on *Lex Rhodia de iactu*, the Rhodian law that regulated the loss of cargo at sea. According to this law, if a ship's captain decided to jettison part of the cargo in order to save the ship from danger, the loss was borne jointly by the owners of the ship and those of the cargo.

Between the 5th and 15th centuries, mutuality developed and most communities of craftspeople and merchants created relief funds. For example, the first medieval guilds were formed during this period. Their purpose was to establish relief funds that would compensate members in the event of theft, fire, flood, or death of livestock (Tanzi and D'Argenlieu, 2013). This period was also marked by a major turning point in the development of insurance. During the 14th century, Pope Gregory XI decided to prohibit usurious interest rates, which were considered contrary to good morals. Shipowners of the time would get around this law by creating a kind of bill of sale in which the merchant had bought the owner's cargo and, therefore, owed them the equivalent amount. The merchant would pay some kind of premium not mentioned in the contract, while a clause in the contract provided that it was void if the ship did not reach its destination (Brulhart, 2017). This is how the first insurance contracts were born. There seems to be a consensus that a contract dated October 23, 1347, in Genoa was the very first insurance contract, although some authors mention an earlier contract dated 1343 (Nelli, 1972).

The merchant cities of northern Italy were the birthplaces of both banking and insurance. The expansion of the latter was driven by maritime powers such as Flanders, England, Spain, and Portugal. The legislation established in the "Five Ordinances" of Barcelona, adopted in the middle of the 15th century, was the first official insurance regulation (Brulhart, 2017). In 1681, the Colbert Ordinance, also known as the "Great Ordinance of Marine," was the first draft of a social contract, as it established the legal basis for marine insurance throughout Europe. Among other things, these texts established the shipowner's obligations towards sailors who were injured or ill on board (France, 1715). In 1720, an edict defined more general rules for the allocation of retirement and invalidity pensions to injured sailors.

The insurance contracts most similar to those that exist in our 21st-century economy appeared in Italy between the 12th and 13th centuries: according to a Florentine historian named Villani, insurance was born in Lombardia in 1182. As for contracts tied to survival, the tontine—a contract by which several people agree to leave the invested capital to the survivors in the event of death—was created in 1653 by the Italian banker Lorenzo Tonti. It was one of the first contracts to provide for death (Mckeever, 2009). In the same period, in 1688, Lloyd's of London was founded (Grey, 1893). This was a marketplace where insurers—whether individuals or corporations—gathered to jointly insure risks. The name is a reference to Lloyd's Coffee House in London, a meeting place where insurance contracts were discussed.

In 1654, Blaise Pascal developed the law of large numbers, the first step in formalizing probability theory, a theory that is now essential in characterizing a risk (Pradier, 2006). Then came the first actuarial table (Kreager, 1993; see section 6.2) in 1657, followed in 1660 by the first calculation of life annuities (Hebrard, 2004; see section 6.3). The development of mathematics, especially statistics and probability, has provided actuaries with the tools they need to evaluate the funding of insurance company liabilities. At the same time, risk management has seen the development of quantitative risk management (QRM), which focuses on the numerical evaluation of risk (McNeil et al., 2015).

Year	Description
Around 2000 BCE	First traces of risk sharing
Around 1400 BCE	First relief organizations for stone masons
Around 700 BCE	Maritime loan with risk redistribution
From the 5th to the 15th centuries	Development of mutuality for craftspeople and merchants
1347	First insurance contract in Genoa
Around 1400	Pope Gregory XI's prohibition on usurious interest rates
Around 1450	Adoption of the Barcelona Ordinances
1653	First tontine
1654	Blaise Pascal's law of large numbers
1657	First actuarial tables
1660	First life annuity calculation
1666	Great Fire of London
1681	Colbert Ordinance
1688	Creation of Lloyd's of London
1720	Regulations on retirement and invalidity pensions for sailors
1842	Great Fire of Hamburg
1861	Glarus fire
1906	Earthquake and fire of San Francisco

Table 1.3: Milestones in the historical development of insurance.

The role of fires in the development of insurance Several major disasters have driven more recent developments and regulations in the insurance industry (Swiss Re, 2014). The first of these was the Great Fire of London in 1666, which burned for four days and destroyed over 70,000 houses across the city. After this event, a Londoner named Nicholas Barbon made a fortune rebuilding the city and later turned to insuring homes. He founded the first company offering house insurance, also known as fire insurance. In 1842, the Great Fire of Hamburg was the first to affect the financial viability of the insurance companies of the time. Many British insurers suffered huge losses and withdrew from the German market. The disaster heightened the industry's awareness of risk and gave rise to professional reinsurance. The oldest independent reinsurance company in the world, Cologne Re, was founded in connection with this event. Later, the Glarus fire of 1861 destroyed much of the canton and was highly publicized (Hauser, 2011). The fire led to the creation of the reinsurance company Swiss Re and ultimately to the creation of fire insurance in Switzerland, which is now mandatory for every building owner in most cantons. In the canton of Vaud, fire insurance is mandatory for both landlords and tenants. Finally, the San Francisco earthquake of 1906 caused fires throughout the city, destroying the homes of some 200,000 of the city's 450,000 inhabitants (The Museum of the City of San Francisco, 2020). The event was one of the most remarkable in the history of fire insurance and was the starting point for the calculation of individual premiums, i.e., premiums that depend on specific risk situations (see section 6.5). Table 1.3 presents a timeline of important events in the history of the insurance industry. Further details and illustrations can be found in Swiss Re (2013).

A historical overview of the insurance industry in Switzerland Switzerland currently has one of the most highly developed insurance systems in the world (see chapter 5). Here are some of the major events that contributed to this development (Swiss Re, 2017). The year 1806 saw the appearance of the first cantonal institution offering fire insurance in Switzerland, in the canton of Aargau (Körner and Degen, 2014). ECA Vaud was created in 1811 as the 11th such institution in the country. In the years that followed, the first insurance companies that we still know today were founded. In the canton of Vaud, we can mention two important years: 1895, with the establishment of Vaudoise Assurances—one of the ten largest insurers on the Swiss market—, and 1907, with the creation of the *Caisse cantonale vaudoise des retraites populaires*, since renamed Retraites Populaires.

The first social insurance was the military insurance, with the corresponding federal law adopted in 1902 (Federal Social Insurance Office, 2014). Mandatory accident insurance (AA) was introduced in 1918, the same year that Suva was founded, while loss of earnings compensation (APG) appeared in 1940. A major reform was the approval of the old age and survivors' insurance (AVS) in 1948, which guaranteed a pension to retirees and formed what we now call the first pillar. In 1959, the motor vehicle insurance ordinance came into force, requiring minimum insurance coverage. Later, invalidity insurance (AI) was introduced in 1960 (Fracheboud, 2015) and supplementary benefits (PC) in 1966. The three-pillar model was approved by the people in 1972, and unemployment insurance (AC) in 1976. The law on occupational pensions (LPP) was passed in 1985, as was the law on health insurance (LAMal). Lastly, health insurance began to include maternity insurance in 2004.

Regarding the supervision of private insurance companies, the Federal Assembly of the Swiss Confederation passed the first insurance supervision act (LSA) in 1885 and created the Federal Office of Private Insurance (FOPI) in 1978. In 2006, FOPI decided to create a tool to test the solvency of private insurance companies, the Swiss Solvency Test (SST). More recently, FOPI was integrated into the Swiss Financial Market Supervisory Authority (FINMA) in 2009. Table 1.4 presents key dates in the development of the Swiss insurance industry.

Year	Description
1806	First cantonal institution offering fire insurance (ECA)
1811	Creation of ECA Vaud
1826	First personal property insurance (La Mobilière)
1863	First reinsurance company in Switzerland (Swiss Re)
1872	First civil liability insurance (Zurich Assurances)
1885	First law on insurance supervision (LSA)
1893	Federal law on mandatory livestock insurance
1895	Foundation of Vaudoise Assurances
1902	Military insurance (first social insurance in Switzerland)
1907	Creation of Retraites Populaires
1918	Mandatory accident insurance (AA)
1940	Mandatory insurance against loss of income (APG)
1948	Old age and survivors' insurance (AVS)
1959	Mandatory vehicle insurance
1960	Invalidity insurance (AI)
1966	Supplementary benefits (PC)
1972	Three-pillar old age pension system
1976	Unemployment insurance (AC)
1978	Creation of the Federal Office of Private Insurance (FOPI)
1985	Law on occupational pensions (LPP)
1994	Law on mandatory health insurance (LAMal)
2004	Introduction of maternity insurance
2006	Introduction of the Swiss Solvency Test (SST)
2009	Integration of FOPI into the Swiss Financial Market Supervisory Authority (FINMA)

Table 1.4: Timeline of insurance in Switzerland.

1.5 Further reading and resources

This book is not the first one to discuss risk management, and we occasionally refer to the existing literature in order to expand on our examples. While few books have been published in French, the English language literature is abundant, especially if we include all the books that cover the implementation of ERM concepts. In table 1.5, we provide some suggestions for additional reading.

We also provide in table 1.6 the names and websites of a number of academic societies and professional associations. In particular, this list includes the Swiss Insurance Association, the umbrella organization for private insurance companies, and the Swiss Association of Actuaries, which brings together specialists in actuarial science. Finally, table 1.7 provides an overview of the most relevant scientific journals.

- Borghesi and Gaudenzi, 2013, *Risk Management*.
- Darsa, 2016, *La gestion des risques en entreprise* [in French].
- Denuit and Charpentier, 2004, *Mathématiques de l'Assurance Non-Vie* (Tome I) [in French].
- Doherty, 2000, *Integrated Risk Management*.
- Dorfman and Cather, 2012, *Introduction to Risk Management and Insurance*.
- Fraser and Simkins, 2011, *Enterprise Risk Management*.
- Frenkel et al., 2005, *Risk Management: Challenge and Opportunity*.
- Gaultier-Gaillard and Louisot, 2014, *Diagnostic des risques* [in French].
- Head and Horn, 1997, *Essentials of Risk Management*.
- Hull, 2018, *Risk Management and Financial Institutions*.
- Lam, 2014, *Enterprise Risk Management: From Incentives to Controls*.
- Louisot, 2014, *Gestion des risques* [in French].
- Maquet, 1991, *Des primes d'assurance au financement des risques* [in French].
- Rejda and McNamara, 2017, *Principles of Risk Management and Insurance*.
- Trieschmann et al., 2004, *Risk Management and Insurance*.
- Vaughan and Vaughan, 2013, *Fundamentals of Risk and Insurance*.

Table 1.5: Selected further reading.

• American Risk and Insurance Association (ARIA)	☑ www.aria.org
• Swiss Association of Actuaries (SAA/ASA/SAV)	☑ www.actuaries.ch
• Swiss Insurance Association (SIA/ASA/SVV)	☑ www.svv.ch
• Casualty Actuarial Society (CAS)	☑ www.casact.org
• Certified Entreprise Risk Analyst Association (CERA)	☑ www.ceraglobal.org
• Risk and Insurance Management Society (RIMS)	☑ www.rims.org
• Society of Actuaries (SOA)	☑ www.soa.org
• Swiss Risk Association (SRA)	☑ www.swiss-risk.org
• The Institute of Risk Management (IRM)	☑ www.theirm.org

Table 1.6: Selected academic societies and professional societies.

- Annals of Actuarial Science
  ⬀ www.cambridge.org/core/journals/annals-of-actuarial-science

- ASTIN Bulletin
  ⬀ www.cambridge.org/core/journals/astin-bulletin-journal-of-the-iaa

- European Actuarial Journal
  ⬀ link.springer.com/journal/13385

- Insurance: Mathematics and Economics
  ⬀ www.journals.elsevier.com/insurance-mathematics-and-economics

- Journal of Insurance Issues
  ⬀ www.jstor.org/journal/jinsuissu

- Journal of Insurance Regulation
  ⬀ https://content.naic.org/prod_serv_jir.htm

- Journal of Risk and Financial Management
  ⬀ www.mdpi.com/journal/jrfm

- Journal of Risk and Uncertainty
  ⬀ www.link.springer.com/journal/11166

- Journal of Risk Finance
  ⬀ www.emeraldinsight.com/loi/jrf

- North American Actuarial Journal
  ⬀ www.tandfonline.com/loi/uaaj20

- Risk Management
  ⬀ www.palgrave-journals.com/rm

- Risk Management and Insurance Review
  ⬀ https://onlinelibrary.wiley.com/journal/15406296

- Risks
  ⬀ www.mdpi.com/journal/risks

- Scandinavian Actuarial Journal
  ⬀ www.tandfonline.com/loi/sact20

- The Geneva Papers on Risk and Insurance – Issues and Practice
  ⬀ www.palgrave.com/de/journal/41288

- The Journal of Risk and Insurance
  ⬀ https://onlinelibrary.wiley.com/journal/15396975

Table 1.7: Selected scientific journals.

CHAPTER 2

Risk

The term "risk" can be found in many sentences that we use every day, such as "that's risky" or "let's not risk that happening." In this chapter, we will familiarize ourselves with the concept of risk and introduce the term's definition. We define the term "risk" in section 2.1 and introduce the concept of reference framework in section 2.2. In section 2.3, we illustrate the strategic, operational, and external risks a company is exposed to. We propose a characterization of risks in section 2.4 and of risk exposure in section 2.5. Among all the characteristics of a risk exposure, it is important to identify the perils and the exposed values. In section 2.6, we present a definition and classification of perils and hazards. Lastly, in section 2.7, we introduce a categorization of exposed values. The insights gained through this classification will provide the basic knowledge needed to identify and analyze a risk. This is a critical step before moving on to the evaluation of risk exposure (see chapter 3).

2.1   Definition of the term "risk"

Daily use and improper use   On the surface, risk seems to be a fairly simple concept that can be delineated and illustrated as we have done in the introduction (chapter 1). By using the word "risk," we associate uncertainty with the realization of an event and emphasize its potential negative consequences. However, this is not a true definition; rather, it is a series of concepts linked to that of risk. Several precise definitions are possible, which may differ somewhat depending on the area in question. For instance, a certain definition of the term "risk" may be appropriate for an economist but not necessarily for a statistician or an actuary.

In addition, the terminology of risk is often used improperly. "Risk" can refer to the cause of a loss—"you are not covered for this risk," meaning that your contract does not cover the cause of the event that resulted in the loss—, the object of the risk— "young men are bad risks," meaning that young men statistically cause larger potential losses—, or the financial loss associated with the risk—"there is a 1,000-franc risk," meaning that the potential loss is 1,000 francs. In everyday language, we often use various forms of the term in many situations, for example, "to risk arriving late" or "to risk an activity." Even among experts in many different fields, the term "risk" has become very popular and is now often used to simply describe the uncertainty of a situation. In this book, we will examine the traditional concept of "measurable" risk, which we will define and assess below.

Dictionary definitions   Risk and related concepts need to be formally defined. Let us begin by looking at the definitions found in dictionaries. The Webster (2010) dictionary suggests an origin of the word "risk" that is different from the one we have seen in the previous chapter, stating that it originates from the Greek *rhiza*, meaning "cliff," referring to hazardous sea travel. The dictionary offers the following definitions:

Definitions of the word "risk" in Webster's dictionary

- the chance of injury, damage, or loss; dangerous chance; hazard

- the chance of loss

- the degree of probability of loss

- the amount of possible loss to the insuring company

According to the Cambridge (2023) dictionary, the word's definitions are the following:

Definitions of the word "risk" in the Cambridge dictionary

- the possibility of something bad happening

- something bad that might happen

- *(Phrase)* at risk: in a dangerous situation

- *(Phrase)* take a risk: to do something that might be dangerous

We note that some of these definitions are improper uses of the term, as mentioned above. However, these definitions have two features in common with those we can find in the literature: uncertainty and the event's potentially unwelcome aspect. However, our definition of risk does not mention insurance coverage.

ISO standard definitions The ISO Guide 73:2009 standard, defined by the International Organization for Standardization (2009), provides definitions of generic terms related to risk management. Its purpose is to ensure consistent use of terminology. In section 1.1, it defines the term "risk." This definition refers to deviations from expectations, such as those defined in a business plan. The definition is followed by several notes that provide more specific information.

Definition of the word "risk" according to the ISO Guide 73:2009 standard

Effect of uncertainty on objectives.

- An effect is a deviation from the expected — positive and/or negative.

- Objectives can have different aspects (such as financial, health and safety, and environmental goals) and can apply at different levels (such as strategic, organization-wide, project, product and process).

- Risk is often characterized by reference to potential events and consequences, or a combination of these.

- Risk is often expressed in terms of a combination of the consequences of an event (including changes in circumstances) and the associated likelihood of occurrence.

- Uncertainty is the state, even partial, of deficiency of information related to, understanding or knowledge of, an event, its consequence, or likelihood.

The International Organization for Standardization (2018) also defines the principles and guidelines of risk management as part of the ISO 31000:2018 standard. Section 3.1 also offers a definition that reproduces that of the ISO Guide 73:2009 standard, specifying the elements that characterize a risk. These include risk sources (elements that can cause risk), potential events (the occurrence of a particular set of circumstances), their consequences (the impact of the event on objectives), and likelihood (probability that the event will occur).

Definition of the word "risk" according to the ISO 31000:2018 standard

Effect of uncertainty on objectives.

- An effect is a deviation from the expected. It can be positive, negative or both, and can address, create or result in opportunities and threats.

- Objectives can have different aspects and categories, and can be applied at different levels.

- Risk is usually expressed in terms of risk sources, potential events, their consequences and their likelihood.

The vocabulary, concepts, and principles (see also the definition 4.1 in section 4.1 on risk management) defined by the International Organization for Standardization are widely used in professional practice. However, and although risk management is a mature field, a full consensus has not yet been reached, as evidenced by the discussions within the scientific community (Aven, 2011, 2012).

Our definition of risk Considering the aspects outlined above, we now propose the following definition of risk:

Definition 2.1 (*Risk*)

Risk *is a condition characterized by the possibility of the occurrence of an event that causes an adverse deviation from the expected or desired results.*

By definition 2.1, a number of conditions must be met for a risk to exist. First, the occurrence of the condition or event must be uncertain. This means that it must be possible to characterize it with a probability that is between zero and 100%: the event must be neither impossible nor certain. This means that the concept of uncertainty is linked to that of risk. It is a consequence of the non-deterministic nature of risk but also of the knowledge and perception of the likelihood of the adverse event occurring.

Second, an adverse deviation or loss must result from the occurrence of the event in question. That is, the event must result in an adverse deviation from what was expected. Therefore, our definition links risks to the objectives of the entity under consideration. It is intuitively clear that there are situations where the risk is greater than in other situations: this is the idea behind the concept of degree of risk, which we will explore when we discuss risk appreciation (see chapter 3).

2.2 Reference framework for risk analysis

Implementing a risk management system typically begins with identifying the risks to which an organization is exposed. However, in order to properly define the context, it is important to consider the reference framework and decide on a perspective to take. In this context, we refer to the perspective used to identify and examine risks as the "reference framework."

Definition 2.2 (*Reference framework*)

The **reference framework** *refers to the point of view from which the risk is analyzed.*

Indeed, the risks to which a private individual is exposed are different from those to which a business is exposed. For example, the risk of business failure is not relevant when the reference framework is a private individual, nor is the risk of death when the reference framework is a business.

Examples of reference frameworks

- *World (global scale)*: We identify the Earth, the terrestrial globe in its entirety, as the reference framework. In this case, the relevant risks are called global risks. These are, for example, those we discussed in section 1.1, i.e., risks related to the environment, technology, society, geopolitics, and economics.

- *State (national scale)*: At the national level, we consider all the risks to which a country or region is exposed. These risk analyses are conducted by governments for their internal affairs. This reference framework often includes the same types of risks as at the global level. Examples of risks include those related to road safety and protection against fire and natural hazards, which we discussed in section 1.3.

- *Enterprise*: The "enterprise" reference framework includes public and private companies, as well as associations. Enterprises can be very different in size, ranging from a one-person business to a multinational corporation operating around the world. In this context, enterprise risks are very important, and the risks identified are highly dependent on the industry.

- *Private individual*: In this reference framework, we look at individuals and how they interact with their environment. The relevant risks are those to which a person is exposed on a daily basis, such as those related to illness, accident, disability, or death, as well as those related to the family environment.

Since certain types of risk are only relevant in certain reference frameworks, it is essential to identify the reference framework before conducting a risk analysis. In section 2.4, we look at risk characterization, then we look at risk exposure (see section 2.5).

2.3 Risks within a company

Depending on the perspective taken, the types of risks to be analyzed are different. We have seen that from a global perspective, there are environmental, technological, social, geopolitical, and economic risks. From the perspective of a company—which is the perspective that we take most often— the three main categories of risk are strategic, operational (or internal), and external risks (Kaplan and Mikes, 2012). Some of these are within the company's control, while others are beyond its control. External risks include some of the risks we have mentioned in the global reference framework but from a perspective that analyzes only their impact on the company. The purpose of this chapter is to describe these enterprise risks in more detail.

Strategic risks Strategy is essential for all businesses. Regardless of their size, they create a strategic plan and adjust it over time in response to developments in their macroeconomic environment. Strategic risks are those that result from fundamental decisions made by non-executive and executive management. They relate to a company's objectives and can be divided into business risks and non-business risks. Their control is essential to ensure the long-term viability of the company.

Non-business risks are risks that are not directly related to the goods or products offered by the company. Examples include financial risks related to long-term funding sources, image risks, knowledge management risks, and integrity risks. The level of strategic risk depends on the position of the company as a whole in relation to its environment; it is not only influenced by the individual decisions of its managers.

Examples of non-business strategic risks
(adapted from Darsa, 2016)

- *Financial risks*: This family of risks includes risks that directly affect the company's health and financial performance. There are more than 10,000 financial risks within a company. Without covering them all, we will list below some financial risks that may belong to the category of strategic risks.

  - *Liquidity risk or treasury risk*: A shortfall in cash flow that could lead to a cessation of payments.

- *Financial loss risk*: Losses resulting from poor investment, operational or management decisions.

- *Accounting risk*: Risks associated with the misinterpretation or misapplication of accounting standards.

- *Tax risk*: Penalties resulting from non-compliance with tax regulations.

- *Financing risk*: Risks associated with the company's financing or debt structure.

- *Image and/or reputation risk*: Warren Buffett (CEO of Berkshire Hathaway) is often quoted as having said: "It takes twenty years to build a reputation and five minutes to ruin it." Reputation risk is a major concern in an economy where 70-80% of market value is based on intangible assets that are difficult to value (Eccles et al., 2007). Image risk is the risk of potential damage to a company's brand and reputation that could affect its earnings, assets, or liquidity as a result of an association, action, or inaction that could be perceived by stakeholders as inappropriate, unethical, or inconsistent with the company's values and beliefs. Although difficult to measure, it is estimated that reputation accounts for a quarter of a company's value.

- *Knowledge management risk*: Knowledge management risks are related to the potential losses resulting from the identification, storage, or protection of knowledge that could diminish the organization's operational or strategic advantage (Perrott, 2007; Durst and Zieba, 2019).

- *Integrity risk*: This risk is closely related to fraud, corruption, and the financing of illegal activities. It includes all risks that could result in a loss of customer confidence and financial sanctions due to improper or unethical behavior by the organization (OECD, 2013).

Business risks are risks that result from decisions made by an organization's management. These decisions may relate to, for instance, products, services and pricing. Business risks include risks associated with the development and marketing of goods and services, economic risks that affect product sales and costs, and risks resulting from changes in the technological environment that affect sales and production. More specifically, these risks are often associated with poorly thought-out product diversification, inconsistent or inappropriate offerings, poorly controlled growth or geographic expansion, or technological disruption.

Competitors' actions also affect the level of risk: competition in product markets and technological developments can make certain production processes or products themselves quickly obsolete, resulting in losses. Business risks are diverse and vary greatly by industry.

Examples of strategic financial business risks
(adapted from Darsa, 2016)

- *Investment error risk*: This risk is related to a deterioration in operating conditions as a result of an error, with consequences for financial capacity.

- *Underinvestment risk*: A financial inability to renew or maintain its equipment can cause a company to become uncompetitive.

- *Operating risk*: This is the risk of an imbalance between revenues and costs.

- *Outsourcing opportunity risk*: This is the risk of a deterioration in the cost structure as a result of a strategy to locate certain centers of competence in areas with high social costs.

- *Supplier risk*: The loss of a critical supplier can disrupt business relationships and affect the production of goods or the provision of services.

- *Business interruption risk*: This risk refers to the partial or total cessation, temporary or permanent, of all or part of a company's activities, leaving it unable to maintain its business cycle or cover operating expenses such as salaries, rent, and insurance.

Operational or internal risks Unlike strategic risks, which are related to the vision of the company's strategic plan, operational risks are related to what happens "on the ground." The concept of operational risk is very broad and directly related to the day-to-day activities of the organization. Operational risk can be defined as the risk of loss resulting from inadequate or failed internal processes, people and systems or from external events (Basel Committee on Banking Supervision, 2006). This definition includes legal risks but excludes strategic risks and reputational risks.

By way of illustration, we can mention the following operational risks: disrupted production due to machine failure, resignation of disgruntled key employees, lost sales due to product quality issues, and non-delivery of ordered equipment. All of these are operational risks because they involve the company's internal resources, systems, processes, and people. The categories listed below provide further examples.

Examples of operational risks (adapted from Darsa, 2016)

- *Risk of internal fraud*: These risks relate to potential losses resulting from misappropriation of assets, tax fraud, abuse of a dominant position, and corruption.

- *Risk of external fraud*: Unlike internal fraud, the potential losses here are related to interactions with elements outside the organization: information theft, hacking, third-party theft, and counterfeiting.

- *Risk related to work practices and safety*: These risks are related to discrimination and workers' compensation, health, and safety.

- *Risk related to clients, products and business practices*: Examples include the risk of manipulation, abusive business practices, product defects, breach of fiduciary duty, and churning.

- *Property loss risk*: These risks relate to potential losses due to natural disasters, terrorism, or vandalism.

- *Business disruption and systems failure risk*: These are risks associated with disruptions caused by the interruption of public services or software or hardware failures.

- *Risk related to the process execution, delivery, and management*: Losses can result from data entry errors, accounting errors, failure to report required information, or loss of client assets due to carelessness.

- *Industrial risk*: Any risk associated with the use of production tools that can affect operational performance, productivity, the supply cycle, storage, distribution, and the safety of people.

- *Legal risk*: These are potential events related to operations, including contractual relationships with customers, suppliers, and employees, that could result in the company being taken to court.

- *Technological risk*: These risks relate to the company's inability to adapt to technological developments in production or operations. They are often related to the company's strategic plan and its investment in research and development.

- *IT risk*: The use of computer systems can result in losses due to cybercrime, failure of digital components, viruses infecting computers, and website hacking.

- *Human resources risk*: There are four categories of human resource risk: personnel, personnel health, management, and human capital (Kessler, 2009). These are social and psychosocial risks related to the management of the company and the individual, respectively. In the case of personnel, examples include the increasing number of claims, low productivity, and personnel management costs. In terms of employee health, the main issue is the increase in absenteeism, followed by absenteeism related to psychosocial risks. In terms of human capital, the risks are increased by the inefficiency of human resources, the increase in turnover, and an unfavorable corporate culture. Lastly, in terms of management, the risks include non-compliance and reduced attractiveness as an employer.

- *Financial risk*: Some of the strategic financial risks listed above may, depending on the company, be operational in nature.

External risks Finally, external risks arise from events outside the company's control. Sources of such risks include major macroeconomic changes, natural disasters, and political changes. External risks require a different approach than internal risks. Because companies cannot prevent these types of events, managing these risks means focusing on identifying them (they tend to be obvious in hindsight) and mitigating their impact through proactive management.

Examples of external risks (see section 1.1 and Darsa, 2016)

- *Environmental risk*: Risks related to losses from natural disasters, weather events, and, in the longer term, climate change.

- *Technological risk*: Rapid technological advances and cyber dependencies can create these risks.

- *Geopolitical risk*: This risk includes potential losses due to interstate conflict and the failure of a country's government.

- *Social risk*: Sources of this risk include the uncontrolled spread of infectious diseases causing disruptions that affect society and the economic health of the company.

- *Economic risk*: This family of risks includes asset bubbles in financial markets, fiscal crises, and structural unemployment.

- *Financial risks*: There are many financial risks, some of which are external to the company. Below is a list of some of the more common risks.

  - *Credit risk*: Financial costs resulting from customer default.
  - *Interest rate risk*: Potential losses related to changes in interest rates and their effect on the company's debt.
  - *Exchange rate risk*: Losses resulting from adverse movements in foreign exchange rates that cause foreign exchange losses.
  - *Financial markets risk*: Losses in the value of investments made with surplus cash as a result of developments in the financial markets.
  - *Risk of takeover*: Change in shareholder base resulting in loss of power.
  - *Risk of sell-off*: This risk can occur as a result of strong disagreement with the company's strategy or financial performance.

We will revisit the risks listed above as we illustrate the various concepts involved, especially when it comes to characterizing the risks in concrete terms.

2.4 Characterization of risks

Many risk classification systems have been developed in Europe and the United States since the first half of the 20th century. The choice of a classification system depends on the circumstances and especially on the reference framework. We introduce here a terminology for risk characterization (Vaughan and Vaughan, 2013), similar to a list of characteristics for a car (make, color, engine size) or a house (number of rooms, size, location).

The guiding principles of this characterization allow us to better understand risks and determine the most appropriate measures to manage them (see chapter 4). The characteristics that we list do not apply equally to all the reference frameworks identified in section 2.2. Other characterizations may be considered. In practice, additional categories may be introduced if this contributes to a more effective assessment or process improvements. The following distinctions are made in this section:

- risks with and without financial consequences,
- dynamic and static risks,
- pure and speculative risks,
- fundamental and particular risks.

Risks with and without financial consequences A risk can be characterized by the nature of its consequences: does it have economic consequences or not? In the broadest definition of the term, a risk exists even if there are no financial consequences. For instance, the risk of death is the potential loss of life that obviously outweighs any associated financial consequences. However, human, emotional, and psychological aspects are often difficult, if not impossible, to quantify, even though they are potentially significant. We primarily examine risks with financial consequences from the point of view of a company and an individual.

Dynamic and static risks There is an important distinction between a dynamic risk and a static risk. Willett (1901) distinguishes between these two classes and emphasizes their importance for risk theory and insurance techniques. The distinction is important to an entrepreneur and his or her positioning with respect to risk. Our understanding of dynamic and static risk is as follows:

Definition 2.3 (*Dynamic risk and static risk*)

> A **dynamic** risk is a risk that results from changes in the economy.
> By contrast, a **static** risk is one that exists in the absence of changes in the economy.

Dynamic risks are related to economic changes such as price fluctuations, consumer trends, and technological developments. Such changes tend to benefit society in the long run, as they lead to adjustments when resources are misallocated. Dynamic risks typically affect large numbers of people but are more difficult to predict than static risks because they do not occur regularly.

Static risks can refer to losses caused by irregular natural events or by human error or misconduct. Static losses exist in an economy that does not change (i.e., a static economy), and static risk is therefore associated with losses that would occur in an unchanging economy. For instance, if all economic variables remained constant, certain people prone to fraud would continue to steal, embezzle, and abuse their positions; as a result, certain entities would continue to suffer financial losses. In the case of static risks, these losses are caused by factors other than changes in the economy, such as natural disasters and the dishonesty of other people. Losses associated with static risks appear to occur periodically and are therefore generally predictable. In most cases, static risks are pure risks (see below). Table 2.1 summarizes the main characteristics of dynamic and static risks.

Dynamic risks	Static risks
• With economic change	• Even in an unchanging economy
• Hard to predict	• Easy to predict
• Can have benefits	• Have no benefits
• Affect many people	• Affect few or very few people
• Mainly speculative risks	• Mainly pure risks

Table 2.1: Main characteristics of dynamic and static risks.

Pure and speculative risks Pure risks are associated with events whose occurrence has only negative or neutral consequences. These are typically risks related to property, personal liability, or people. Speculative risks, on the other hand, can have either positive or negative consequences. Examples include business decisions and stock market investments. Our definition is as follows:

Definition 2.4 (*Pure risk and speculative risk*)

*A **pure** risk is a risk associated with events whose occurrence can only have negative consequences.*
*By contrast, a **speculative** risk is a risk associated with events whose occurrence can have either positive or negative consequences.*

With pure risks, there is no prospect of benefit or profit—they are generally beyond one's control. They cannot be completely avoided, and at best, they can be mitigated. In the case of a building fire, for example, the owner does not benefit from the risk. Unless a fire occurs, the status quo is maintained. From a risk management perspective, efforts can be made to reduce the likelihood of the risk occurring, as well as the severity of the risk if it does occur. We will discuss risk management techniques in section 4.3. Pure risks can generally be covered by insurance. Individuals and companies are exposed to different types of pure risks that threaten different types of values. We classify pure risks according to the following typology:

- property risks (with direct and indirect losses),

- liability risks,

- personal risks,

- net income,

In section 2.7, as we look at the types of exposed values, we will discuss the values affected by these risks.

Examples of the four types of pure risks

- *Property risk*: This risk relates to direct and indirect losses that may affect movable property (e.g., the risk of theft or damage to a piece of equipment), real estate (e.g., the risk of fire in a building), or intangible assets (e.g., the risk of theft of identity or invention).

- *Liability risk*: This refers to potential losses associated with civil or criminal liability. For example, damage to other people's property or injury caused to other people makes the person who caused the damage or injury civilly liable for compensation.

- *Personal risk*: This refers to damage to a person's physical integrity, such as death, injury, or illness. In certain cases, this results in economic losses: a death results in a significant loss of income for a household—especially if the deceased was the main financial contributor— and a serious injury or illness may prevent a person from working, resulting in a loss of income. Personal risks may also involve direct economic risks, such as the risk of unemployment or inadequate income in retirement.

- *Net income risk*: This type of risk relates to economic losses that affect an organization's income or economic objectives. Examples include risks arising from the failure of a third party (for example, the risk that a borrower will default, i.e., fail to make the required payments) and the risk of business interruption.

Speculative risks, which are associated with events whose occurrence may have negative, positive, or neutral consequences, are risks to which exposure is generally intentional. For example, by investing in the stock market or a company, or by speculating on currencies, one is exposed to the risk of fluctuations in the value of the investment. If the stock price rises or the exchange rate moves in a favorable direction, a profit is made. Conversely, if the situation is unfavorable, a loss occurs. If prices do not change, there are no consequences. Speculative risks cannot generally be covered by insurance. Table 2.2 lists the main characteristics of pure and speculative risks.

Pure risks	Speculative risks
• Negative consequences	• Positive or negative consequences
• Generally no control	• Generally intentional exposure
• Generally insurable	• Generally not insurable
• Often static risks	• Often dynamic risks
• Four types: property, liability, personal, net income	

Table 2.2: Main characteristics of pure and speculative risks.

Fundamental and particular risks Fundamental risks, also known as systemic or systematic risks, arise from the natural, technological, social, or economic environment. These risks are, therefore, non-discriminatory and impersonal in both their origin and their consequences; they generally affect a wide range of people, or even everyone. What is meant by "most people" depends on the reference framework and the context. On a global scale, the risk of a pandemic is certainly fundamental; on the scale of an entire industry, the risk of unemployment may be fundamental. Losses caused by macroeconomic conditions are also related to fundamental risks, as the entire economy and all economic agents are affected at the same time (Louisot, 2014). In finance, the term "systemic risk" refers to a financial risk that affects an entire economy and threatens the stability of a market or of the financial system as a whole, as opposed to a single firm.

Conversely, particular risks—also called specific risks—affect an individual, a company, or a group of specific individuals or companies, but not all individuals or companies. Their impact is, therefore, local, not global. Certain risks are more particular, such as the risk of fire in a carpentry shop.

The line between a fundamental risk and a particular risk may be blurred, and the categorization depends on the context. It is important to know the reference framework on which the analysis is based. For a given risk to be considered fundamental, most of the elements in the reference framework must be affected. The risk of a strong Swiss franc can illustrate our point: from the perspective of the tourism industry or certain industrial activities with significant exports, this risk is fundamental because it affects most companies. However, from the perspective of all companies on the continent or from the perspective of a local company, this risk of a strong Swiss franc is considered to be particular: it only affects certain industries in Switzerland, such as tourism or exports.

Definition 2.5 (*Fundamental risk and particular risk*)

A **fundamental** risk is a risk caused by the environment (whether natural, technological, geopolitical, social, or economic) that affects most people.
By contrast, a **particular** risk is a risk that affects a specific individual, company, or group without affecting all individuals or companies.

From an insurance perspective, a fundamental risk cannot be insured because it cannot be diversified. Because such risks occur simultaneously for everyone rather than randomly, it is impossible to create a diversified portfolio of uncorrelated risks. For example, there are no insurance policies that cover losses due to a deterioration in the economic environment or business interruption caused by a pandemic. By contrast, particular risks are specific to each entity, not systematic and diversifiable (Baranoff et al., 2019). For example, a fire in one building is typically unrelated to a fire in another building some distance away. This allows an insurer to build a balanced portfolio that covers many buildings over a large area. It is the law of large numbers (see chapter 6) that allows the insurer to predict the number of claims with sufficient accuracy to calculate insurance premiums.

Emerging risks In several publications, the Swiss Insurance Association (2018) examines emerging risks. These risks are new or unknown, dynamically evolving, only partially identified, and generally characterized by a high degree of uncertainty. Their costs they are difficult to estimate, posing significant challenges for governments, businesses, and liability insurers. While new technologies and changes in our behavior are seen as opportunities, they also present risks that are difficult to predict. These risks are associated with developments we are seeing in many areas, such as the Internet of Things, autonomous transportation, robotics, nanotechnology, functional foods, and genetically modified organisms.

2.5 Characterization of risk exposures

Now that we have classified risks, we will introduce the concept of risk exposure. Risk exposure, or loss exposure, is any possibility of loss arising from an identified risk, whether pure or speculative.

Definition 2.6 (*Risk exposure*)

A **risk exposure** *is any possibility of loss resulting from a risk.*

We place every risk exposure in a three-dimensional system:

- perils that can cause loss (and hazards that promote loss),
- values exposed to loss,
- potential financial consequences of a loss.

In sections 2.6, 2.7, and 3.1, we provide details on each of these dimensions, along with definitions of relevant terms. The diagram in figure 2.1 provides a synoptic view of the concepts involved in characterizing risk exposure.

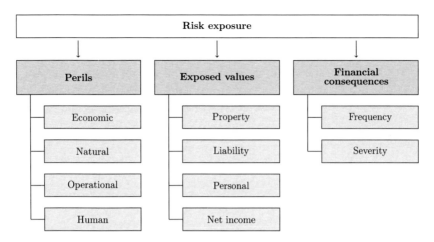

Figure 2.1: Characterization diagram for risk exposure.

Example of a risk exposure analysis

To illustrate the characterization of a risk exposure, consider the following situation: A university professor rides his electric bicycle to campus every day. On his way, he is exposed to the risk of a traffic accident. How can we characterize the risk exposure associated with this commute, taking the professor as a private individual as the reference framework?

The peril, or cause, is obviously an accident. The conditions that increase the likelihood of loss, i.e., the hazards, can be varied, for example, a slippery road, fog, or fatigue.

This is a triple exposure to loss because three types of values are exposed, and the magnitude of the financial consequences is different for each:

- First, in the event of an accident, the professor may be injured, disabled, or even killed. The type of exposed value is his *person*. The consequences can be catastrophic, and the financial losses significant, especially in the case of disability.

- Then, his bicycle may be damaged or destroyed. The type of exposed value here is his *property*. The financial consequences are not negligible, but they remain relatively moderate.

- Finally, he may be civilly liable for the accident. This means that he is responsible for losses that the accident may cause to other people. The type of exposed value here is his *liability* and his wealth. The potential financial consequences can be even more significant than in the first exposed value because several people can be victims of this accident caused by the professor.

We note that the government has already become involved in risk management, at least in part, through regulation, by requiring liability insurance for drivers, as well as accident insurance and affiliation to a pension fund for employees to cover the risk of vital losses for their family.

Keeping the same example, but this time in the reference framework of the university as an institution, this commute by electric bicycle is also an exposure to losses for the university, with the same peril. In this case, the exposed value is that of a person, a member of the organization's staff. In this case, the potential financial consequences are the costs incurred as a result of the professor's long-term absence.

In the next section, we will look at the classification of perils and hazards and specify the types of exposed values.

2.6 Perils and hazards

The terms "peril" and "hazard" are often confused and used interchangeably. They are also sometimes confused with the term "risk." In this section, we will explain what these terms refer to and how to clearly distinguish between them.

Definition of the term "peril" Having defined risk (definition 2.1 in section 2.1) and risk exposure (definition 2.6 in section 2.5), we now introduce the concept of peril. It refers to the cause or source of the adverse event that results in a loss. In other words, it is the event that causes the loss. There can be no loss without an identifiable peril. However, a single loss can have multiple perils. There are many examples of this, including fire, earthquake, road accident, sabotage, etc. Our definition is as follows:

Definition 2.7 (*Peril*)

Peril *is the cause of the adverse event that results in a loss.*

The words "peril" and "causes" can be used interchangeably when associated with the concept of risk. For example, in the case of death, multiple perils are possible: a person may die from a disease, an accident, suicide, an act of war, and so on. In the case of a house burning down, the peril is the fire itself. In winter, if a person is caught in an avalanche, the avalanche is the peril or cause of the accident.

Classification of perils Like Louisot (2014), who provided the inspiration for this section, we use a two-dimensional system to classify perils. Our approach is to analyze:

- the location of the origin,
- the nature of the phenomenon.

The origin location criterion means classifying the peril based on whether it is endogenous or exogenous. This definition refers to the entity's control and aims to determine whether the cause is within or outside the entity's control.

> **Definition 2.8 (*Endogenous and exogenous peril*)**
>
> *A peril is said to be **endogenous** when it is created by the entity or individual within its sphere of control.*
> *By contrast, a peril is called **exogenous** when it is created outside the control of the entity or individual.*

A fire that starts in an individual's home or on the premises of a business is an endogenous peril to the individual or the business. An exogenous cause of business interruption risk for a company is, for example, a neighboring business being affected by a sit-in strike that blocks the entire area in which the company is located. A strike is an endogenous peril for the neighboring business but an exogenous peril for the company in question. We note here the importance of the reference framework chosen.

The second dimension has to do with the nature of the phenomenon involved in the peril. We identify four classes:

> **Definition 2.9 (*Economic, natural, operational, and human peril*)**
>
> – *An **economic** peril is a sudden change in an economic parameter that affects the individual's or company's environment and causes an immediate and significant constraint.*
> – *A **natural** peril is a cause resulting from the action of the forces of nature.*
> – *An **operational** peril is not the direct cause of human action but of productive activities driven by human action.*
> – *A **human** peril is a cause triggered by human action or inaction.*

Thus, an economic peril may involve the action or inaction of a large number of people or a government, causing a sudden change in a parameter that affects the economic environment. Examples include a strike, a boycott, a civil war, and a change in consumer preferences. The removal of the CHF/EUR exchange rate cap by the Swiss National Bank in 2015 (see section 1.3) was an economic cause that resulted in immediate financial losses.

The forces of nature lead to natural perils. Humans have little or no control over these forces, which include earthquakes, hurricanes and cyclones, hail, floods, and wildfires. Other phenomena, such as lightning strikes, tsunamis, and epidemics, sometimes add to the devastating power of these natural catastrophes. For a given peril (e.g., an earthquake), such phenomena may be considered either as a secondary peril or as a physical hazard, i.e., a condition that increases the probability of loss (see below). For instance, in the context of an earthquake, a tsunami may be considered as a separate peril or as a condition that aggravates losses, particularly in coastal locations.

Operational perils include all events caused by a malfunction in the operation of production systems, such as a fire or a machine breaking or failing. This class typically includes most of the causes of accidents that occur in companies.

Losses can be caused by the action or inaction of a single person or a small group of people. A theft, an accident due to negligence or incompetence, and a fire due to arson or negligence are all caused by individuals. That is, they are human perils. However, it should be noted that a human peril can be intentional or unintentional. Therefore, we present a more precise definition:

Definition 2.10 (*Intentional and unintentional human peril*)

> An **intentional** human peril is the result of a deliberate or conscious act by an individual or group of individuals.
> By contrast, an **unintentional** human peril is the result of an error, omission, or negligence.

An unintentional human peril can result from an action, error, or negligence either at the time of the event—for example, a lit cigarette butt discarded near flammable material—or before the event—for example, a flood caused by poorly sealed walls in a basement surrounded by wet ground.

In the case of intentional human perils, the person causing the peril typically wants to cause harm or take someone's property. Their intent may or may not be malicious. If there is no malicious intent, the actor might be called a "crafty actor." For example, this type of peril can result from legitimate actions by a user who makes undocumented changes to a system to improve its performance or facilitate the work of other users. A subsequent user may be unaware of the changes and follow the original process, causing an accident. Another illustration of this concept is as follows: A truck driver must take a 45-minute break after driving for 4.5 hours. He asks his or her employer to end the shift one hour earlier for personal reasons. To make this possible, the employer exceptionally allows the driver to take a shorter break so that the final performance is not affected. There is no malicious intent, but this action increases the likelihood of an accident caused by the driver's inattention. As we will see later, we can also think of the behavior as increasing the likelihood of loss and, therefore, call this behavior a moral hazard that increases the potential loss associated with the risk of an accident.

When an intentional human peril is called malicious, it emphasizes the intent to cause harm or to take an asset that does not belong to you. These are illegal acts. We distinguish between malicious acts committed for profit, such as industrial espionage, and those committed without a profit motive, such as arson committed for revenge. The former is an illegal act that follows the traditional economic model; in the latter, the perpetrators act for a cause, such as vandalism or terrorism, whose motives are more difficult to identify. The cause of the WTC attacks of September 11, 2001, referred to in section 1.2, can be characterized as human, intentional, malicious, but without a profit motive. Intentional human peril is one of the most difficult to manage. It must be recognized and requires frequent action and adaptation. A particularly striking example is the fight against computer viruses, which requires constant vigilance.

Figure 2.2 provides a table to help classify perils.

Nature of the phenomenon

Location of the origin	economic	natural	operational	human			
				intentional			unintentional
				crafty actor	malicious with …		
					profit motive	no profit motive	
endogenous							
exogenous							

Figure 2.2: Peril classification table (adapted from Louisot, 2014).

Definition of the term "hazard" A hazard is a danger that creates or increases the likelihood that a loss will occur. Unlike a peril, a hazard is not the element that triggers the loss; it is not the cause. Rather, it is a condition or context that makes the situation riskier. In other words, a hazard can exist without a cause ever occurring.

Definition 2.11 (*Hazard*)

> A **hazard** is a condition that creates or increases the probability of occurrence of the adverse event that causes a loss.

Obviously, the concept of hazard is closely related to that of peril: depending on the peril being analyzed, the hazard is different. We have seen earlier that sometimes, in order to describe a risk exposure, a particular element can be considered either a peril or a hazard. For example, in road traffic, if the relevant peril for the risk of death is an accident, the hazards that increase the probability of suffering a loss include an icy road, high speed, and driver inattention. Depending on the goal of the analysis, it could also be argued that the icy road, high speed, or driver inattention is ultimately the cause of death and, therefore, the peril.

The choice of a reference framework and a peril is key to determining the presence of hazards. In practice, the risk manager sets the framework for his or her analyses, and it is essential to follow the logic of his or her reasoning to its conclusion. Lastly, it should be noted that—as in the road traffic example above—there are often multiple hazards associated with a given loss.

Types of hazards Like Vaughan and Vaughan (2013) and Borghesi and Gaudenzi (2013), we identify two main types of hazards:

> **Definition 2.12 (*Physical hazards and moral hazards*)**
>
> A **physical hazard** *is an objective physical condition that increases the probability of occurrence of the adverse event.*
>
> *By contrast, a* **moral hazard** *consists of a person's dishonesty or personality problem that increases the probability of occurrence of the adverse event.*

Examples of physical hazards include, for the peril of a traffic accident, an icy road, and, for the peril of a fire, the presence of flammable products in a storage area. Examples of moral hazards include the behavior of a disloyal employee, a highly negligent person, or a driver who frequently speeds. While our definitions state that the likelihood of the adverse event occurring is increased by a hazard, the severity of the event may also be increased (e.g., by a speeding driver).

For insurance specialists, there is an important difference in moral hazards. They make a subtle distinction between "moral hazard" and "morale hazard." Morale hazards are related to indifference or carelessness toward the possibility of loss because of the existence of insurance coverage. An example is a person who leaves their laptop computer in their car without hiding it, knowing that the insurance will pay if the laptop is stolen. Another example is the owner of a house with fire insurance who is having financial difficulties and decides to deliberately burn down their house in order to receive compensation. If this carelessness is the result of insurance coverage, then it is a morale hazard.

In addition to the above hazards, there is also legal hazard. This refers to the increased likelihood of loss as a result of legislation, legal doctrine, and case law. This legal risk is significant in the area of civil liability in certain jurisdictions. It also exists in the case of property risks. For instance, if building codes require new buildings to comply with certain legal requirements, demolition of an older, non-compliant building may require an owner to incur additional rebuilding costs, thereby increasing their exposure to loss.

Distinction between risk, peril, and hazard Although it may sometimes seem difficult to distinguish between them, the terms "risk," "peril," and "hazard" refer to very different concepts. To make the distinction clear, we present a three-level hierarchy. "Risk" is the top level and includes the other two. A risk is associated with its perils and hazards. The risk also defines the exposed values and the potential financial consequences, both of which we will cover later (see also figure 2.1). At the second level of the hierarchy are the perils. Each peril has a number of hazards. These are the final levels of the analysis. As a practical example, consider the risk of a building catching fire. In this case, there are many perils: for example, a fire or an explosion. For each of these perils, we can imagine a number of hazards. For example, for the peril of explosion, the hazards could be an employee mishandling a product or terrorism.

In the example given at the end of section 2.5, and depending on the context, the peril may be specified to some extent. In the analysis of the example, one could have specified the peril by providing more information about the accident's origin, which could be related to high speed or inattention. When the peril is specified, the hazards must also be reviewed. The role of the risk manager is to adjust and reframe the analysis. There are often multiple ways to interpret and specify a given situation.

2.7 Types of values exposed to losses

When we refer to risk exposure (definition 2.6 in section 2.5), the type of exposed value determines what is affected by the realization of the risk.

Definition 2.13 (*Exposed value*)
The **exposed value** refers to the type of loss resulting from the realization of the adverse event.

Of course, a single event can cause losses that belong to more than one type of value. In general, economic values exposed to risk can be classified into one of the following four categories:

- property,
- liability,
- person,
- net income.

Property Property values can be divided into tangible values, which have a physical reality, i.e., things, and intangible values, which have no physical reality. Tangible values include real property—for example, land, buildings, and man-made structures—and movable assets—for example, equipment, machinery, furniture, hardware, and raw materials. Intangible values include information, patents, and manufacturing and operating licenses.

Property losses can be direct, i.e., losses caused primarily by the total or partial destruction or deterioration of property values. Losses can also be indirect. In this case, they are the consequences of direct losses, such as the costs of demolition and removal of debris and unusable property, increased construction costs, and the diminution in value of undamaged property.

Liability This type of loss is closely related to the concept of civil and criminal liability. Generally speaking, civil liability is the obligation to compensate for damages caused to others by one's fault or in cases established by law. However, the concept of liability depends on both legislation and case law. It varies from country to country and over time. Each individual or company must, therefore, be aware of the specifics of the countries with which they are in contact.

Civil and criminal liability in Switzerland

In Switzerland, a distinction is made between civil and criminal liability. In civil law, liability is defined by the Swiss Code of Obligations (Swiss Confederation, 2023, article 41, paragraph 1): "Any person who unlawfully causes damage to another, whether wilfully or negligently, is obliged to provide compensation." All persons, whether natural or legal, are bound by this law. The conditions for liability are an unlawful act, damage, a fault—which is presumed in the case of contractual liability—, and a natural and adequate causal link between the fault and the damage.

According to article 42, the claimant, i.e., the injured part, bears the burden of proving the damage and a sufficient causal relationship between the fault and the damage. The claimant must also prove that a fault has been committed in cases of criminal liability. The fault may be intentional or the result of negligence or breach of the duty of care. Negligence may be gross or slight. Gross negligence occurs when a person failed to take reasonable precautions or measures when the circumstances were such that they should have taken such precautions or measures. Negligence is slight if the fault could have been committed by anyone in the same circumstances.

With respect to criminal liability, the goal is to sanction an act rather than to remedy a loss. Involuntary homicide, unintentional injury, and property damage are criminal offenses punishable by a fine or imprisonment. A criminal can be committed intentionally, negligently, or recklessly.

There are different types of civil liability, depending on the nature of the damage. In the examples of civil liability listed below, it is possible to reduce the amount you have to pay out of pocket by purchasing liability insurance (see section 5.4).

Examples of civil liability

- *Personal liability*: This liability applies to any natural person and relates to damage caused either by the person as an individual or by their children or pets, for example.

- *Landlord's civil liability*: Losses caused by a landlord's property—for example, tiles falling from the roof and causing injury or a leak in the oil tank polluting the groundwater—involve the landlord's civil liability.

- *Vehicle owner's liability*: The owner of a vehicle is liable for any damage caused by an accident involving the vehicle.

- *Professional liability*: This liability is linked to errors made by a lawyer, notary, editor, or doctor in the performance of their duties.

- *Commercial liability*: This includes any damage caused by a company to a third party or to the property of a third party.

- *Product liability*: Product liability relates to losses caused by products sold by a company, such as food, drugs, machinery, and software.

Person Losses suffered by an individual may be related to his or her total or partial inability to work due to illness, accident, death, retirement, resignation, or unemployment. In this context, both the person's employer and family suffer a loss. For the company, the loss consists primarily of lost production, costs associated with filling the vacancy, and administrative costs. For the individual and his or her family, the costs are divided between the medical expenses, if necessary, and the loss of earnings in terms of income and consumption.

The losses suffered by the family may be partially compensated by personal, social, or private insurance. Depending on the cause, the losses may be partially covered by health insurance (LAMal), loss of earnings compensation (APG), accident insurance (AA), invalidity insurance (AI), unemployment insurance (AC), old age and survivors' insurance (AVS), and the pension fund (see sections 1.4 and 5.2). For instance, in the event of death, the AVS pays a widow's or widower's pension to the surviving spouse and an orphan's pension to the children. Accident insurance covers the financial consequences of both occupational and non-occupational accidents.

Net income A company's net income is equal to its revenues minus its costs over a given period. A loss of net income can therefore be caused by lower revenues, higher costs, or both. It affects the company's economic objective or profit. Potential losses can result from a variety of situations.

Examples of loss of net income situations

- *Business interruption*: An accident can force a company to suspend all or part of its activities. The potential loss is then mainly related to the decrease in production.

- *Contingent business interruption*: A contingent business interruption is the interruption of a company's activities as a result of an event outside the company. For example, this interruption may be the result of an accidental event at a neighboring company or the bankruptcy of a major supplier.

- *Loss of expected profit on finished goods*: The destruction of finished goods, for example, by fire, is a loss of both property value—through the cost of replacing the goods—and net income—through the profit that would have been earned on those goods.

- *Loss of rental income*: The deterioration or destruction of movable or immovable property that could have been rented out if it had not been damaged results in a loss of rental income. This is an obvious consequence of, for example, a fire in a rental building.

- *Loss of active debt recovery*: This potential loss can occur when a business is unable to bill its customers. A business interruption can also cause a contingent business interruption among key customers, leaving them unable to pay their bills.

- *Increase in operating expenses*: As a result of an accidental event, a company may be forced to reorganize its production processes, move production to a new location, or hire additional personnel, thereby increasing its operating costs.

- *Decision-making error related to a speculative risk*: With a broad understanding of the term "accidental" event, which refers to any event not planned by the entity, any decision that involves some degree of uncertainty—for example, which products and services to offer, which technologies to use, which business strategy to adopt—can be considered to be an earnings-related risk exposure because it may affect the entity's economic objective.

As noted above, a single event can cause the loss of multiple types of value. Considering the examples of the Sandoz warehouse fire in Basel in November 1986, the WTC attacks of September 11, 2001 (section 1.2), the explosion and subsequent fire at the AZF plant in Toulouse in the same year, the explosion of the Deepwater Horizon offshore oil rig in the Gulf of Mexico in April 2010, the crash of the Germanwings plane in the Alps in March 2015, or the explosions at the port of Beirut in August 2020, we see that in addition to direct property damage (buildings, machinery, products), losses also occurred in other categories. Indirect losses (property), such as the costs associated with evacuation and land rehabilitation, are much more significant in many cases. In each case, losses are recorded in terms of liability, i.e., civil liability towards all persons and organizations directly or indirectly affected by the event. The loss of value associated with people injured or killed was particularly significant in the above examples. Finally, these events caused business interruption losses to the affected companies: these indirect losses are not classified as property losses but as loss of net income.

CHAPTER 3

Risk appreciation

Having defined the concept of risk in chapter 2, it is time to take a closer look at the appreciation of risks. The first step in appreciating risks is to identify them. This consists of understanding their causes and determining the exposed values (see chapters 2 and 4). Then comes the analysis and assessment of the risks. One of the elements that characterizes a risk exposure (see figure 2.1 and section 2.5) is the potential financial impact of a risk. Risk analysis begins with knowing the potential frequency and severity of the risk. This information is essential for risk assessment in order to select the most appropriate risk management technique (see section 4.3). This is because these techniques work by attempting to limit the probability of an adverse event occurring and to reduce the severity of the losses incurred. Knowing how to measure a risk also makes it possible to evaluate the effect of measures taken to manage it.

We begin this chapter by introducing the basic elements needed to analyze a risk exposure (see section 3.1), then discuss how to measure the indicators and what criteria are relevant for assessing the financial consequences (see section 3.2). If we describe the exposure to loss using random variables, then there are several criteria available for a risk assessment that aims to produce a deterministic value. In section 3.5, we examine and discuss the assessment using the expected value criterion and then present the expected utility criterion, which takes into account risk aversion, among other factors. Lastly, we go beyond the study of average loss to look at extreme losses and conclude the chapter by presenting the value-at-risk criterion and related criteria. For this purpose, we recall mathematical concepts related to random variables, probability theory, and utility (see sections 3.3 and 3.4).

3.1 Analysis of a risk exposure

Frequency and severity   There are two parameters to consider when analyzing a risk exposure. The first is frequency, which measures the probability of the event occurring. Frequency can be expressed as the number of events per unit of time. Here, we establish a direct relationship with the measure of probability and consider it to be a value between 0 and 1: a value of 0 means a zero percent probability, i.e., the event cannot possibly occur; a value of 1 means a one-hundred-percent probability, i.e., the event is certain to occur. We use the following definition:

Definition 3.1 (*Frequency*)

Frequency *is the probability of occurrence of the adverse event causing a loss.*

In the simplest model, frequency is a number between 0 and 1. We often exclude the bounds 0 and 1 to focus on situations where the event is neither impossible (frequency of 0%) nor certain (frequency of 100%). Note that there are more advanced models in which frequency is described by a random variable and thus a probability distribution (see section 3.3). The frequency gives information about the probability of an event. It can apply to past events as well as potential future events.

The second parameter is known as severity and refers to the amount of potential loss for a given adverse event. It is a measure of the consequences—i.e., the impact—of an event on objectives. Our definition of severity is as follows:

Definition 3.2 (*Severity*)

Severity *is the amount of loss incurred if the adverse event occurs.*

Severity is most often described in terms of a random variable. It is, therefore, characterized by a probability distribution that describes the occurrence of each amount of loss. Describing the severity of a risk exposure as high is a statement about the distribution of that random variable. In other words, if the event occurs, there is a higher probability of significant losses than for a risk exposure with low severity (see section 3.5).

Risk exposure mapping   The frequency and severity parameters are not of the same nature, and together, they define risk exposure. In other words, to evaluate the level of risk or the significance of a risk, the combination of frequency and severity must be evaluated. Saying that the frequency is high says nothing about the severity. Similarly, to say that the severity of a risk exposure is high is to evaluate the distribution of potential losses, not the frequency of the event.

Many events can have a high frequency but low severity, such as minor manufacturing defects in a mass production process or individuals in the population catching a cold. Conversely, certain events—such as a nuclear accident or a plane crash—can have major consequences and therefore high severity, but fortunately their probability of occurrence is quite low, often due to reinforced risk management.

At first, a traditional approach is to classify risk exposures based on their frequency and severity, using a matrix or diagram as in figure 3.1.

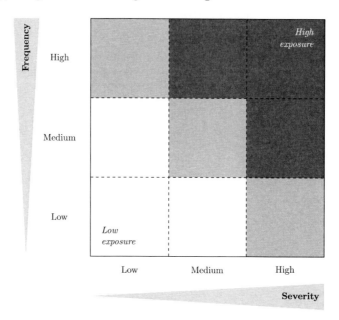

Figure 3.1: Frequency – severity diagram for a risk exposure.

This diagram provides a canvas on which to place risk exposures along two axes: frequency (vertical) and severity (horizontal). Our first approach is to divide the severity axis into three groups: "low," "medium," and "high." We do the same with the frequency axis, with the groups "low," "medium," and "high." The diagram thus shows nine areas that can be used to group risk exposures. These areas are often shaded or colored to represent high, medium, and low absolute risk. In the upper right corner of the graph are risk exposures that are characterized by both high frequency and high severity. We call these risk exposures "high." In the other corner, at the bottom left of the graph, are low-severity and low-frequency risk exposures. We call these exposures "low."

In practice, low risk exposures are acceptable without special measures, but high risk exposures are unacceptable and require measures to manage and control the risks (see chapter 4). These techniques can reduce the absolute level of risk. Thus, a risk exposure that is considered high in the overall risk mapping (figure 3.1) may be considered medium or low in the net risk mapping, i.e., after risk control measures have been implemented. It should be noted that the decision to consider a risk exposure as acceptable or not depends on risk acceptance. This is the level of overall risk that one is willing to accept. We characterize this aspect using the risk aversion coefficient introduced in section 3.4.

Ideally, risk management measures should be taken for all identified risks. However, in the real world, with its associated constraints—for example, economic and budgetary limitations—, risk owners must prioritize which risk exposures to address and make decisions about how to manage each risk. The position of a given risk exposure in this diagram indicates the level of priority it should be given when implementing a risk management program. These matrices are designed to be practical, and they can initially be created without highly accurate calculations to quantify frequency values and severity distributions. An example of this type of analysis is shown in figure 1.1, where certain global risks were placed in the matrix based on responses to a survey.

The canvas we present uses qualitative labels for the frequency and severity axes. In the absence of numerical values, the distinction between the terms used ("low," "medium," etc.) can lead to uncertainty and debate about the categories, depending on the context and culture of the reader. Several studies have investigated the different ways in which such scales are understood and interpreted. For example, the experimental and linguistic study conducted by Blum et al. (2019) analyzes the correspondence between the terminology used to refer to probability and the actual numerical probabilities in different contexts.

However, it should be noted that it is sometimes difficult to make objective assessments of risks for which no data are available. There could also be discussions about what is meant by a "high frequency" or "high severity" risk exposure. What are the thresholds at which we decide that a given severity is "low," "medium," or "high"? For frequency, since its value is between 0% and 100%, some might be tempted to suggest the following division: "low" frequencies are between 0% and 33%, "medium" frequencies are between 33% and 67%, and "high" frequencies are between 67% and 100%. However, this division does not make much sense. Can you really say that a risk that has a 30% probability of occurring has a "low" frequency? For this reason, the categories are typically not quantified precisely in the first step. The second step is to work in depth to define the relevant thresholds for each axis. Occasionally, the time horizon of the study can help to agree on the thresholds for the frequency classes (e.g., by distinguishing between events that occur once a month, once a year, or once a century). Establishing links between severity classes and the organization's revenues or net income can also be helpful. In professional practice, we find similar frequency-severity matrices, though sometimes with more or fewer sections, the idea being that the risk manager can tailor the canvas to the organization's needs (for an illustration, see the example in figure 3.2).

Correlations between risk exposures

The approach outlined above considers each risk exposure separately and ig-
nores correlations between different exposures. These correlations can exist
between different risk exposures but also for the same exposure at different
points in time. Here are some examples.

- *Correlations over time*: Natural catastrophes such as earthquakes and
  floods are often followed by similar events over a period of time. If a risk
  exposure is described as centennial, i.e., if its frequency is such that an
  event occurs on average once every 100 years, this does not mean that
  the next event will occur in 100 years and the next in 200 years. The
  occurrence of two events in a relatively short period of time cannot be
  ruled out, especially in the case of natural disasters. For example, an
  earthquake is often followed by several aftershocks.

- *Frequency between exposures*: There may be a relationship between the
  frequencies of different risk exposures. For example, an objective probability of a workplace accident in a construction company can be observed
  based on statistics published by insurers or official bodies. If the prevention measures implemented by a particular company are not in line with
  industry standards, the frequency of accidents is likely to be significantly
  higher than indicated by the statistics for the industry as a whole. It can
  be assumed that a company's inability to implement effective prevention
  measures will have consequences in other areas, and therefore, its overall
  risk exposure will be higher than generally accepted in the industry.

Despite the inaccuracies mentioned above and the qualitative nature of the approach, this type of canvas can help highlight risks that need to be prioritized, i.e.,
those that are located in the top and right areas of the chart.

Example of risk mapping

As a concrete example, figure 3.2 illustrates the mapping of risks for a
pharmaceutical company. The risks listed are all the major risks identified
during the company's risk identification process (see section 4.2). First, there
are the civil liability (CL) risks, whose type of exposed value belongs to the
"liability" category (see section 2.7). These are CL risks related to motor
vehicles (1), products (2), clinical trials (3), operations (4), the fiduciary
role (5), the environment (6), and patent violations (7). Then, people-related
risks refer to losses resulting from the actions of natural persons. These
include workplace accidents (8), third-party CL (9), directors and officers'
CL (10), employer's CL (11), the defection of key managers (12), and theft
committed by an employee (13). Then come risks in the "terror," "damage,"
and "operating losses" categories. These include the intentional deterioration
of products (14) and unlawful acts such as theft, kidnapping, or terrorist

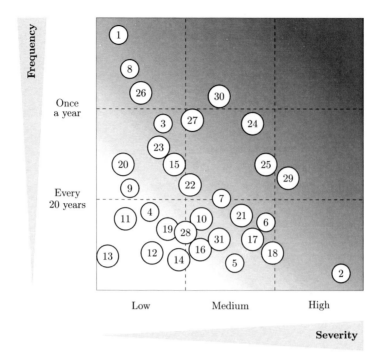

Civil liability (CL)
1. CL motor vehicles
2. CL products
3. Clinical trials
4. Operational CL
5. Fiduciary
6. Environmental CL
7. Patent violation

Persons
8. Workplace accidents
9. Third-party CL
10. Directors and officers CL
11. Employers CL
12. Defection of key managers
13. Theft committed by an employee

Malicious risks
14. Intentional product deterioration
15. Theft, kidnapping, terrorist attack, etc.

Damage, operating losses
16. Fire, explosion, etc.
17. Natural catastrophes
18. Operating losses
19. Machinery breakdown
20. Transportation
21. Product recall
22. Loss of data

Financial risks
23. Credit risk
24. Foreign exchange rate
25. Investment in research
26. Interests
27. Negative publicity
28. Pension funds

Risks related to new regulations
29. Mandatory recall
30. Denial or delay of approval

Political risks
31. Political risks, conflicts

Figure 3.2: Illustration of risk exposure mapping for a pharmaceutical company (adapted from Swiss Re, 1999).

attacks (15). Then there are the risks of fire and explosion (16), natural catastrophes (17), operating losses (18), machinery breakdown (19), transportation (20), product recalls (21), and loss of data (22). There are also financial risks related to credit (23), foreign exchange rates (24), investment in research (25), interests (26), negative publicity (27), and pension funds (28). We also identify risks related to new regulations and, in particular, to drug approvals by the relevant national authorities. Notable among these are the risk of mandatory recall (29) and the risk of denial or delay of approval (30). Finally, there are political risks and conflicts (31). This is not an exhaustive list, but it illustrates the variety of risks that must be considered in practice.

The graph gives an idea of the magnitude of the exposures associated with each of the risks listed above. The vertical axis indicates the frequency of occurrence, with three categories ranging from "once a year" to "every 20 years." These values refer to the average probability of an adverse event occurring over a given period of time, once a year and once every 20 years, respectively. The horizontal axis indicates the severity, which in this case can be expressed as a percentage of annual profits.

Of the risk exposures shown, we note that risks (29) and (30), as well as risks (24) and (25), are among the highest. Risks related to drug approvals in various markets are very significant, as any delay, expiration, revocation, or suspension of approval has a direct impact on earnings. In the case of an international company, exchange rates (24) often present a risk of volatility. With respect to investments in research (25), it should be noted that a pharmaceutical company initiates costly research programs to develop new drugs with no prior assurance that the investments will yield a return. Many therapeutic products do not pass clinical trials and are not approved for sale, in which case part of the investment is lost.

Finally, let us take a closer look at risk exposures (1) and (2). Motor vehicle CL is an exposure that is very frequent due to the high number of traffic accidents, but that results in low severity losses at the level of a company. This is because motor vehicle CL is covered by mandatory insurance policies, which means that the main cost incurred by the company is related to the deductible provided in the policy (see risk financing techniques, which we will study in section 4.3). For the product CL related to drugs, it can lead to enormous costs and threaten the existence of the company if, for example, a drug is ineffective or has quality problems or side effects. The level of severity is high, but fortunately, the frequency can be limited by extensive clinical trials and quality control.

Objective probability and subjective probability To determine the probability of loss for a given risk exposure, we must evaluate the probability of an adverse event occurring. An individual uncertain event can be characterized by two types of probability: objective probability and subjective probability.

Definition 3.3 (*Objective probability*)

Objective probability *is the relative frequency with which an event occurs in the long term, based on the hypothesis of an infinite number of independent observations made under identical conditions.*

The definition of objective probability refers to an "infinite" number of observations made "in the long term" of "independent" events under "identical" conditions. These factors are difficult to obtain in the real world. In practice, a probability is considered objective if statistics are available over a (very) large ($\neq$infinite) number of events over several years (how many years is long term?). This is the case, for example, with observations on the prevalence of certain diseases or traffic accidents (see section 1.3): statistics are available over several decades and make it possible to estimate the number of events and, therefore, the probability of their occurrence, with a fair degree of accuracy. However, although the observations are (relatively) independent, the conditions are often only (very) approximately identical. For example, car accidents may have occurred under similar conditions, on the same type of road, at the same time of day, or in similar weather, but the significant improvements in car safety equipment over the years may introduce bias into the assessment. Despite these practical issues, objective probability is clearly distinct from subjective probability.

Definition 3.4 (*Subjective probability*)

Subjective probability *is a personal estimate of the probability of loss.*

Subjective probability is an individual's estimate of the frequency based on his or her own perception and information about the situation. As we will discuss below in light of figure 3.3, subjective and objective probabilities can be very different. Most often, low probabilities of occurrence are overestimated, while high probabilities of occurrence are underestimated.

In the graph in figure 3.3, we compare the subjective perception of the number of deaths per year for various risk exposures on the one hand and the actual numbers on the other hand (Zweifel and Eisen, 2012). For various causes of death, the graph shows the actual number of deaths per year in the United States (horizontal axis) and the estimated number of deaths (vertical axis). The subjective numbers are based on a survey in which participants provided their personal estimates. To better illustrate the values associated with different risks, both axes use a logarithmic scale, meaning that the increments are powers of ten: each step on the scale represents a tenfold increase in value. The 45-degree diagonal line shows perfectly accurate estimates. This means that if a data point is on or near this line, the average subjective estimate is quite accurate and close to the actual value. This is the case, for example, for deaths due to accidents and car accidents. Note that the standard deviation for subjective estimates is relatively small. This is illustrated by adding confidence intervals to some of the data points.

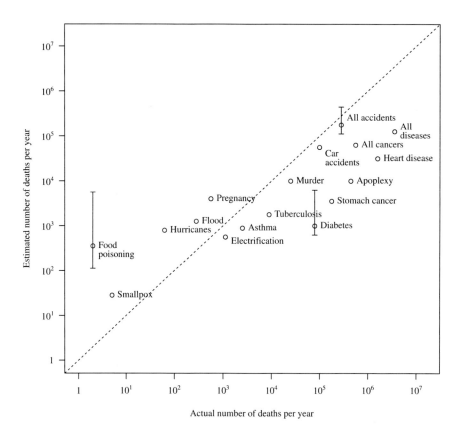

Figure 3.3: Subjective perception of risk of death by cause of death (adapted from Zweifel and Eisen, 2012, paragraph 2.2.1, figure 2.4).

Points above the diagonal indicate that these causes of death are overestimated, while points below the diagonal represent underestimated frequencies. For example, for the risk of death from food poisoning, the estimates are off by two orders of magnitude, i.e., 100 times higher than the actual frequency. We see that the risks that cause the fewest deaths are generally overestimated, with a high standard deviation (and a high confidence interval) between the estimates of different individuals. In contrast, the risks of death from diabetes and stomach cancer are significantly underestimated. For these "more common" risks, which have more deaths per year, the subjective estimates are lower than the actual numbers.

3.2 Valuation of consequences

In this section, we discuss several ways to measure a risk exposure. First, it is important to know how to evaluate frequency and severity in practice. Then, we need to find a criterion that allows us to evaluate risks by adding financial and utility values to them. To this end, we introduce the principle of risk assessment using a random variable that describes potential losses.

Measuring risk in terms of frequency and severity The impact of a risk exposure in terms of losses, such as the ability of an organization to achieve its goals, determines which risk management techniques should be used. It is, therefore, essential to be able to measure or estimate this impact, including not only direct losses but also indirect losses (see section 2.7). The assessment of the frequency and severity of risks can be qualitative and quantitative. Qualitative risk management is based on subjective evaluation methods, which are sometimes the only alternative when data is not available. In contrast, quantitative risk management relies on statistical methods such as stochastic modeling, projection, and simulation. Stochastic modeling of risk involves, among other things, determining the distributions of risk severity and frequency. A more detailed presentation of quantitative risk management can be found in McNeil et al. (2015).

Risk measurement, especially the modeling of the severity of an event, uses models from probability theory. The probability distributions of a random variable are used to describe the probability of occurrence of an adverse event or the amount of potential loss (see section 3.3). In the simpler models, statistics are then used to estimate the average probability of occurrence or the expected value of potential losses. Modeling can also be done using subjective or objective probability distributions. In principle, only purely random risks, such as the risk of losing a game of dice, are modeled using this method.

In the case of a pure risk, introduced in definition 2.4 in section 2.4, losses can be described by a positive random variable; the density plot shows the probabil-

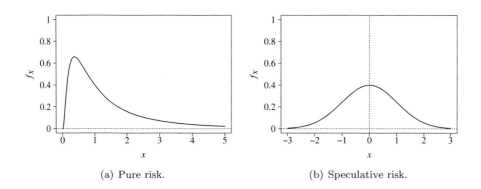

(a) Pure risk. (b) Speculative risk.

Figure 3.4: Illustration of probability densities for the severity of a pure risk and a speculative risk.

ity for each severity value. Graph (a) in figure 3.4 shows this probability density associated with a pure risk. Note that small losses are often more likely than large losses, as shown on the graph. In the case of a speculative risk, the random variable can take positive or negative values, and a sign convention makes it possible to distinguish between losses and gains relative to the expected outcome. A severity of zero, or no loss, is associated with a situation where there is no adverse deviation from the expected outcome. The case of a speculative risk is illustrated in figure 3.4(b).

Estimating potential losses is tantamount to evaluating random variables. There are a number of technical and mathematical tools that can be used to make estimates. However, they must be used correctly, appropriate interpretations must be offered, and correct conclusions must be drawn. Errors can occur in the choice of a model or in the estimation of the parameters used. The assessment of a risk exposure is subject to the many challenges of modeling, including errors due to randomness, diagnostic errors, and prediction errors.

Challenges when modeling a risk exposure

- *Errors related to randomness*: There is an error due to the random nature of the event, even with full knowledge of the characteristics of the hazard. Chance, or the non-deterministic nature of the risk, makes it impossible to predict the outcome of a risk exposure over a given period of time. Probability theory is the tool that allows us to understand the dimensions of this problem and, in a way, to reduce the remaining uncertainty about the future.

- *Diagnostic error*: This type of error is related to inappropriate specification of the model. Modeling is used to infer general characteristics from an often limited number of observations. Therefore, the key question is: does the chosen model adequately describe all the data, and is it suitable to answer the question under investigation? The concept of statistical inference is the control tool that can provide information about the likelihood of error.

- *Prediction error*: This problem is related to the calibration or parameters of the model: in order to use a model, it must be "configured" by setting the values of the various parameters it uses. This is often done using historical data. However, it is not certain that such estimates based on historical data will remain accurate in the future, especially in rapidly evolving areas. Cyber risk is an example of such an area, as cyberattack techniques change from year to year; see section 4.7. To mitigate this error, a number of forecasts or scenarios can be used.

One technique that is often used is to define possible scenarios—for example, the most realistic scenario and favorable, unfavorable, and catastrophic scenarios—and to evaluate the potential future losses that could result in each of these scenarios. The idea behind this approach is that each scenario uses a different set of

63

parameters for the models. There are two methods: projection and simulation. In the deterministic projection method, the risk manager calculates the amount of expected future losses for each scenario considered. Using available statistics and historical data, they project these values into the future based on a number of hypotheses. The result is a value that represents the estimated potential loss for each scenario.

By using the stochastic method of simulation, richer information can be obtained. Instead of working with a limited number of hypotheses, each with specific values for the parameters relevant to the scenario in question, the risk manager generates each parameter using a random variable with a specified distribution. A random number generator is then used to produce possible values for all the parameters involved in the scenario. Such a simulation is typically repeated a large number of times (in the thousands), which makes it possible to generate a value for potential losses based on different sets of parameters. The result is a distribution of all the estimated loss values. In principle, it is then possible to make a comprehensive estimate of the distribution, expected value, and standard deviation of the potential losses.

Risk estimation and modeling

The difference between measuring risk in a company and analyzing risk in the financial markets, for example, is that the fair value of liquid financial products that are traded is equal to their actual market price. The market also offers higher returns for riskier investments, providing an indication of the amount of risk taken in a given investment. The measurement of risk can be interpreted as the determination of the fair price for a risk. For risks that are covered by insurance policies, the insurance company assesses the risk and sets the price, i.e., the premium, for covering a given risk. However, when the risk is not transferred to an insurer or when a financial product is not negotiated, the value or price must be determined using a mathematical model.

In the context of an organization, there are often multiple risk exposures. While it is relatively easy to model a risk on a single time series, i.e., a variable on a single series of data points, risk aggregation is much more difficult. When more than three or four univariate models need to be combined, the computations become cumbersome, increasing the likelihood of diagnostic or prediction errors. Real-world situations are often difficult to predict. An illustration of this is the unfolding of the financial crisis that began in 2007: before the crash, international markets were moving relatively independently, and then they suddenly acted in unison (Rockinger, 2012). Proper analytical tools must be combined with a broader perspective on the risk environment to mitigate these challenges.

Another issue is the way in which risk is determined. Value-at-risk (see definition 3.27 in section 3.5) is currently the preferred measure, but it is not a very good one. It gives the minimum expected loss over a period of time for a given probability, but it does not evaluate the dangers of a combined group of risks. A better, though less popular, measure is the expected shortfall, which is the average loss that will occur if things go wrong (see definition 3.29).

Risk assessment criteria To perform a risk assessment (sometimes called a risk evaluation), the first objective is to define a criterion that can be used to estimate the potential loss resulting from a risk exposure and to compare different risk management techniques for that risk exposure and the associated potential loss. After the initial assessment of a risk exposure, the critical step is to choose the most effective and appropriate techniques for a given exposure (see section 4.4). Three evaluations are necessary to compare different management techniques:

- the evaluation of the frequency and severity of potential losses,

- the evaluation of the impact of various risk management techniques on the frequency, severity, and predictability of potential losses,

- the evaluation of the costs associated with implementing the various risk management techniques.

Assessing a risk exposure requires translating risks into values, especially financial values and utility values. To make this translation, we need to have evaluation criteria and principles that allow us to measure a risk and compare it to another risk. This requires a discussion of different criteria that can be applied. It should be noted that valuation is not always easy, as there are multiple criteria available (see section 3.5), and, in particular, implementation requires knowledge of modeling and mathematics. For example, the concept of conditional probability is often poorly understood in practice. To illustrate this point, we can use the famous Monty Hall problem (see below).

Monty Hall problem

The Monty Hall problem is a probability puzzle inspired by the American game show *Let's Make a Deal*. The game pits the host against a contestant—the player—, who is placed in front of three closed doors. Behind one of them is the main prize (a car in the original game), and behind each of the other two is a consolation prize (a goat). The contestant first chooses one of the doors. Then, the host opens a door that is neither the player's choice nor the one with the main prize behind it. Finally, the contestant can either open the door they originally chose or switch to the other unopened door.

The question facing the player is: what should they do to maximize their chances of winning the grand prize? Should they stay with their original choice or switch to the third door? The puzzle is simple to state, but its solution is not intuitive: the game describes a conditional probability problem (the

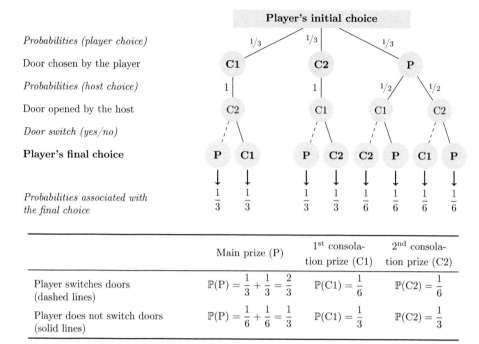

Figure 3.5: Illustration of the probability tree for the Monty Hall problem.

host opens a door), and we propose a solution using a probability tree, a tool commonly used in decision theory.

The probability tree of the Monty Hall problem is shown in figure 3.5. We denote the door with the main prize as "P" and the doors with the consolation prizes as "C1" and "C2", respectively. On the first level of the tree, we find the player's initial probabilities for each door: since there are three doors and the player chooses one, the initial probability for each prize is $1/3$.

The second level of the tree represents the moment when the host opens a door that is neither the one with the main prize nor the one the player chose. Thus, if the player chooses door C1, the host will open door C2 with a probability of 1, i.e., 100%, since the other door has the main prize. By the same logic, if the player chooses door C2, the host will open door C1 with a probability of 1. If the player initially chooses the door with the main prize, the host will open one of the two remaining doors at random, i.e., C1 or C2, each with a probability of $1/2$.

The third level of the tree is the final step, where the player is given the opportunity to switch doors. In each scenario, the left branch represents the candidate's decision to switch doors (dashed line), for example, ending up with door P in the first scenario. The right branch means they stay with their original door, ending up with door C1 in the first scenario, and so on. Now, for each branch, we specify the probability of the outcome. For the first branches, multiplying the probabilities at each intersection gives $1/3$ each time. For the four branches on the right, the same process gives $1/6$.

Finally, we look at the overall probability of winning the main prize, P, depending on whether the player switches doors in the final step. By summing the probabilities associated with the outcome P after switching doors (dashed lines), we find that $\mathbb{P}(P) = 1/3 + 1/3 = 2/3$, while the sum of the probabilities leading to P after not swapping doors (solid lines) is $\mathbb{P}(P) = 1/6 + 1/6 = 1/3$. Thus, if the contestant decides not to switch doors, their situation does not change, and they retain their initial probability of $1/3$ of winning the main prize. However, if the contestant switches doors, their probability of winning the main prize becomes $2/3$. This can be explained by the fact that when the contestant switches doors, it is as if they had two doors to choose from, to begin with, or the host eliminated one "bad" door among those two. In other words, the second step of the game, when the host opens a door, gives the contestant an important piece of information that changes the game. This idea of an additional piece of information introduces the concept of conditional probability, that is, a probability that changes with new information. In section 3.3 we review the main concepts of probability theory.

Modeling losses using the random variable S   A fundamental part of risk assessment is the modeling of potential losses. We refer to these losses using a random variable that we call S, which represents the potential losses associated with a risk exposure. We look at the total potential losses and use the present value of all future payments resulting from the adverse event. We can represent the financial consequences of a risk exposure over a given period of time by using a family of random variables. These variables relate to the following times and future amounts:

- T_0, the random future time at which the adverse event occurs,

- $T_1, T_2, \ldots$, the random future times at which payments are made,

- $S_1, S_2, \ldots$, the amounts of each payment made at $T_1, T_2, \ldots$.

If we consider an entire year as the exposure period, the observation time t will be between 0 and 1. Two outcomes are possible: either the adverse event occurs during the observation period, or it does not.

- If the adverse event occurs during the considered period (year), i.e., if the realization of T_0, noted t_0, verifies $t_0 \leq 1$, then the event is considered, and the random variable S is equal to the current value of all future payments $s_1, s_2, \ldots$, which are the realizations of the random variables $S_1, S_2, \ldots$ at times $t_1, t_2, \ldots$, which are the realizations of the random variables $T_1, T_2, \ldots$. These payments may be made during the period under consideration or much later.

- Otherwise, if the adverse event does not occur during this period, i.e., if $t_0 > 1$, then $S = 0$. The loss is zero because the event did not occur during the period observed.

The illustration in figure 3.6 shows an example where the adverse event occurs at t_0 within the interval $[0; 1]$. Three payments are considered: payments s_1 and s_2, which must be made during the period, i.e., before the end of the year at $t_1, t_2 \leq 1$, and a third payment, s_3, which must be made later ($t_3 > 1$). The random variable S representing the total losses associated with this risk exposure is the sum of the current values of payments s_1, s_2, and s_3.

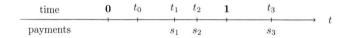

Figure 3.6: Illustration of the losses associated with a risk exposure.

The concept of a risk assessment principle   The goal is to define a criterion that allows us to evaluate this random variable in order to make comparisons with other random variables. In section 3.5 (definition 3.24), we establish that a principle of risk assessment or risk measurement consists of associating to each random variable S a deterministic value $\Pi(S)$. Several criteria, i.e., several applications Π, are possible. For example, the principle of equivalence or expected value uses the expected value as its Π function. Other principles are related to expected utility or value-at-risk (see section 3.5).

The application of a risk management technique will have the effect of transforming the random variable S into a new random variable. Two types of fundamental questions arise with respect to this potential loss S and are evaluated before and after applying a risk management technique:

- What deterministic value should be assigned to the random variable S? This is the "price tag" or risk pricing problem.

- What is the "maximum loss" to be assumed? In other words, how much capital must be available to survive the adverse event, i.e., the potential loss S? This is the solvency problem.

These questions will guide us as we introduce various concepts and examine different ways of valuing potential losses. In sections 3.3 and 3.4, we introduce theoretical aspects of random variables and the concept of utility, respectively. Then, in section 3.5, we provide more details about different risk assessment principles.

Notes before going further

- *Risk vs. loss terminology*: In some works, the random variable is identified with risk exposure itself and is referred to as "risk S." We use the term "loss S" to refer to the risk exposure.

- *Values of S*: In the case of a pure risk, the variable S is a random variable that can be positive or zero. In principle, a random variable can also be introduced for a speculative risk. The difference lies in the range of values for the loss S: positive values are typically associated with an effective loss, while negative values are interpreted as a gain (see figure 3.4).

- *Duration of the losses*: In certain cases, the period over which future payments must be made may be longer than the period of risk exposure. For example, in the case of a liability exposure in the current year, an accident causing a disability will result in a pension being paid for the rest of the victim's life. This is longer than the exposure period.

- *Types of exposure*: Depending on the type of risk exposure, one or more adverse events may occur during the time period considered. For example, for the risk of death of a person, there is a single event. In most cases, however, multiple events are possible. For example, the risk of an accident to a vehicle in a company's fleet and the risk of an employee's death in a large company are events that may occur multiple times during the period considered. In this case, the random variable S represents the sum of the present values of all losses associated with adverse events that occur during the exposure period.

- *Exposure "volume"*: When multiple adverse events can occur, it is often possible to define a measure that represents the volume of risk exposure. Returning to the examples above, the number of vehicles or employees can indicate the volume of risk exposure. In these cases, the frequency of the risk exposure can be expressed per unit of volume, i.e., the probability of a vehicle being involved in an accident or the probability of an employee dying during the exposure period.

3.3 Random variables and probability theory

In section 3.2, we saw that when assessing a risk exposure, potential losses are described by a random variable, say X. Assessing a risk exposure, therefore, means studying that random variable, i.e., its mathematical properties or possible realizations. In this section, we will cover a number of definitions and mathematical tools from the fields of probability theory and statistics.

Random variable A random variable X is a variable that can take different values x in a given range. These values are called realizations of the random variable and are real numbers. They depend on the realized event ω, and we call Ω the universe of all events that could be realized. We will not go into the formal details of constructing the probability space and measuring the probability $\mathbb{P}$. However, it should be noted that the information available at any given time plays a key role in analyzing risk in a dynamic framework.

We now formalize the basic model for risk assessment and formally distinguish two cases: the case where this random variable X is discrete and the case where X is continuous. For a discrete random variable, the set of values it can take is finite and countable, a discrete subset of the set of real numbers. If, on the other hand, the random variable is continuous, it can take any real numerical value in a given interval or a family of intervals. We use the following definition:

Definition 3.5 (*Random variable*)

A **random variable** X *is an application from the set of possible events* Ω *to* $\mathbb{R}$, *which associates a real number* x *with each possible event* ω,

$$X \ : \ \Omega \to \mathbb{R}$$
$$\omega \mapsto x = X(\omega).$$

The set of possible values x *is called the support of* X *and is denoted* $\mathcal{X}$.

By convention, we use capital letters to denote random variables (for example, X, Y, S, and N). Realizations are denoted by lowercase letters. Thus, $(X = x)$ represents the event for which the realization of the random variable X is the number x, and $\mathbb{P}(X = x)$ is the probability of that event, i.e., the probability that the random variable X takes the value x.

Distribution function When analyzing a random variable, and in our specific case, a potential loss, it is important to determine how that variable is distributed. In this context, the distribution function of a loss can be used to determine the probability that a loss is less than or equal to a certain amount. Formally, it is defined as follows:

Definition 3.6 (*Distribution function*)

The **distribution function** F_X *of a random variable* X *is defined as*

$$F_X(x) = \mathbb{P}(X \le x), \ \forall x \in \mathbb{R}.$$

We interpret the expression $F_X(x)$ as the probability that the random variable X takes a value less than or equal to x. This distribution function satisfies three conditions:

(a) $\lim_{x \to -\infty} F_X(x) = 0$ and $\lim_{x \to +\infty} F_X(x) = 1$,

(b) F_X is an increasing function,

(c) F_X is right continuous.

Based on the first two conditions, we can conclude that the values $F_X(x)$ are between 0 and 1, that is:

$$0 \leq F_X(x) \leq 1, \ \forall x \in \mathbb{R}.$$

From the definition, $\forall a, b \in \mathbb{R}$, $a < b$, we have the following identity:

$$\mathbb{P}(a < X \leq b) = \mathbb{P}(X \leq b) - \mathbb{P}(X \leq a) = F_X(b) - F_X(a).$$

We will see later what the distribution function curve looks like for the most commonly used probability distributions.

Continuous and discrete random variable Next, we distinguish between continuous and discrete random variables:

Definition 3.7 (*Continuous and discrete random variables*)

*A random variable X is **continuous** if its distribution function F_X is a continuous function; X can then take an infinite number of values. By contrast, a **discrete** random variable takes a finite number of values, and its distribution function is a step function.*

These two types of random variables have many properties in common, and the concepts that we examine apply similarly to both. However, their support is different, finite for discrete variables and infinite for continuous variables. This means that there are formal differences between the expressions used. In particular, we use finite sums for the realizations of a discrete random variable but an integral for a continuous random variable.

Probability mass and probability density functions In the case of a discrete random variable, the probability mass function evaluated at x gives the probability that the random variable X takes a value equal to x. In particular, it differs from the distribution function, which considers the probability that the random variable takes a value that is less than or equal to a given value. This leads us to the following formal definition:

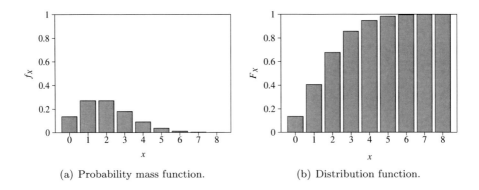

(a) Probability mass function.   (b) Distribution function.

Figure 3.7: Illustration of the probability mass and distribution functions of a discrete random variable (based on a Poisson distribution with parameter $\lambda = 2$).

Definition 3.8 (*Probability mass function*)

The **probability mass function** f_X of a discrete random variable X is defined as

$$f_X(x) = \mathbb{P}(X = x), \ \forall x \in \mathcal{X}.$$

Thus, for a discrete variable, the distribution function has the following characteristic:

$$F_X(x) = \mathbb{P}(X \le x) = \sum_{k:x_k \le x} f_X(x_k), \ \forall x \in \mathbb{R},$$

where the $x_k \in \mathcal{X}$ correspond to k realizations of the random variable X. We see that the sum of the values of the probability mass function for all realizations x_k less than or equal to x gives the value of the distribution function F_X in x. The graph of the distribution function is a step function whose step is $f_X(x_k)$ at each realization x_k of X. Figure 3.7 illustrates the probability mass function (graph a) and the distribution function (graph b) of a discrete variable, using the example of a Poisson distribution with parameter $\lambda = 2$.

In the case of a continuous random variable X, the distribution function F_X is continuous and differentiable. Therefore, for an increase of the random variable by $\Delta x > 0$, we have

$$\mathbb{P}(x < X \le x + \Delta x) = F_X(x + \Delta x) - F_X(x) \approx f_X(x) \cdot \Delta x,$$

where $f_X(x) = F'_X(x)$. If we look at this equation in terms of derivatives, we have

$$\mathbb{P}(x < X \le x + dx) = f_X(x)\, dx = dF_X(x).$$

The function f_X is called the probability density function. By analogy with the relationship between the distribution function and the probability mass function for discrete random variables, we can replace the sum with an integral in the case of a continuous random variable, which gives the following relationship:

Definition 3.9 (*Probability density function*)

The **probability density function** f_X of a continuous random variable X is given by

$$F_X(x) = \int_{-\infty}^{x} f_X(y)\, \mathrm{d}y, \ \forall x \in \mathbb{R}.$$

Figure 3.8 illustrates the probability density function (graph a) and the distribution function (graph b) of a continuous variable using a gamma distribution with parameters $k = 2$ and $\theta = 1$ (see below for a definition of the gamma distribution).

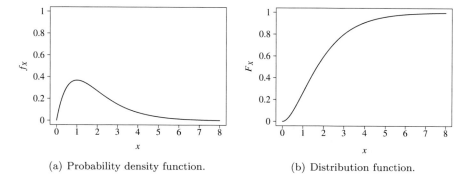

(a) Probability density function.   (b) Distribution function.

Figure 3.8: Illustration of the probability density and distribution functions of a continuous random variable (based on a gamma distribution with parameters $k = 2$ and $\theta = 1$).

Note that the function f_X is a mass function in the case of a discrete random variable or a density function in the case of a continuous random variable if and only if it satisfies the following two conditions:

(a) $f_X(x) \geq 0, \ \forall x,$

(b) $\sum_{x \in \mathcal{X}} f_X(x) = 1$ or $\int_{-\infty}^{+\infty} f_X(x)\, \mathrm{d}x = 1.$

The first condition is that f_X takes only positive values. The second condition requires that the sum of the probabilities over all possible realizations of the random variable X is equal to 1.

Expected value The expected value of a random variable X is the weighted average of its possible realizations. The realizations are weighted by probability, i.e., by the values of their respective mass or density functions.

Definition 3.10 (*Expected value*)

The **expected value** $\mathbb{E}(X)$ of a random variable X is defined as

– If X is a discrete random variable:

$$\mathbb{E}(X) = \sum_{x \in \mathcal{X}} x \cdot f_X(x) = \sum_{x \in \mathcal{X}} x \cdot \mathbb{P}(X = x),$$

– If X is a continuous random variable:

$$\mathbb{E}(X) = \int_{-\infty}^{+\infty} x \cdot f_X(x) \, \mathrm{d}x.$$

The expected value has certain important properties:

(a) For any constant c:

$$\mathbb{E}(c) = c.$$

(b) For a random variable X and two real parameters a and b:

$$\mathbb{E}(a + b \cdot X) = a + b \cdot \mathbb{E}(X).$$

(c) For two random variables X and Y and two real parameters a and b:

$$\mathbb{E}(a \cdot X + b \cdot Y) = a \cdot \mathbb{E}(X) + b \cdot \mathbb{E}(Y).$$

(d) For two random variables X and Y:

$$\text{If } X \leq Y, \text{ then } \mathbb{E}(X) \leq \mathbb{E}(Y).$$

Transformation of a random variable If we consider a random variable X and a real function $u : x \mapsto u(x)$, then $u(X)$ represents a new random variable.

The expected value $\mathbb{E}(u(X))$ for the random variable $u(X)$ is calculated as follows:

- If X is a discrete random variable:

$$\mathbb{E}(u(X)) = \sum_{x \in \mathcal{X}} u(x) \cdot f_X(x) = \sum_{x \in \mathcal{X}} u(x) \cdot \mathbb{P}(X = x),$$

- If X is a continuous random variable:

$$\mathbb{E}(u(X)) = \int_{-\infty}^{+\infty} u(x) \cdot f_X(x) \, \mathrm{d}x.$$

Jensen's inequalities Jensen's inequalities are mathematical results that, for a function u, give an ordering relationship between the expected value of the transformed random variable $\mathbb{E}(u(X))$ and the function applied to the expected value of the random variable $u(\mathbb{E}(X))$. The order relationship depends on the concavity of the function u.

As a reminder, a function u is said to be convex, or concave upwards if $d^2 u(x)/dx^2 \doteq u''(x) \geq 0$. Conversely, a function u is concave, or concave downwards, if $u''(x) \leq 0$.

We have the following inequalities:

Theorem 3.1 (*Jensen's inequalities*)

- If u is a convex function $(u''(x) \geq 0)$, then for any random variable X we have

$$\mathbb{E}(u(X)) \geq u(\mathbb{E}(X)).$$

- If u is a concave function $(u''(x) \leq 0)$, then for any random variable X we have:

$$\mathbb{E}(u(X)) \leq u(\mathbb{E}(X)).$$

We offer a demonstration of the first of these two inequalities (the second can be demonstrated using the same reasoning).

In the case where u is a convex function, we have for any $x, y \in \mathbb{R}$

$$u(y) \geq u(x) + u'(x) \cdot (y - x).$$

Graphically, this equation corresponds to that of the tangent at point x to the graph of the function u. By defining $y = X$ and $x = E(X)$, we have

$$u(X) \geq u(\mathbb{E}(X)) + u'(\mathbb{E}(X)) \cdot (X - \mathbb{E}(X)).$$

Taking the expected value of both sides of this inequality, we get:

$$\begin{aligned}
\mathbb{E}(u(X)) &\geq \mathbb{E}[u(\mathbb{E}(X)) + u'(\mathbb{E}(X)) \cdot (X - \mathbb{E}(X))] \\
&= \mathbb{E}[u(\mathbb{E}(X))] + \mathbb{E}[u'(\mathbb{E}(X))] \cdot \mathbb{E}[X - \mathbb{E}(X)] \\
&= u(\mathbb{E}(X)) + u'(\mathbb{E}(X)) \cdot (\mathbb{E}(X) - \mathbb{E}(X)) \\
&= u(\mathbb{E}(X)).
\end{aligned}$$

Therefore, $\mathbb{E}(u(X)) \geq u(\mathbb{E}(X))$.

Moments, variance, and standard deviation Moments are measures of the dispersion of a random variable. For a non-zero natural number $n \in \mathbb{N}^*$, the moment of order n and the central moment of order n, written μ'_n and μ_n respectively, of a random variable X are defined as follows:

Definition 3.11 (*Moment and central moment of order n*)

The **moment of order** n, $n \geq 1$, of a random variable X is defined as

$$\mu'_n = \mathbb{E}(X^n).$$

The **central moment of order** n, $n \geq 1$, of a random variable X is defined as

$$\mu_n = \mathbb{E}[(X - \mathbb{E}(X))^n].$$

We note that the expected value is equal to the moment of order 1, since $\mu'_1 = \mathbb{E}(X)$. We also note that the central moment of order 1 is zero by construction since $\mu_1 = \mathbb{E}(X - \mathbb{E}(X)) = \mathbb{E}(X) - \mathbb{E}(X) = 0$.

The second central moment corresponds to the variance. Going beyond the simple calculation of an average or an expected value, the variance is a first measure of the variability. For two random variables expressed in the same unit of measurement, the one with the highest variance will, therefore, have higher variability, i.e., less stability, than the other. The definitions of variance and standard deviation are as follows:

Definition 3.12 (*Variance and standard deviation*)

The **variance** $\text{Var}(X)$ of a random variable X is the second central moment given by

$$\text{Var}(X) = \mu_2 = \mathbb{E}[(X - \mathbb{E}(X))^2].$$

The **standard deviation** $\sigma(X)$ of a random variable X is the square root of the variance given by

$$\sigma(X) = \sqrt{\text{Var}(X)}.$$

Below, we summarize a selection of the properties of variance:

(a) For a random variable X:

$$\text{Var}(X) = \mathbb{E}(X^2) - \mathbb{E}(X)^2.$$

(b) For any constant c:

$$\text{Var}(c) = 0.$$

(c) For a random variable X and two real parameters a and b:

$$\text{Var}(a + b \cdot X) = b^2 \cdot \text{Var}(X).$$

The definitions and properties of variance and expected value can be used to determine $\text{Var}(x)$:

- If X is a discrete random variable:

$$\text{Var}(X) = \sum_{x \in \mathcal{X}} (x - \mathbb{E}(X))^2 \cdot f_X(x) = \left(\sum_{x \in \mathcal{X}} x^2 \cdot \mathbb{P}(X = x) \right) - \mathbb{E}(X)^2,$$

- If X is a continuous random variable:

$$\text{Var}(X) = \int_{-\infty}^{+\infty} (x - \mathbb{E}(X))^2 \cdot f_X(x) \, \mathrm{d}x = \left(\int_{-\infty}^{+\infty} x^2 \cdot f_X(x) \, \mathrm{d}x \right) - \mathbb{E}(X)^2.$$

The expressions above also show the calculations, in particular finite sums and integrals, that should be used to determine the variance when the distribution of the random variable is provided.

Covariance and correlation   Two measurements are especially important when there are multiple risk exposures described by multiple random variables. The initial examination of the dependencies and relationships between random variables is often done using covariance and correlation. Although these two measures may seem similar, there are notable differences between them. Covariance measures how two variables change in relation to each other; it is an extension of the concept of variance, which measures how a single variable changes. The measure can take any real value and is defined as follows:

Definition 3.13 (*Covariance*)

If X and Y are two random variables with expected values μ_X and μ_Y, respectively, the **covariance** of X and Y is given by

$$\text{Cov}(X, Y) = \mathbb{E}((X - \mu_X) \cdot (Y - \mu_Y)).$$

The higher the absolute value of the covariance, the more related and interdependent the two variables are. A positive value means that an increase in one variable leads to an increase in the other, while a negative value indicates an inverse relationship between the two random variables. Although this measure is very useful in defining the nature of the relationship between two variables, it does not measure its magnitude because it depends on the unit of measurement used. The unit of measurement for the covariance is that of the product of the units of measurement of the two random variables considered.

For two random variables X and Y:

$$\text{Var}(X + Y) = \text{Var}(X) + \text{Var}(Y) + 2 \cdot \text{Cov}(X, Y).$$

To compare the scales of multiple interactions between random variables, we need a normalized measure of dependence, and that is correlation: a unit measure of the way random variables interact with each other. Correlation is a normalized measure of covariance:

Definition 3.14 (*Correlation*)

If X and Y are two random variables with standard deviations σ_X and σ_Y, respectively, the **correlation** *between X and Y is given by*

$$\rho(X,Y) = \frac{Cov(X,Y)}{\sigma_X \cdot \sigma_Y}.$$

The correlation takes values between -1 and $+1$. A correlation close to $+1$ means that there is a strong positive relationship between the two random variables, while a correlation close to -1 indicates a strong negative relationship.

For random variables X and Y with respective expected values μ_X and μ_Y, we have the following properties:

(a) $Cov(X,Y) = \mathbb{E}(X \cdot Y) - \mu_X \cdot \mu_Y$,

(b) $Cov(X,X) = Var(X)$,

(c) $-1 \leq \rho(X,Y) \leq 1$,

(d) $\rho(X,X) = 1$.

Here, we consider only the linear correlation between two random variables. In reality, the dependency between risk exposures and the random variables describing them results in a more complex correlation structure. In this context, we use copula functions to characterize the dependency relationships in a more general way.

Independent random variables   Having looked at how to measure the dependence between two random variables using covariance and correlation, it is equally useful to examine the concept of independence, which we will formalize in this section. In fact, determining whether two random variables are independent means determining whether the realizations of one affect the values taken by the other. From a probability perspective, the joint probability (see below) of two independent random variables is simply equal to the product of the probabilities of each variable.

Definition 3.15 (*Independent random variables*)

Two discrete random variables X and Y are **independent** *if, for all realizations x and y, we have*

$$\mathbb{P}(X = x, Y = y) = \mathbb{P}(X = x) \cdot \mathbb{P}(Y = y).$$

The independence property is particularly interesting because it leads to the next property. Two random variables X and Y are independent if and only if for all functions u and v, we have

$$\mathbb{E}(u(X) \cdot v(Y)) = \mathbb{E}(u(X)) \cdot \mathbb{E}(v(Y)).$$

To illustrate this property, consider the following example. If X and Y are two independent random variables, then we can write

$$\mathbb{E}(X \cdot Y) = \mathbb{E}(X) \cdot \mathbb{E}(Y).$$

In particular, their covariance and correlation coefficient are zero. For covariance $\mathrm{Cov}(X, Y)$, using property (a) above, we find

$$\mathrm{Cov}(X, Y) = \mathbb{E}(X \cdot Y) - \mathbb{E}(X) \cdot \mathbb{E}(Y) = 0.$$

From this result, we obtain the correlation coefficient $\rho(X, Y) = 0$.

Lastly, if X and Y are two independent random variables, we have seen that their covariance is zero and therefore

$$\mathrm{Var}(X + Y) = \mathrm{Var}(X) + \mathrm{Var}(Y).$$

The independence definitions and properties can be generalized to any number of random variables.

Joint and marginal distributions In the presence of families of discrete random variables, i.e., several discrete random variables describing different risk exposures, it is often useful to have information about the probability of certain combinations of realizations. First, we define a joint distribution:

Definition 3.16 (*Joint distribution*)

*The **joint distribution** of two discrete random variables X and Y with respective realizations x and y and respective supports $\mathcal{X}$ and $\mathcal{Y}$ is defined by*

- *the domain of the combinations of possible realizations of X and Y, i.e., $\mathcal{X} \times \mathcal{Y}$,*

- *the joint probability of each combination of realizations, i.e., $\mathbb{P}(X = x, Y = y)$, $\forall (x, y) \in \mathcal{X} \times \mathcal{Y}$.*

Based on the joint distribution of the two random variables, we can determine the marginal distribution of X.

Definition 3.17 (*Marginal distribution*)

Let two discrete random variables X and Y have x and y as their respective realizations and $\mathcal{X}$ and $\mathcal{Y}$ as their respective supports. The **marginal distribution** of X is defined by

$$\mathbb{P}(X = x) = \sum_{y \in \mathcal{Y}} \mathbb{P}(X = x, Y = y).$$

Similarly, the marginal distribution of Y is

$$\mathbb{P}(Y = y) = \sum_{x \in \mathcal{X}} \mathbb{P}(X = x, Y = y).$$

Table 3.1 shows the joint and marginal densities for two discrete random variables X and Y with possible realizations $\mathcal{X} = \{x_1, x_2, \ldots, x_n\}$ and $\mathcal{Y} = \{y_1, y_2, \ldots, y_m\}$. For each combination of realizations (x_i, y_j), $1 \leq i \leq n$, $1 \leq j \leq m$, we present the joint probability $p_{ij} \doteq \mathbb{P}(X = x_i, Y = y_j)$. By adding all realizations of the random variables Y and X, respectively, we present the marginal distributions $\mathbb{P}(X = x_i)$ and $\mathbb{P}(Y = y_j)$ of X and Y, respectively. Note that the sum of the marginal distributions, i.e., $\sum_{x_i \in \mathcal{X}} \mathbb{P}(X = x_i)$—the sum in the rightmost column of the table—and $\sum_{y_j \in \mathcal{Y}} \mathbb{P}(Y = y_j)$—the sum in the bottom row of the table—is always equal to 1.

X \ Y	y_1	y_2	$\cdots$	y_m	$\sum_{y_j \in \mathcal{Y}}$
x_1	$p_{11} = \mathbb{P}(X = x_1, Y = y_1)$	$p_{12} = \mathbb{P}(X = x_1, Y = y_2)$	$\cdots$	$p_{1m} = \mathbb{P}(X = x_1, Y = y_m)$	$\mathbb{P}(X = x_1)$
x_2	$p_{21} = \mathbb{P}(X = x_2, Y = y_1)$	$p_{22} = \mathbb{P}(X = x_2, Y = y_2)$	$\cdots$	$p_{2m} = \mathbb{P}(X = x_2, Y = y_m)$	$\mathbb{P}(X = x_2)$
$\vdots$	$\vdots$	$\vdots$	$\ddots$	$\vdots$	$\vdots$
x_n	$p_{n1} = \mathbb{P}(X = x_n, Y = y_1)$	$p_{n2} = \mathbb{P}(X = x_n, Y = y_2)$	$\cdots$	$p_{nm} = \mathbb{P}(X = x_n, Y = y_m)$	$\mathbb{P}(X = x_n)$
$\sum_{x_i \in \mathcal{X}}$	$\mathbb{P}(Y = y_1)$	$\mathbb{P}(Y = y_2)$	$\cdots$	$\mathbb{P}(Y = y_m)$	1

Table 3.1: Illustration of joint and marginal distributions for two random variables X and Y.

To illustrate the concepts outlined above, we present two examples of numerical applications.

Application using a discrete random variable

Let the discrete random variable S represent the amount of a potential loss associated with a risk exposure. We do not know the future amount of this loss, but we do have information about the distribution of the loss through its probability mass function. We know that the loss has a 90% chance of being zero, $S = 0$, and a 10% chance of being $S = 1$.

In this example, the possible realizations of the random variable S are 0 and 1. The probability of each of these realizations (probability mass function) is 90% for the value $S = 0$ and 10% for the value $S = 1$. The probability mass function of the random variable S is $f_S(s) = \mathbb{P}(S = s)$. The distribution of the discrete random variable S can be represented in various ways. First, we can use a table showing all possible realizations with their respective probabilities (see table 3.2).

Realizations of S	Realization probability
$s_1 = 0$	$f_S(s_1) = \mathbb{P}(S = s_1) = \mathbb{P}(S = 0) = 0.90$
$s_2 = 1$	$f_S(s_2) = \mathbb{P}(S = s_2) = \mathbb{P}(S = 1) = 0.10$

Table 3.2: Representation of the realizations of S and their respective probabilities.

Application with a discrete random variable (cont.)

The second way to represent the distribution of S is to plot the probability mass function f_S with the possible realizations on the horizontal axis and their associated probabilities on the vertical axis, as shown in figure 3.9(a). For a plot to represent the probability mass function of a discrete random variable or the probability density of a continuous random variable, it is obvious that the probability of each realization s must be between 0 and 1 and that the sum of the probabilities of all realizations s must be equal to 1. Graph (b) in figure 3.9 illustrates the distribution function F_S. Notice that at each point, the distribution function F_S—which starts at zero—is incremented by the value of the probability mass function at that point. At the last point, F_S reaches the value of 1.

Application with a discrete random variable (conclusion)

By definition 3.10, we compute the expected value of S,

$$\mathbb{E}(S) = \sum_{s \in \mathcal{S}} s \cdot f_S(s) = \sum_{s \in \mathcal{S}} s \cdot \mathbb{P}(S = s) = 0 \cdot 0.90 + 1 \cdot 0.10 = 0.1.$$

By definition 3.12, the variance of S is equal to

$$\mathrm{Var}(S) = \left(\sum_{s \in \mathcal{S}} s^2 \cdot \mathbb{P}(S = s) \right) - \mathbb{E}(S)^2 = 0^2 \cdot 0.90 + 1^2 \cdot 0.10 - 0.1^2 = 0.09.$$

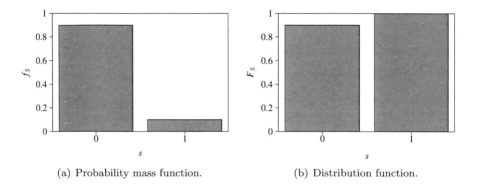

(a) Probability mass function.　　　　　(b) Distribution function.

Figure 3.9: Representation of the probability mass and distribution functions of S.

Application with two discrete random variables

Let N be a random variable representing the number of accidents of a cyclist. The probability mass function is the following:

$$f_N(n) = \begin{cases} 0.80 & \text{for } n = 0, \\ 0.16 & \text{for } n = 1, \\ 0.04 & \text{for } n = 2. \end{cases}$$

The amount of potential losses A resulting from a single accident is distributed as follows:

$$f_A(a) = \begin{cases} 0.50 & \text{for } a = 1{,}000, \\ 0.50 & \text{for } a = 2{,}000. \end{cases}$$

Note that the loss resulting from an accident A is independent of the number of accidents N. Let S be the total amount of potential losses for all accidents that occur.

The joint distribution of the number of accidents N and the total amount of potential losses S is given in table 3.3. For the realizations of N, which gives the number of accidents, we consider possible values 0, 1, and 2. For each of these values, we look at the total amount of losses S. For $N = 0$, i.e., no accidents, there are no losses, so $S = 0$. For $N = 1$, an accident has occurred, resulting in a loss of $A = 1{,}000$ or $A = 2{,}000$, so S can take these two values. For $N = 2$, in the same way, the amount of losses can be 2,000 (two accidents worth 1,000), 3,000 (one accident worth 1,000 and another worth 2,000), or 4,000 (two accidents worth 2,000).

Once we have listed the realizations of N and S, we can evaluate the joint probabilities in the 3rd column of table 3.3. The probability of the event $(N = 0, S = 0)$ is 0.80, which is directly derived from $\mathbb{P}(N = 0) = 0.80$. There is no realization of A to consider. Then, we find the probability $\mathbb{P}(N = 1, S = 1{,}000)$ by multiplying the two factors $\mathbb{P}(N = 1) = 0.16$ and $\mathbb{P}(A = 1{,}000) = 0.50$, which gives 0.08. This product gives the joint probability because random variables N and A are independent (see definition 3.15). The same reasoning applies to $\mathbb{P}(N = 1, S = 2{,}000)$.

For $N = 2$, we specify the possible losses for each accident. For the event $(N = 2, S = 2{,}000)$, we have $\mathbb{P}(N = 2) = 0.04$, and we report two accidents worth 1,000. For the first accident, we have $\mathbb{P}(A = 1{,}000) = 0.50$, and for the second accident, we similarly have $\mathbb{P}(A = 1{,}000) = 0.50$. The product of the three probabilities is $\mathbb{P}(N = 2, S = 2{,}000) = 0.04 \cdot 0.50 \cdot 0.50 = 0.01$. For $\mathbb{P}(N = 2, S = 4{,}000)$ we can use the same reasoning, replacing 1,000 with 2,000 as the loss for each accident. Finally, we evaluate $\mathbb{P}(N = 2, S = 3{,}000)$. We still have $\mathbb{P}(N = 2) = 0.04$. However, for $S = 3{,}000$ there are two possibilities, whose probabilities we add together. We must consider a first scenario in which the first accident causes a loss of 1,000 with $\mathbb{P}(A = 1{,}000) = 0.50$, and the second accident causes a loss of 2,000 with $\mathbb{P}(A = 2{,}000) = 0.50$. Then, we consider a second scenario in which the first accident causes a loss of $A = 2{,}000$, and the second accident is less severe with $A = 1{,}000$. These two scenarios are separate possibilities and must be added together as follows: $\mathbb{P}(N = 2, S = 3{,}000) = \mathbb{P}(N = 2) \cdot [\mathbb{P}(A = 1{,}000) \cdot \mathbb{P}(A = 2{,}000) + \mathbb{P}(A = 2{,}000) + \mathbb{P}(A = 1{,}000)] = 0.02$. As a final step, we check that the sum of all joint probabilities is 1.

Realizations of N	Realizations of S	Joint probabilities
0	0	0.80
1	1,000	0.08
1	2,000	0.08
2	2,000	0.01
2	3,000	0.02
2	4,000	0.01

Table 3.3: Representation of the joint distribution of N and S.

Application with two discrete random variables (conclusion)

Table 3.4 shows the marginal distribution of S, which is the sum of all possible realizations of N for each realization of S (see definition 3.17). Looking at table 3.3, we see that the realization $S = 2{,}000$ is the only realization associated with two different values of N. By adding $\mathbb{P}(N = 1, S = 2{,}000)$ and $\mathbb{P}(N = 2, S = 2{,}000)$, we get $\mathbb{P}(S = 2{,}000) = 0.08 + 0.01 = 0.09$.

We can now summarize all probabilities for the joint distribution and the marginal distributions of N and S in table 3.5.

Realizations of S	Marginal probability of S
0	0.80
1,000	0.08
2,000	0.09
3,000	0.02
4,000	0.01

Table 3.4: Representation of the marginal distribution of S.

N \ S	0	1,000	2,000	3,000	4,000	$\sum_{s \in S}$
0	0.80					0.80
1		0.08	0.08			0.16
2			0.01	0.02	0.01	0.04
$\sum_{n \in N}$	0.80	0.08	0.09	0.02	0.01	1

Table 3.5: Representation of the joint distribution and marginal distributions of N and S.

Law of large numbers and central limit theorem Before concluding this section, we will mention two other theorems that are important in risk assessment and insurance pricing. The law of large numbers states that as the size of a sample increases, its statistical properties become closer to those of the population. This means that the empirical mean calculated from an observed sample converges to the expected value as the sample size tends to infinity. This result is particularly important in risk management. There are several versions of this theorem, and we use the weak law of large numbers here.

Theorem 3.2 (*Law of large numbers*)

Let X_n be a series of n independent and identically distributed random variables with the same expected value $\mu = \mathbb{E}(X_i)$. The empirical mean is $\mu_n = \frac{1}{n} \sum_{i=1}^{n} X_i$.

The **law of large numbers** states that the empirical mean μ_n converges in probability to the expected value μ as n tends to infinity:

$$\forall \epsilon > 0, \quad \lim_{n \to +\infty} \mathbb{P}\left(|\mu_n - \mu| \geq \epsilon\right) = 0.$$

The central limit theorem is probably one of the most widely used theorems in probability theory. It places special emphasis on the standard normal distribution (see below). This theorem gives an indication of the convergence of the sum of a series of random variables.

Theorem 3.3 (*Central limit theorem*)

Let X_n be a series of n independent and identically distributed random variables with the same mean $\mu = \mathbb{E}(X_i)$ and the same standard deviation $\sigma = \sigma(X_i)$. The empirical mean is $\mu_n = \frac{1}{n}\sum_{i=1}^{n} X_i$.
The **central limit theorem** states that the random variable

$$Z_n = \frac{\mu_n - \mu}{\sigma/\sqrt{n}}$$

converges to the standard normal distribution as n tends to infinity:

$$\lim_{n \to +\infty} \mathbb{P}(Z_n \leq x) = \Phi(x),$$

where Φ is the distribution function of the standard normal distribution. In other words, the series Z_n converges to the standard normal distribution.

The series Z_n of theorem 3.3 can be interpreted as a measure of the deviation of the empirical mean μ_n (calculated based on n random variables) from the expected value μ. As n takes increasing values, the series Z_n tends to the standard normal distribution, whose expected value is equal to 0. Thus, the error of the empirical mean μ_n relative to the expected value μ tends to 0 as n tends to infinity.

The theorem then allows us to determine confidence intervals for estimating the expected value using the empirical mean. Using the quantile q of the standard normal distribution (see above), we have

$$\mu - q \cdot \frac{\sigma}{\sqrt{n}} < \mu_n < \mu + q \cdot \frac{\sigma}{\sqrt{n}}.$$

This relation provides a confidence interval for the empirical mean μ_n if the expected value μ and the standard deviation σ are known. In practice, however, we typically try to estimate a confidence interval for the expected value μ based on observations. Using the theorem, we can obtain the confidence interval

$$\mu_n - q \cdot \frac{\sigma}{\sqrt{n}} < \mu < \mu_n + q \cdot \frac{\sigma}{\sqrt{n}}.$$

This second relationship provides a confidence interval for the expected value μ as a function of the empirical mean μ calculated from observations. Since the standard deviation σ in this latter relationship is generally not known, we use an estimate based on empirical data, $\sigma_n = \sqrt{\frac{1}{n}\sum_{i=1}^{n}(X_i - \mu_n)^2}$, which gives

$$\mu_n - q \cdot \frac{\sigma_n}{\sqrt{n}} < \mu < \mu_n + q \cdot \frac{\sigma_n}{\sqrt{n}}.$$

To estimate a symmetric confidence interval with 95% accuracy, we choose $q = \Phi^{-1}(0.975) \approx 1.96$. We then have

$$\mathbb{P}\left(\mu \in \left[\mu_n - 1.96 \cdot \frac{\sigma_n}{\sqrt{n}}; \mu_n + 1.96 \cdot \frac{\sigma_n}{\sqrt{n}} \right] \right) \approx 95\%.$$

Examples of discrete probability distributions   In this section, we introduce some discrete probability distributions that will be useful later. In particular, we look at the Bernoulli distribution, the Poisson distribution, the binomial distribution, the negative binomial distribution, and the geometric distribution. For each of these, we present their probability mass function and characterize their expected value and variance as a function of the parameters of the distribution in table 3.6.

Probability distribution	$f_X(k)$	$\mathbb{E}(X)$	$\mathrm{Var}(X)$
Bernoulli distribution (p) $0 < p < 1$	$\begin{cases} \mathbb{P}(X = k = 1) = p \\ \mathbb{P}(X = k = 0) = 1 - p \end{cases}$	p	$p \cdot (1 - p)$
Poisson distribution (λ) $\lambda > 0$	$\mathbb{P}(X = k) = \dfrac{e^{-\lambda}\lambda^k}{k!}$ $\forall k \in \mathbb{N}$	λ	λ
Binomial distribution (n, p) $n \in \mathbb{N},\ 0 < p < 1$	$\mathbb{P}(X = k) = \dbinom{n}{k} \cdot p^k \cdot (1 - p)^{n-k}$ $\forall k \in \{0, 1, 2, \ldots, n\}$	$n \cdot p$	$n \cdot p \cdot (1 - p)$
Negative binomial distribution (n, p) $n \in \mathbb{N},\ 0 < p < 1$	$\mathbb{P}(X = k) = \dbinom{k + n - 1}{k} \cdot p^n \cdot (1 - p)^k$ $\forall k \in \mathbb{N}$	$\dfrac{n \cdot (1 - p)}{p}$	$\dfrac{n \cdot (1 - p)}{p^2}$
Geometric distribution (p) $0 < p < 1$	$\mathbb{P}(X = k) = p \cdot (1 - p)^{k-1}$ $\forall k \in \mathbb{N}^*$	$\dfrac{1}{p}$	$\dfrac{1 - p}{p^2}$
Geometric distribution* (p) $0 < p < 1$	$\mathbb{P}(X = k) = p \cdot (1 - p)^k$ $\forall k \in \mathbb{N}$	$\dfrac{1 - p}{p}$	$\dfrac{1 - p}{p^2}$

* Alternative definition.

Table 3.6: Examples of discrete probability distributions.

In our comments, we provide examples of how to use the various distributions. This is because certain distributions are often used to describe the frequency of claims. This is the case of the Poisson distribution, which is used to describe the number of events that occur within a given time interval. The expected value of this variable is equal to the parameter λ, which specifies the distribution. This parameter is relatively easy to evaluate by studying historical statistics and determining the average number of events that occur by time interval. However, the Poisson distribution is equidispersed, and the parameter λ alone does not allow the variance to be calibrated independently from the mean. In many situations, especially for risk exposures covered by non-life insurance (see figure 5.7 in section 5.4), the annual number of claims is empirically overdispersed. This means that the variability is higher than predicted by the model. This observation demonstrates the interest in using distributions such as the negative binomial distribution.

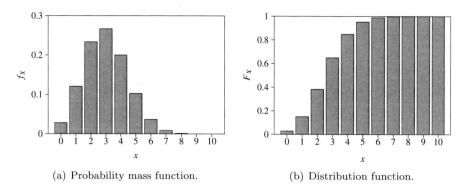

(a) Probability mass function.   (b) Distribution function.

Note: The vertical axes of graphs (a) and (b) are not on the same scale.

Figure 3.10: Illustration of the probability mass and distribution functions of a binomial distribution with parameters $n = 10$ and $p = 0.3$.

Comments on the examples of discrete probability distributions

- *Bernoulli distribution*: This distribution is used in binomial trials. The two outcomes, often interpreted as success and failure, or the realization and non-realization of an event A, have probabilities of p and $(1 - p)$, respectively.

- *Poisson distribution*: This distribution is used, for example, to count the number of accidents, claims, or people in a queue. For an event A, the probability distribution with parameter λ gives the number of occurrences of A (within a given time interval). The probability mass and distribution functions of a Poisson distribution with parameter $\lambda = 2$ are shown in figure 3.7.

- *Binomial distribution*: This distribution is used to count the number of realizations within n trials. Thus, for an event A whose probability of occurrence is p, the random variable X indicates the number of realizations of A within n trials. The probability mass and distribution functions of a binomial distribution with parameters $n = 10$ and $p = 0.3$ are shown in figure 3.10.

- *Negative binomial distribution*: This distribution is used to count the number of non-realizations before the nth realization. Thus, for an event A whose probability of occurrence is p, the random variable X indicates the number of non-realizations of A before n realizations of A occur.

- *Geometric distribution*: This distribution is used to count the number of trials required before the first realization occurs. Thus, for an event A, whose probability of occurrence is p, the random variable X indicates the number of trials required before the first realization of A occurs.

- *Geometric distribution (alternative definition)*: This alternative formulation of the geometric distribution is used to count the number of failures before the first realization. This is an alternative formulation with a unit shift in k (counting failures, as opposed to counting the number of trials before the first realization). It is a special case of the negative binomial distribution with $n = 1$. Thus, for an event A whose probability of occurrence is p, the random variable X indicates the number of non-realizations of A before the first realization occurs.

Examples of continuous probability distributions   After reviewing discrete probability distributions, we will now summarize some continuous probability distributions. In this section, we look specifically at the uniform distribution, the exponential distribution, the normal distribution, the standard normal distribution, the log-normal distribution, the Pareto distribution, and the gamma distribution. We present an overview of their parameters, probability density and distribution functions, and expected value and variance in table 3.7.

Continuous probability distributions are particularly useful for describing phenomena that can take continuous values, such as elapsed time or amount of damage. For example, the exponential distribution is used to qualify the time elapsed between two events. The gamma distribution is often used to describe the distribution of potential losses resulting from an adverse event. In practice, the parameters of these distributions are calibrated using empirical observations. Note again that the normal distribution is used in many financial models, most notably for the log return on assets in the Black–Scholes model used to calculate the theoretical value of options.

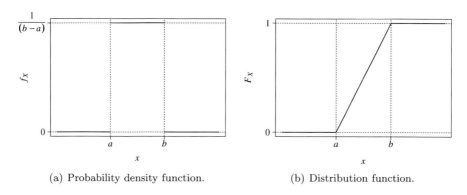

(a) Probability density function.   (b) Distribution function.

Figure 3.11: Illustration of the probability density and distribution functions of a uniform distribution with parameters a and b.

Probability distribution	$f_X(x)$	$F_X(x)$	$\mathbb{E}(X)$	Var(X)
Uniform distribution (a,b) $a,b \in \mathbb{R},\ a < b$	$\begin{cases} \frac{1}{b-a} & \text{if } a \le x \le b \\ 0 & \text{else} \end{cases}$ $\forall x \in \mathbb{R}$ (support $[a;b]$)	$\begin{cases} 0 & \text{if } x < a \\ \frac{x-a}{b-a} & \text{if } a \le x \le b \\ 1 & \text{if } x > b \end{cases}$	$\frac{a+b}{2}$	$\frac{(b-a)^2}{12}$
Exponential distribution (λ) $\lambda \in \mathbb{R}_+^*$	$\begin{cases} \lambda \cdot \exp(-\lambda x) & \text{if } x \ge 0 \\ 0 & \text{else} \end{cases}$ $\forall x \in \mathbb{R}$ (support $\mathbb{R}_+$)	$\begin{cases} 1 - \exp(-\lambda x) & \text{if } x \ge 0 \\ 0 & \text{else} \end{cases}$	$\frac{1}{\lambda}$	$\frac{1}{\lambda^2}$
Normal distribution (μ,σ^2) $\mu \in \mathbb{R},\ \sigma^2 \in \mathbb{R}_+^*$	$\frac{1}{\sigma\sqrt{2\pi}} \cdot \exp\left(-\frac{1}{2}\left(\frac{x-\mu}{\sigma}\right)^2\right)$ $\forall x \in \mathbb{R}$	$\frac{1}{\sigma\sqrt{2\pi}} \cdot \int_{-\infty}^{x} \exp\left(-\frac{1}{2}\left(\frac{t-\mu}{\sigma}\right)^2\right)\,dt$	μ	σ^2
Standard normal distribution	$\frac{1}{\sqrt{2\pi}} \cdot \exp\left(-\frac{1}{2}x^2\right)$ $\forall x \in \mathbb{R}$	$\frac{1}{\sqrt{2\pi}} \cdot \int_{-\infty}^{x} \exp\left(-\frac{1}{2}(t-\mu)^2\right)\,dt$	0	1
Log-normal distribution (μ,σ^2) $\mu \in \mathbb{R},\ \sigma^2 \in \mathbb{R}_+^*$	$\frac{1}{x\sigma\sqrt{2\pi}} \cdot \exp\left(-\frac{(\ln(x)-\mu)^2}{2\sigma^2}\right)$ $\forall x \in \mathbb{R}_+^*$	$\frac{1}{2} + \frac{1}{2} \cdot \mathrm{erf}\left(\frac{\ln(x)-\mu}{\sigma\sqrt{2}}\right)$	$\exp(\mu+\sigma^2/2)$	$(\exp(\sigma^2)-1) \cdot \exp(2\mu+\sigma^2)$
Pareto distribution (x_m, k) $x_\mathrm{m} \in \mathbb{R}_+^*,\ k \in \mathbb{R}_+^*$	$k \cdot \frac{x_\mathrm{m}^k}{x^{k+1}}$ $\forall x \in [x_\mathrm{m};+\infty[$	$1 - \left(\frac{x_\mathrm{m}}{x}\right)^k$	$\dfrac{k \cdot x_\mathrm{m}}{k-1}$ si $k > 1$ ∞ si $k \le 1$	$\dfrac{k \cdot x_\mathrm{m}^2}{(k-1)^2 \cdot (k-2)}$ si $k > 2$ ∞ si $k \le 2$
Gamma distribution (k,θ) $k \in \mathbb{R}_+^*,\ \theta \in \mathbb{R}_+^*$	$\frac{x^{k-1} \cdot \exp\left(-\frac{x}{\theta}\right)}{\Gamma(k) \cdot \theta^k}$ $\forall x \in \mathbb{R}_+$	$\frac{\gamma(k,x/\theta)}{\Gamma(k)}$	$k \cdot \theta$	$k \cdot \theta^2$

Note: $\mathrm{erf}(x) = \frac{2}{\sqrt{\pi}} \int_0^x \exp(-t^2)\,dt$ is the Gauss error function, $\Gamma(k) = \int_0^\infty t^{k-1} \cdot \exp(-t)\,dt$ is the Euler gamma function, $\gamma(k,x) = \int_0^x t^{k-1} \cdot \exp(-t)\,dt$ is the lower incomplete gamma function.

Table 3.7: Examples of continuous probability distributions.

Comments on the examples of continuous probability distributions

- *Uniform distribution*: This distribution, whose support is a bounded interval $[a; b]$, has the same probability density at every point in that interval. Sub-intervals of equal length have the same probability. The probability density and distribution functions of a uniform distribution with generic parameters a and b are shown in figure 3.11.

- *Exponential distribution*: The exponential distribution is often used to model the time between two events. Its parameter is the intensity λ. Thus, for an event A, the random variable X indicates the time until the event occurs—such as an accident or a claim. If the elapsed times follow an exponential distribution, the number of realizations per time interval can be described by a Poisson distribution. The probability density and distribution functions of an exponential distribution with parameter $\lambda = 1$ are shown in figure 3.12.

- *Normal distribution*: The normal distribution, also known as the Gaussian distribution, is used to describe random phenomena. A normal random variable is characterized by its expected value μ and its variance σ^2 (or its standard deviation σ). The normal distribution has a special place in mathematics because of the central limit theorem (see theorem 3.3). Any normal random variable can be decomposed as $X = \mu + \sigma \cdot Z$, where Z is a random variable that follows a so-called standard normal distribution, with expected value $\mu = 0$ and standard deviation $\sigma = 1$.

- *Standard normal distribution*: This is a special type of normal distribution with an expected value of 0 and a standard deviation of 1. If X is normal with an expected value μ and variance σ^2, then $Z = (X - \mu)/\sigma$ is standard normal. The probability density and distribution functions of a standard normal distribution are shown in figure 3.13.

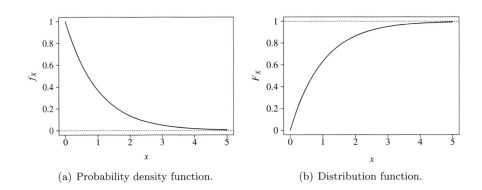

(a) Probability density function.　　　　　(b) Distribution function.

Figure 3.12: Illustration of the probability density and distribution functions of an exponential distribution with parameter $\lambda = 1$.

- *Log-normal distribution*: The log-normal distribution is often used in financial analysis to describe the price of financial instruments such as stocks, foreign exchange rates, and interest rates. A random variable X follows a log-normal distribution with expected value μ and variance σ^2 (or standard deviation σ) if the variable $\ln(X)$ follows a normal distribution with expected value μ and variance σ^2. The probability density and the distribution functions of a log-normal distribution with parameters $\mu = 0$ and $\sigma = 1$ are shown in figure 3.14.

- *Pareto distribution*: The Pareto distribution is a special type of power-law distribution with applications in physics and social sciences. Among other uses, it can provide a theoretical basis for the "80–20 principle," also known as the Pareto principle, and is often used in non-life reinsurance. The Pareto distribution considers two parameters: the variable x_m, which also characterizes the support $[x_m; +\infty[$, and the parameter k, often called the Pareto index.

- *Gamma distribution*: The gamma distribution is useful for measuring probabilities related to positive values, such as elapsed time—for example, as part of a survival analysis—and loss amounts. It is characterized by two parameters, k and θ, which affect the shape and scale of its graph. The probability density and distribution functions of a gamma distribution with parameters $k = 2$ and $\theta = 1$ are shown in figure 3.8.

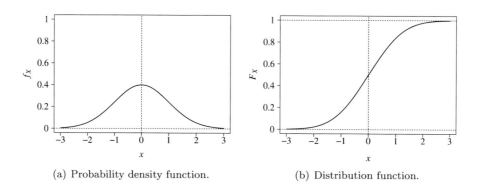

(a) Probability density function.   (b) Distribution function.

Figure 3.13: Illustration of the probability density and distribution functions of a standard normal distribution.

3.4 Utility and utility functions

In section 3.5, when we study the principles of risk assessment, we will see that analyzing risks using the expected value of losses is not adequate. This is because the same amount may be perceived differently depending on the individuals or

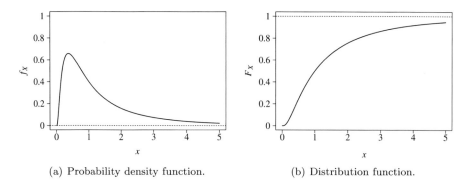

(a) Probability density function. (b) Distribution function.

Figure 3.14: Illustration of the probability density and distribution functions of a log-normal distribution with parameters $\mu = 0$ and $\sigma^2 = 1$.

companies. This perception depends, in particular, on the company itself and its risk preferences. For example, a loss of one million Swiss francs may be catastrophic for a small company, whereas a multinational corporation with revenues in the billions of Swiss francs may consider it a trivial amount. To account for these preferences, we transform values of wealth, profit, and loss into quantities of utility that reflect individual attitudes toward risk. In this section, we will introduce the concepts of utility and certainty equivalent. We will illustrate the most common utility functions and relate risk aversion to the parameters of these functions.

Definition and hypotheses Utility is a measure of the "satisfaction" gained from obtaining a good. We represent the utility of having an amount of money x as the value $u(x)$. As we will see below, the shape of the graph of the function u varies depending on each individual's preferences. Formally, a utility function assigns a utility value $u(x)$ to a monetary value x:

Definition 3.18 (*Utility function*)

A **utility function** u *is an application that assigns a utility value $u(x)$ to any amount of money x,*

$$u : x \mapsto u(x).$$

Using this measure, an individual can rank various options available to them based on their own preferences. This function u is different for each person and each company. We assume that the utility function is n times differentiable. It must also satisfy two important additional hypotheses:

- *Hypothesis 1*: Every individual would rather have more money than less money: the utility function u is an increasing function. Thus, for any two amounts of money x and y,

$$x > y \quad \Rightarrow \quad u(x) \geq u(y).$$

In other words, the first derivative of the utility function u is positive:

$$\frac{\mathrm{d}u}{\mathrm{d}x} = u'(x) \geq 0.$$

Note that u is an increasing function, i.e.,

$$u'(x) \geq 0.$$

- *Hypothesis 2*: The richer a person is, the less they value an increase in their wealth: marginal utility is a decreasing function. Utility u is a concave function. For any positive amount h we have

$$x > y \quad \Rightarrow \quad u(x + h) - u(x) \leq u(y + h) - u(y).$$

In other words, the second derivative of the utility function u is negative:

$$\frac{\mathrm{d}^2 u}{\mathrm{d}x^2} = u''(x) \leq 0.$$

Note that marginal utility is decreasing, i.e.,

$$u''(x) \leq 0.$$

Expected utility   The expected value of utility $u(X)$, that is, the utility u of a random variable X, is obtained by applying the definition of the expected value. If X is a random variable representing wealth, then the value of that wealth in terms of utility is given by expected utility.

Definition 3.19 (*Expected utility*)

*The **expected utility** of a random variable X is given by*

– If X is a discrete random variable:

$$\mathbb{E}(u(X)) = \sum_{x \in \mathcal{X}} u(x) \cdot \mathbb{P}(X = x),$$

– If X is a continuous random variable:

$$\mathbb{E}(u(X)) = \int_{-\infty}^{+\infty} u(x) \cdot f_X(x) \, \mathrm{d}x.$$

If v is another utility function, defined as $v(x) = \alpha \cdot u(x) + \beta$, with $\alpha > 0$, the order of preference is not changed. Thus, for random variables X and Y, we have the following relationship:

$$\mathbb{E}(v(X)) > \mathbb{E}(v(Y)) \quad \Longleftrightarrow \quad \mathbb{E}(u(X)) > \mathbb{E}(u(Y)).$$

This means that the utility function actually defines an order of preference.

Attitude towards risk The utility function of an individual or company reflects their preferences. In particular, it includes an aspect of attitude toward risk. We distinguish three types of risk behavior: neutrality, aversion, and preference. What allows us to classify preferences between these categories is the slope of the marginal utility $u'(x)$, i.e., $u''(x)$.

More specifically, an individual or a company with a neutral attitude toward risk ($u''(x) = 0$) has a linear utility function. Risk aversion is expressed by a concave utility function ($u''(x) < 0$), while risk preference is expressed by a convex utility function ($u''(x) > 0$). We summarize the different attitudes toward risk based on the shape of the graphical representation of $u(x)$ in table 3.8.

Finally, using Jensen's inequalities mentioned in section 3.3 (see theorem 3.1), we determine ordering relationships between the expected utility $\mathbb{E}(u(X))$ and the utility of the expected value $u(\mathbb{E}(X))$. These inequalities depend on the concavity of the function u, i.e., on the sign of $u''(x)$. In the case of risk aversion, we note that $u''(x) < 0$, and we have $\mathbb{E}(u(X)) < u(\mathbb{E}(X))$; therefore, the expected utility is less than the utility of the expected value.

Attitude	Condition	Shape of $u(x)$	Ordering relationship
Risk aversion	$u''(x) < 0$	Concave	$\mathbb{E}(u(X)) < u(\mathbb{E}(X))$
Risk neutrality	$u''(x) = 0$	Linear	$\mathbb{E}(u(X)) = u(\mathbb{E}(X))$
Risk preference	$u''(x) > 0$	Convex	$\mathbb{E}(u(X)) > u(\mathbb{E}(X))$

Table 3.8: Attitudes toward risk, utility function plot forms, and ordering relationships between expected utility and expected value utility.

Certainty equivalent In risk theory, when faced with choices guided by measures of utility, the certainty equivalent is an important concept. This measure reflects how much a situation of certainty is worth compared to an uncertain alternative. Depending on one's attitude toward risk, this amount may differ substantially from the expected value of the amounts involved in the possible outcomes.

As an example, consider the following choice: an agent can either receive a certain amount x or participate in a lottery in which this amount x can increase to y_1 with a probability of p or decrease to y_2 with a probability of $1 - p$. To get a more concrete idea, we can imagine that the amounts x, y_1, and y_2 represent a fortune or a bank account balance.

How can we determine whether a rational individual would prefer the lottery or the certainty? To do this, we need to determine the certainty equivalent of the lottery and compare it to the amount promised with certainty. This certainty equivalent will, of course, depend on the amounts y_1 and y_2 and the probability p, but also on the individual making the decision. If the certainty equivalent of the lottery is higher than the amount offered with certainty, then the individual will prefer the lottery. Otherwise, they will prefer to take the certainty. If the certainty equivalent is equal to the amount offered with certainty, the individual will be indifferent to the choice to be made.

Definition 3.20 (*Certainty equivalent*)

> *In decision theory, the* **certainty equivalent** *is the amount an individual or company would be willing to pay or accept to avoid being in a given situation of uncertainty.*

It follows that the value of the certainty equivalent is the amount that makes the decision maker indifferent to the choice to be made. In the case of an amount to be paid, it is the maximum amount; in the case of an amount to be received, it is the minimum amount. The value is different for each individual or company, and this allows us to characterize the individual's or company's attitude to risk.

Certainty equivalent and lottery ticket

Imagine you are faced with the following decision: "You have a lottery ticket that gives you a 50% chance of winning CHF 1,000. How much, at least, would you have to be paid to sell it?"
In this situation, you have a choice between (a) a 50-50 chance of winning CHF 1,000 and (b) getting a certain amount by selling your ticket. The certainty equivalent is the price at which you are willing to sell your lottery ticket. This amount depends on each individual, i.e., it is "your" certainty equivalent.

Certainty equivalent and insurance premium

Imagine you are faced with the following decision: "You park and lock your bicycle at the train station in the morning. There is a 5% chance that your bicycle, worth CHF 2,000, will be stolen when you return at the end of the day. How much, at most, would you be prepared to pay for theft insurance for your bike?"
In this situation, you have a choice between (a) a one in twenty chance of losing your CHF 2,000 bicycle and (b) paying a fixed amount for an insurance policy that covers the potential loss of your bicycle. The certainty equivalent is the price you are willing to pay to insure your bicycle. This amount varies from person to person.

Formally, we use the random variables X and Y to illustrate the certain and uncertain situations, respectively. For realizations $x, y_1, y_2 \in \mathbb{R}_+$, with $y_1 > y_2$, we set

$$X = x \quad \text{with certainty (probability 1)},$$

and

$$Y = \begin{cases} y_1 & \text{with probability } p, \\ y_2 & \text{with probability } 1 - p. \end{cases}$$

In the graph in figure 3.15, we show the points y_1, y_2, the expected value of the lottery Y, i.e., $\mathbb{E}(Y)$, and the values of utility at points y_1, y_2, and $\mathbb{E}(Y)$ for a risk-averse person. Note the concave shape of u, which corresponds to a risk-averse attitude.

The expected value of the utility $u(Y)$, i.e., the average utility weighted by the probabilities of the alternatives $u(y_1)$ and $u(y_2)$, is given by

$$\overline{u} = \mathbb{E}(u(Y)) = p \cdot u(y_1) + (1 - p) \cdot u(y_2).$$

This is the utility associated with the lottery. For given values of y_1 and y_2, the certainty equivalent is the amount $x = x_0$, which must be determined, at which the decision maker is indifferent to the choice between the certain amount and the lottery. This amount, x_0, is such that $u(x_0) = \overline{u}$. Formally, the equality of expected utilities gives

$$\mathbb{E}(u(X)) = \mathbb{E}(u(Y)) \iff u(x_0) = \overline{u}.$$

In our case, this means that the certainty equivalent x_0 can be determined by the following formula:

$$x_0 = u^{-1}(\overline{u}) = u^{-1}(\mathbb{E}(u(Y))) = u^{-1}[(p \cdot u(y_1) + (1 - p) \cdot u(y_2)].$$

The graph in figure 3.15 illustrates the relationships between the expected value of the lottery $\mathbb{E}(Y)$ and the certainty equivalent. First, we find the graphical representation of a utility function for a risk-averse individual or company. Then, the amounts y_1, y_2, and $\mathbb{E}(Y)$ are plotted on the horizontal axis. The graph illustrates the case where $p = 0.5$ so that $\mathbb{E}(Y)$ is at the midpoint between y_1 and y_2. To each of these three amounts, y_1, y_2, and $\overline{y} = \mathbb{E}(Y)$, we assign a utility on the vertical axis: $u(y_1)$, $u(y_2)$, and $u(\overline{y}) = u(\mathbb{E}(Y))$, respectively. We calculate the expected value $\overline{u} = \mathbb{E}(u(Y))$ based on the values $u(y_1)$ and $u(y_2)$. With $p = 0.5$, we find $\overline{u} = \mathbb{E}(u(Y))$ at the midpoint between $u(y_1)$ and $u(y_2)$. Finally, we look for the amount corresponding to this average utility by applying the inverse function u^{-1}. This step is indicated by the arrows on the graph. The result is the certainty equivalent, $x_0 = u^{-1}(\overline{u}) = u^{-1}(\mathbb{E}(u(Y)))$. Note that $x_0 < \overline{y}$, which is a consequence of the concavity of the utility function.

The certainty equivalent yields results that are easy to interpret. The difference between the expected value of the random variable $\overline{y} = \mathbb{E}(Y)$ and the certainty equivalent $x_0 = u^{-1}(\overline{u}) = u^{-1}(\mathbb{E}(u(Y)))$ gives us a first way to evaluate a risk

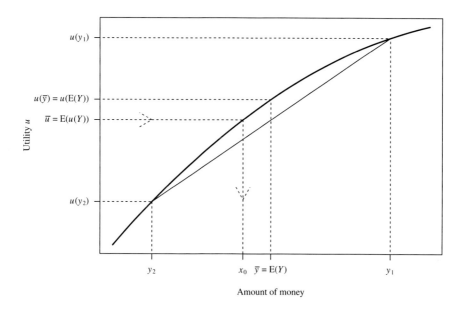

Figure 3.15: Illustration of the certainty equivalent in a risk-averse attitude.

premium. This is because the expected value $\mathbb{E}(Y)$ gives the amount expected by an agent who is indifferent to risk. If an agent is risk-averse, the certainty equivalent is less than the expected value because the agent assigns a lower value to the lottery than to the certain amount. Thus, the "risk premium" is positive: the agent is willing to give up some of the uncertain amount (expected value) in order to receive a certain amount (certainty equivalent). The "risk premium" is given by the difference $\mathbb{E}(Y) - x_0$. If the agent has a preference for risk, the certainty equivalent is higher than the expected value, and so the "risk premium" is negative: the agent must be paid not to play. The example of a gambler in a casino is often used to illustrate this second scenario. In the context of risk management and insurance, we often deal with risk-averse agents who are willing to invest in risk mitigation. The difference $\mathbb{E}(Y) - x_0$ gives an indication of the willingness to pay for such measures, which we will discuss in more detail below.

Risk aversion coefficient In order to evaluate the differences in utility seen above, it is important to choose the correct utility function and parameters, as this function must reflect the agent's attitude toward risk. This attitude is often characterized by a risk aversion coefficient. In this section, we will relate the risk aversion coefficient to the utility function. We will illustrate the approach in the case of small variations and use Taylor series expansions.

As above, we will use a situation with a certain outcome and an uncertain outcome; specifically: an agent is given the choice between receiving a certain amount x and participating in a lottery in which this amount can either increase to $x + h$ with a probability of p or decrease to $x - h$ with a probability of $1 - p$. In this example, h is a positive constant. Formally, we describe the choice of the certain amount with the variable X,

$$X = x \quad \text{with certainty (probability 1)},$$

and the uncertain choice with the random variable Y,

$$Y = \begin{cases} x + h & \text{with probability } p, \\ x - h & \text{with probability } 1 - p. \end{cases}$$

The agent's choice is strongly influenced by the amounts x and h in play, as well as by the probability p of winning the lottery. Especially large deviations h or a low probability p can be prohibitive. Here, we consider the following question: For given values of x and h, what is the lottery probability p at which the agent is indifferent between choosing the certain amount x and the lottery Y?

To express this problem, we define the probability $p = p(x, h)$ as a function of x and h, and we search for p such that the agent is indifferent to both possibilities; in other words, we must find

$$p = p(x, h) \quad \text{such that} \quad \mathbb{E}(u(X)) = \mathbb{E}(u(Y)).$$

For given values of x and h, the value of this probability quantifies risk aversion. The higher it is, the more risk-averse the agent is. For people who are very risk-averse, the probability of winning, p, must be high in order for them to accept the lottery, i.e., for them to be indifferent to the certain alternative.

We have $\mathbb{E}(u(X)) = u(x)$, because $X = x$ with certainty. With the definition of the expected value $\mathbb{E}(u(Y)) = p \cdot u(x + h) + (1 - p) \cdot u(x - h)$, the above condition $\mathbb{E}(u(X)) = \mathbb{E}(u(Y))$ may be written as

$$u(x) = p \cdot u(x + h) + (1 - p) \cdot u(x - h).$$

Solving this equation for p, we get

$$p = p(x, h) = \frac{u(x) - u(x - h)}{u(x + h) - u(x - h)}$$

For small values of h, we use the Taylor series expansions of $u(x + h)$ and $u(x - h)$:

$$u(x + h) = u(x) + \frac{h}{1!} \cdot u'(x) + \frac{h^2}{2!} \cdot u''(x) + \ldots + \frac{h^n}{n!} \cdot u^{(n)}(x) + \ldots,$$

$$u(x - h) = u(x) - \frac{h}{1!} \cdot u'(x) + \frac{h^2}{2!} \cdot u''(x) + \ldots + (-1)^n \frac{h^n}{n!} \cdot u^{(n)}(x) + \ldots,$$

and consider the following second-order approximations:

$$u(x + h) \approx u(x) + h \cdot u'(x) + \frac{1}{2} h^2 \cdot u''(x),$$

$$u(x - h) \approx u(x) - h \cdot u'(x) + \frac{1}{2} h^2 \cdot u''(x),$$

which we substitute in the earlier formula for $p(x, h)$:

$$p(x, h) \approx \frac{h \cdot u'(x) - \frac{1}{2}h^2 \cdot u''(x)}{2h \cdot u'(x)} = \frac{1}{2} + \frac{1}{4}h \cdot \left(\frac{-u''(x)}{u'(x)} \right).$$

To interpret this result, we introduce the following definition:

Definition 3.21 (*Absolute risk aversion coefficient*)

The **absolute risk aversion coefficient** $A(x)$ of a utility function u is defined as

$$A(x) = \frac{-u''(x)}{u'(x)} = -\frac{\mathrm{d}}{\mathrm{d}x} \ln(u'(x)).$$

Introduced by Pratt (1964), the coefficient $A(x)$ measures the curve of the utility function normalized by its derivative. It establishes a relationship between the utility function and risk aversion. Thus, it measures sensitivity. For example, an agent is less risk-averse as their wealth increases if and only if their absolute risk aversion decreases. This is because risk aversion translates into $A(x) > 0$ as, in this case, $u''(x) < 0$. As a reminder, $u'(x)$ is positive for any utility function according to Hypothesis 1 presented at the beginning of section 3.4. Similarly, we have $A(x) < 0$ in cases of preference for risk, as $u''(x) > 0$.

Using the definition of the absolute risk aversion coefficient $A(x)$, the result for the probability $p(x, h)$ is

$$p(x, h) \approx \frac{1}{2} + \frac{1}{4}h \cdot A(x).$$

This result deserves some comment. For a risk aversion of zero, we find that $p \approx 1/2$. This is explained by the fact that the expected utility and expected value of X and Y are identical. A risk-neutral agent does not take into account the variations h in the lottery and values a lottery with a 50-50 chance of winning as equivalent to a certain alternative with the same expected value. Starting with $p \approx 1/2$, for a risk-averse agent, i.e., one whose attitude is characterized by $A(x) > 0$, we see that the probability of winning p must be higher. Likewise, p must increase if the lottery's variations h are larger, i.e., if the potential gains or losses are larger. Finally, p depends on x through the absolute risk aversion coefficient $A(x)$.

In general, we classify utility functions into one of the following three categories, depending on the absolute risk aversion coefficient, which is a function of x:

- If $A(x)$ is a constant, we call the utility function "constant absolute risk aversion" (CARA),

- If $A(x)$ is decreasing in x, we call the utility function "decreasing absolute risk aversion" (DARA),

- If $A(x)$ is increasing in x, we call the utility function "increasing absolute risk aversion" (IARA).

One drawback of the absolute risk aversion coefficient is that it does not take into account an agent's initial wealth. It is easy to imagine that less wealthy individuals are more sensitive to increases in wealth than those who already have significant wealth. The relative risk aversion coefficient $R(x)$ highlights this point. It is defined as follows:

Definition 3.22 (*Relative risk aversion coefficient*)

The **relative risk aversion coefficient** $R(x)$ of a utility function u is defined as

$$R(x) = x \cdot A(x) = x \cdot \frac{-u''(x)}{u'(x)} = -x \cdot \frac{\mathrm{d}}{\mathrm{d}x} \ln(u'(x)).$$

The coefficient of relative risk aversion is proportional to wealth. There are three families of utility functions:

- If $R(x)$ is a constant, we call the utility function "constant relative risk aversion" (CRRA),
- If $R(x)$ is decreasing in x, we call the utility function "decreasing relative risk aversion" (DRRA),
- If $R(x)$ is increasing in x, we call the utility function "increasing relative risk aversion" (IRRA).

Examples of utility functions   In table 3.9, we present some examples of commonly used utility functions. These are the exponential utility function, the power utility function, the logarithmic utility function, and the quadratic utility function. We present the definition of each function, as well as the absolute and relative risk aversion coefficients that characterize it.

In economic terms, an exponential utility function is associated with individuals of modest means. Depending on the value chosen for the parameter λ, utility "saturation" is reached more or less quickly. With an already significant amount of wealth, an increase in wealth results in only an infinitesimal increase in utility. Examples are given in figure 3.16(a). Conversely, a quadratic utility function is appropriate to describe a "Scrooge" type of behavior: in this case, even for a very rich individual, an increase in wealth results in a significant increase in utility. Examples of these functions are shown in figure 3.16(b).

Valuation of the risk premium   We saw above (see figure 3.15) that the certainty equivalent is lower than the expected value: a risk-averse agent is willing to give up some of their wealth in order to reach a given situation with certainty. We call this difference $\mathbb{E}(Y) - x_0$, the risk premium. Thus, in the context of valuing

Utility function	$u(x)$	$A(x)$	$R(x)$	Type of utility
Exponential utility (λ, c) $\lambda \in \mathbb{R}_+^*, c \in \mathbb{R}$	$u(x) = -\exp(-\lambda \cdot x) + c$ $x \in \mathbb{R}_+$	λ	$x \cdot \lambda$	CARA, IRRA
Power utility (γ) $\gamma \in]0;1[\cup]1;+\infty[$	$u(x) = \dfrac{x^{1-\gamma}}{1-\gamma}$ $x \in \mathbb{R}_+^*$	$\dfrac{\gamma}{x}$	γ	DARA, CRRA
Logarithmic utility	$\ln(x)$ $x \in \mathbb{R}_+^*$	$\dfrac{1}{x}$	1	DARA, CRRA
Quadratic utility (α) $\alpha \in \mathbb{R}_+^*$	$x - \alpha \cdot x^2$ $x \in \left[0; \dfrac{1}{2\alpha}\right]$	$\dfrac{2\alpha}{1-2\alpha x}$	$\dfrac{2\alpha x}{1-2\alpha x}$	IARA, IRRA

Table 3.9: Examples of utility functions.

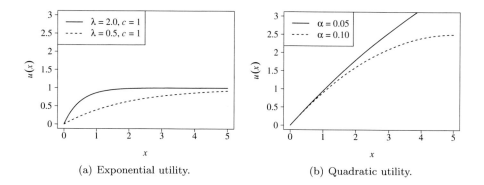

(a) Exponential utility.

(b) Quadratic utility.

Figure 3.16: Illustration of the exponential and quadratic utility functions.

a risk with potential losses S, the use of expected utility leads to the introduction of a safety margin so that the assessment of a risk, or its "price tag" π, is higher than its expected value: $\pi > \mathbb{E}(S)$. In this section, we will take a closer look at the concept of a safety margin.

When valuing a risk premium, i.e., the (maximum) amount one is willing to pay for coverage against a certain risk or the (minimum) amount one is willing to receive for taking on a certain risk, both parties' perspectives must be taken into account. This is easily illustrated in the field of insurance. An insurance policy is a contract that protects the policyholder against losses related to specific risk exposures. The two parties involved are the insurance company, which offers the policy, and the policyholder, who buys the policy. The insurance policy transfers risk from the policyholder to the insurer. Simplifying the problem and assuming that all agents are rational, a contract between both parties is possible if the maximum premium the policyholder is willing to pay is higher than the minimum premium the insurer is willing to offer. From the policyholder's perspective, the problem boils down to calculating the maximum premium they are willing to pay. Conversely, from the insurer's point of view, the problem is calculating the minimum premium that the insurer wants to receive. We use the following definition:

Definition 3.23 (*Risk premium*)

The **risk premium** *π is the amount that (a) an agent is willing to pay, at most, for coverage against a risk, or (b) an agent is willing to be paid for offering coverage against a risk.*

- *Situation (a): If u is the utility function of an agent (e.g., a policyholder) whose initial wealth is w and who faces a risk exposure that could result in losses described by the random variable S, then the risk premium or maximum amount π that the agent is willing to pay for coverage is the solution to the equation*

$$u(w - \pi) = \mathbb{E}(u(w - S)).$$

- *Situation (b): If u is the utility function of an agent (e.g., an insurer) whose initial wealth is w and who is willing to take a risk exposure that could result in losses described by the random variable S, then the risk premium or minimum amount π that the agent is willing to receive to cover that risk is the solution to the equation*

$$u(w) = \mathbb{E}(u(w + \pi - S)).$$

As an illustration, and to comment on the relationships introduced in the definition 3.23, we begin by analyzing the *perspective of a policyholder* who wishes to be insured against the risk of a loss. We use the random variable S to refer to the amount of losses. Let w be the policyholder's wealth, and u be their utility function. The policyholder agrees to buy insurance only if it increases their expected utility. The policyholder has two options: they can buy insurance to cover the risk by paying a premium π, or they can remain uninsured and bear the risk themself. In the first case, their utility is $u(w - \pi)$; in the second case, their utility is $\mathbb{E}(u(w - S))$. The maximum premium π they are willing to pay is the amount at which both options have the same utility, i.e.,

$$u(w - \pi) = \mathbb{E}(u(w - S)).$$

The left-hand side of the equation represents the policyholder's utility if they buy insurance. In this case, they have to pay a premium but do not have to bear the financial consequences S. The utility is deterministic. The right-hand side of the equation is the policyholder's expected utility if they do not purchase insurance. In this case, they must use their own wealth to pay for the consequences S. Since u is a function of the random variable S, we must use the expected value to evaluate the utility.

Risk premium from a policyholder's perspective

Consider a potential policyholder with an exponential utility function

$$u(x) = -e^{-\gamma x},$$

whose initial wealth is w and who is exposed to potential losses represented by the random variable S. From their perspective, the maximum premium π they would pay to insure against S must satisfy the equation

$$-e^{-\gamma(w-\pi)} = \mathbb{E}(-e^{-\gamma(w-S)}).$$

Solving this equation gives us the maximum premium the policyholder is willing to pay,

$$\pi = \frac{1}{\gamma} \cdot \ln(\mathbb{E}(e^{\gamma S})).$$

Note that in this particular case, the premium π does not depend on the policyholder's initial wealth w. Only the exponential utility function has this property.

We can show that if the policyholder is risk-averse, the premium π they are willing to pay is higher than the expected value of the loss. Applying Jensen's inequality to the left-hand side of the above equation, $\mathbb{E}(u(w - S))$, we get

$$\mathbb{E}(u(w - S)) < u(\mathbb{E}(w - S))$$
$$= u(w - \mathbb{E}(S)).$$

Then, using this result in the equation that π must satisfy, we have

$$u(w - \pi) < u(w - \mathbb{E}(S)).$$

Since the utility function u is monotonic and increasing, we have

$$\pi > \mathbb{E}(S).$$

The risk premium π is greater than the expected value $\mathbb{E}(S)$: thus, the risk premium includes a safety margin for risk.

Let us now consider the *perspective of an insurer* covering the risk of loss of an individual or a company. As mentioned above, we use the random variable S to refer to the amount of losses. The insurer's available capital is w, and its utility function is u. The insurer will agree to cover the risk only if doing so increases its expected utility, or at least keeps it at the same level after the risk is transferred. It, therefore, has two options: not to offer insurance, in which case its capital remains unchanged, or to offer insurance, in which case it receives a premium and covers the potential loss S. The minimum premium π that it charges is the solution of the equation where both situations are equal:

$$u(w) = \mathbb{E}(u(w + \pi - S)).$$

The left-hand side of the equation represents the insurer's utility if not covering the risk. It is completely deterministic. The right-hand side of the equation is its expected utility if it decides to cover the risk. In this case, it receives the premium π and pays out the random amount S.

Risk premium from an insurer's perspective

Consider an insurer with an exponential utility function

$$u(x) = -e^{-\gamma x},$$

and a capital w. It is willing to cover losses S for a minimum premium π satisfying the equation

$$-e^{-\gamma w} = \mathbb{E}(-e^{-\gamma(w+\pi-S)}).$$

Solving this equation, we find

$$\pi = \frac{1}{\gamma} \cdot \ln(\mathbb{E}(e^{\gamma S})).$$

This is the same premium we calculated above from the policyholder's perspective. For the policyholder, it is the maximum premium they are willing to pay. For the insurer, it is the minimum premium they are willing to charge the policyholder. In our application, both premiums are equal, and an insurance policy can be signed. Finally, note that in practice, the utility function u, the parameter γ, and the wealth w for the policyholder and the insurer are not identical.

As above, we can show that the minimum premium π charged by a risk-averse insurer is higher than the expected value of the loss S it covers. To do this, we can apply Jensen's inequality to $\mathbb{E}(u(w + \pi - S))$. We have

$$\mathbb{E}(u(w + \pi - S)) < u(\mathbb{E}(w + \pi - S))$$
$$= u(w + \pi - \mathbb{E}(S)).$$

So, the initial equation defining π becomes

$$u(w) < u(w + \pi - \mathbb{E}(S)),$$

and since the utility function u is monotonic and increasing, we conclude that

$$\pi - \mathbb{E}(S) > 0 \quad \Longleftrightarrow \quad \pi > \mathbb{E}(S).$$

The premium π calculated in this case includes a margin for risk.

Approximation of the premium for small risks The calculation of a risk premium is closely related to the concept of utility. The utility function and the characteristics of both the agents and the risk exposure allow an assessment of the risk premium in specific cases. In what follows, we seek a general relationship between the risk premium and the expected value and variance of the loss S while also noting the role of risk attitude. We derive the premium in the case of "small risks," which allows us to use approximations. To do so, we start with an agent (e.g., an insurance company) with wealth w who agrees to cover a risk; we then consider the equation that the minimum premium π must satisfy:

$$u(w) = \mathbb{E}(u(w + \pi - S)).$$

We try to calculate π and ask the following question: What premium $\pi(z)$ should be paid to cover $z \cdot S$, a fraction z of the loss S? We rewrite the equation as follows:

$$u(w) = \mathbb{E}(u(w + \pi(z) - z \cdot S)).$$

Note that if $z = 0$, then $\pi(0) = 0$. This case is trivial because, for $z = 0$, the loss is zero, and there is no coverage. Below, we look at the case where $z \to 0$, i.e., a situation where we can use an approximation of $\pi(z)$ using its second-order Taylor series expansion in the neighborhood of zero.

If we differentiate the above equation with respect to z, we get

$$\frac{\mathrm{d}u(w)}{\mathrm{d}z} = \frac{\mathrm{d}\mathbb{E}(u(w + \pi(z) - z \cdot S))}{\mathrm{d}z}$$
$$\Leftrightarrow \quad 0 = \mathbb{E}(u'(w + \pi(z) - z \cdot S) \cdot (\pi'(z) - S)).$$

Since the utility function is monotonic and increasing in w, this equation is satisfied only if $\mathbb{E}(\pi'(z) - S) = 0$. Therefore, we necessarily have $\pi'(z) = \mathbb{E}(S)$, $\forall z$, and especially in the case where $z = 0$, $\pi'(0) = \mathbb{E}(S)$.

If we differentiate this equation a second time with respect to z, we get

$$\mathbb{E}(u''(w + \pi(z) - z \cdot S) \cdot (\pi'(z) - S)^2) + \mathbb{E}(u'(w + \pi(z) - z \cdot S) \cdot \pi''(z)) = 0.$$

When evaluated at $z = 0$, this equation gives us

$$\mathbb{E}(u''(w + \pi(0)) \cdot (\pi'(0) - S)^2) + \mathbb{E}(u'(w + \pi(0)) \cdot \pi''(0)) = 0,$$

and with $\pi(0) = 0$ and $\pi'(0) = \mathbb{E}(S)$ we have

$$\mathbb{E}(u''(w) \cdot (\mathbb{E}(S) - S)^2) + \mathbb{E}(u'(w) \cdot \pi''(0)) = 0.$$

This can be solved for $\pi''(0)$, resulting in

$$\pi''(0) = -\frac{u''(w)}{u'(w)} \cdot \mathbb{E}((S - \mathbb{E}(S))^2).$$

For small values of z, we introduce the approximation of π using its second-order Taylor series expansion in the neighborhood of zero:

$$\pi(z) = \pi(0 + z) \approx \pi(0) + \frac{z}{1!} \cdot \pi'(0) + \frac{z^2}{2!} \cdot \pi''(0).$$

105

With the previous results, $\pi(0) = 0$, $\pi'(0) = \mathbb{E}(S)$, and $\pi''(0) = -\frac{u''(w)}{u'(w)}$ $\cdot \mathbb{E}\left((S - \mathbb{E}(S))^2\right)$, it follows:

$$\pi(z) \approx \mathbb{E}(S) \cdot z - \frac{1}{2} \cdot \frac{u''(w)}{u'(w)} \mathbb{E}((S - \mathbb{E}(S))^2) \cdot z^2$$

$$\approx \mathbb{E}(z \cdot S) + \frac{1}{2} A(w) \cdot \mathrm{Var}(z \cdot S),$$

where $A(x)$ is the absolute risk aversion coefficient introduced in definition 3.21.

If we define $X = z \cdot S$, then the random variable X is the loss associated with a small risk. We conclude that for this type of risk, the risk premium, π_X, is approximately

$$\pi_X \approx \mathbb{E}(X) + \frac{1}{2} A(w) \cdot \mathrm{Var}(X).$$

The risk premium is essentially the expected value of X, to which we add a margin for risk. This margin is proportional to the variance of X, but it also depends on risk aversion. The higher the risk aversion, the higher the margin for risk. This approximation, which is valid for small risks, highlights the role of the variability of the loss S, here the variance, in determining the premium.

In general, with a risk-averse agent covering a risk exposure with a potential loss of S, we often define

$$\pi \approx \mathbb{E}(S) + \alpha \cdot \mathrm{Var}(S), \quad \alpha \in \mathbb{R}_+.$$

With this approach, $\pi \geq \mathbb{E}(S)$ is checked, and the safety margin is considered proportional to the variance of the loss. Two parameters are then taken into account in evaluating and determining α, namely the *financial capacity* of the agent who will bear the loss and their *individual attitude* to risk, i.e., their risk aversion. Both—wealth w and risk aversion coefficient A—are present in the result that we just derived for small risks.

3.5 Principles of risk assessment

Risk assessment consists of transforming a risk exposure into a (monetary) value. In particular, the goal is to define a criterion that can be used to evaluate potential losses resulting from a risk exposure described by a random variable. Such a criterion must allow comparisons between different risk exposures, analyses of the impact of different risk management techniques, and decisions on which technique is most appropriate in a given situation.

There are several criteria for assessing risk: they are principles-based, for example, on expected value, expected utility, or value-at-risk. In most cases, the use of a metric is necessary to make a decision. How each individual or company acts depends on the situation and their own attitude toward risk. In many cases, there is no "good" or "bad" decision.

Situational risk assessment

We suggest assessing our preferences in the following situations:

- *Situation 1*: Choosing between
  (a) a CHF 30,000 profit with a probability of 25%,
  (b) a CHF 45,000 profit with a probability of 20%.

- *Situation 2*: Choosing between
  (a) a CHF 50,000 profit with a probability of 80%,
  (b) a CHF 30,000 profit with a probability of 100%.

In situation 1, some are attracted to the higher profit of option (b), while others focus on the five percentage point higher chance of profit in option (a). The more mathematically minded say that the expected value of option (a) is CHF 7,500, while that of option (b) is CHF 9,000. In situation 2, such calculations lead to expected values of CHF 40,000 for option (a) and CHF 30,000 for option (b); still, some might prefer the latter because the profit is certain.

Do we use the same criteria when dealing with potential losses?

- *Situation 3*: Choosing between
  (a) a CHF 50,000 loss with a probability of 80%,
  (b) a CHF 30,000 loss with a probability of 100%.

In this case, despite the higher expected value of the loss, some will choose option (a), hoping to benefit from the 20% chance of no loss.

Other situations could be as follows:

- *Situation 4*: Imagine you paid CHF 50 for a concert ticket. When you get to the venue, you realize that you have misplaced the ticket. Do you buy a new ticket?

- *Situation 5*: For the same concert: Imagine that you are about to buy a ticket and you realize that you lost a CHF 50 bill on the way to the venue. Do you still buy a ticket for CHF 50?

These last two examples show how subjective the assessment is, which requires a closer look in the context of utility. The answer will depend on the situation and may be influenced by the other people going to the concert with you.

In order to assess risks, we look at a number of assessment criteria. Assigning an economic value to a risk means using a risk assessment principle, which can be defined as follows:

Definition 3.24 (*Risk assessment principle*)

> A **risk assessment principle** *is an application that assigns a deterministic real number* $\Pi(S)$ *to a random variable S referring to the losses associated with a risk exposure,*
> $$S \mapsto \Pi(S).$$

Thus, a risk assessment principle is a function that assigns a deterministic real number $\Pi(S)$ to each random variable S, representing the loss resulting from a risk exposure. In the following sections, we will look in detail at some of the most commonly used assessment functions.

Expected value criterion The main idea behind using expected value as a criterion is to evaluate the loss represented by the random variable S. Based on this criterion, a risk exposure will be feared the more the expected value of the associated loss will be high. The concept consists of assigning to each random variable S a deterministic number $\mathbb{E}(S)$ that can measure it. Measuring a risk by its expected value is called the equivalence principle.

Definition 3.25 (*Equivalence principle*)

> *The* **equivalence principle** *is a risk assessment principle that assigns to the random variable S describing the losses associated with a risk exposure its expected value* $\mathbb{E}(S)$,
> $$S \mapsto \mathbb{E}(S).$$

The equivalence principle is a special case of a risk assessment principle in which

$$\Pi(S) = \mathbb{E}(S).$$

This criterion is purely economic and has a number of drawbacks. A first criticism can be illustrated by considering the random variable S with the following probability mass function:

$$\mathbb{P}_S(S = s) = \begin{cases} 0.5 & \text{for } s = -1, \\ 0.5 & \text{for } s = +1. \end{cases}$$

The expected value $\mathbb{E}(S)$ of the random variable S is equal to 0. We can interpret S as the outcome of a "heads or tails" game in which the player gains one point if the coin lands on "heads" and loses one point if the coin lands on "tails." The expected return on this game is zero. If each point were worth one franc, it is likely that several people would be willing to play.

Now consider a situation where the points are worth not CHF 1 but CHF 1,000. The expected value has not changed from the previous situation, and yet far fewer people would be willing to play. For most people, these two games are very different. Winning or losing one franc has little impact on one's well-being; however, even though winning a thousand francs is pleasant, losing a thousand francs can have significant negative consequences. We conclude that the equivalence principle is not sufficient to distinguish the *levels of risk* of two situations with the same expected value.

The second drawback can be illustrated using the St. Petersburg paradox.

St. Petersburg paradox

Consider a "heads or tails" game between a player and a bank. In this game, which is intended to be zero-sum, the player places an initial bet. The bank collects the player's initial bet. A coin is then flipped. If it lands on "heads," the bank pays the player one franc, and the game ends. If it lands on "tails," the coin is flipped again. If it lands on "heads" on the second turn, the bank pays the player two francs, and the game ends. If there is a third round, the prize is four francs, and so on. So if the coin lands on "heads" for the first time in the nth round, the bank pays the player 2^{n-1} francs.

The question is: What initial bet should be required of the player in order for the game to be fair, i.e., so that neither the bank nor the player has an advantage?

Finding the answer to this question boils down to determining the player's average expected gain. Thus, for the game to be fair, the player's initial bet must be equal to the expected value of the gain. This can be calculated by summing the potential payoffs $(1, 2, 4, \ldots)$, weighted by their respective probabilities of occurring $(1/2, 1/4, 1/8, \ldots)$:

$$\mathbb{E}(\text{gain}) = \frac{1}{2} \cdot 1 + \frac{1}{4} \cdot 2 + \frac{1}{8} \cdot 4 + \ldots = \sum_{n=1}^{+\infty} \frac{1}{2^n} \cdot 2^{n-1} = \sum_{n=1}^{+\infty} \frac{1}{2} = +\infty.$$

For the game to be fair, the initial bet must be infinite; otherwise, the game is skewed in the player's favor. Thus, if the gain were the only relevant factor, the rational decision would be to bet one's entire wealth (which is finite) on this game, which offers an infinite (and therefore higher) gain. In practice, however, few people are willing to play this game.

Why do individuals refuse to bet all of their money on the game described in the St. Petersburg paradox when the expected payoff is infinite? We can identify two possible answers. First, individuals have risk preferences. In most cases, they are risk-averse and thus less willing to put their money at risk. Second, an assessment based on expected value, even if the formal calculation is clear, is not satisfactory because it excludes certain personal factors.

This paradox was first noted by the mathematician Daniel Bernoulli (Bernoulli, 1954). In 1713, he realized that the measure of risk is not sufficient and that the assessment of individual preferences plays an important role in decision making. He concluded that people assign a value to a sum of money that is different from its numerical value, a kind of *moral value* that depends on various factors, including their personal wealth and their aversion to risk.

These observations about the level of risk and moral value were made over three centuries ago when these questions were raised in the context of games of cards, dice, and heads or tails. Finally, below, we define another principle of risk assessment that incorporates the concept of utility.

Expected utility criterion   Unsatisfied with the ineffectiveness of the equivalence principle in evaluating certain situations, Bernoulli developed in 1632 the foundations of utility theory, which takes into account the individuals' attitude toward risk. We will now consider a criterion based on the concept of utility with which we can define a deterministic value $\Pi(S)$ for the random loss S. Expected utility allows us to introduce the expected utility criterion:

Definition 3.26 (*Expected utility criterion*)

The **expected utility criterion** *is a risk assessment principle that assigns to the random variable S describing the losses associated with a risk exposure its expected utility $\mathbb{E}(u(S))$,*

$$S \mapsto \mathbb{E}(u(S)).$$

We have seen that the utility function defines an order of preference (see section 3.4). Thus, if X and Y are two random variables representing amounts of money, the expected utility criterion states that X is preferred to Y if $\mathbb{E}(u(X)) > \mathbb{E}(u(Y))$. The criterion thus makes it possible to order the preferences of a person faced with choices with uncertain outcomes, which we represent by random variables.

Normative and behavioral economics

Even today, economic models often have a normative aspect, offering absolute judgments and pointing the way to rational behavior. They describe the world as it should be and try to answer the question: How should we act in situations of risk?

Expected value and expected utility are normative criteria. They are called absolute measures. In the case of utility, the measure includes the individual's attitude toward risk since the values of wealth and profit are converted into quantities of utility. Thus, if an individual is rational, it is certain that they will choose the option that maximizes their expected utility.

Risk preferences, risk aversion in particular, and risk assessment are reflected in numerous empirical phenomena:

- The existence of positive interest rates that offer returns on risky investments,

- Risk premiums greater than the expected loss,

- Games in which the required stake is higher than the expected payback for the participants.

These theories are contrasted with more recent research in behavioral economics, which emphasizes the measurement of empirically observable risk and the assessment of risk by individuals themselves. In this case, the theories attempt to describe how people behave in the real world. Nevertheless, both approaches are important, and behavioral economics will not replace normative economics.

Value-at-risk (VaR) criterion   The above criteria can be used to define the deterministic value or "price" of a random loss. Another approach is to determine the capital required so that a random loss does not threaten the survival of the company. This concept is used in particular in the regulatory practice of financial institutions, where it is referred to as the probability of ruin. In our context, value-at-risk refers to situations in which the potential loss resulting from a risk exposure may be greater than the available assets.

Consider a random variable S representing the loss resulting from a risk exposure. In order to assess the value-at-risk, we must choose a confidence level, or a probability of ruin, that is deemed acceptable. For an agent with available capital w, the probability of ruin associated with a given risk exposure is the probability that the amount of loss S is greater than the amount of wealth w, i.e., $\mathbb{P}(S > w)$.

Definition 3.27 (*Value-at-risk*)

*The **value-at-risk** of level α of a potential loss S represented as $\mathrm{VaR}_\alpha(S)$, is the minimum amount of capital an agent must have to cover the potential loss with a probability of α. In other words, it is the minimum capital required for the probability of ruin to be $1 - \alpha$. This capital is given by*

- *If S is a continuous random variable:*

$$\mathrm{VaR}_\alpha(S) \quad \text{such that} \quad \mathbb{P}(S > \mathrm{VaR}_\alpha(S)) = 1 - \alpha,$$

- *If S is a discrete random variable:*

$$\mathrm{VaR}_\alpha(S) = \inf\{x | \mathbb{P}(S > x) \leq 1 - \alpha\}.$$

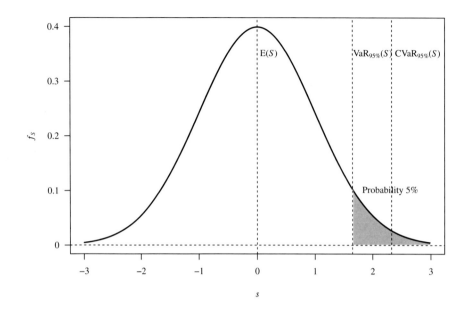

Note: Positive values of S are associated with an effective loss.

Figure 3.17: Illustration of the value-at-risk and the expected shortfall of level $\alpha = 95\%$ of a potential loss S resulting from a speculative risk exposure and described by the standard normal distribution (adapted from McNeil et al., 2015, figure 2.2).

Let α be the confidence level and $1 - \alpha$ the probability of ruin. Typically, the parameter α takes values close to 1, for example, 0.95, 0.99, or 0.995, corresponding to a high confidence level (95%, 99%, and 99.5%, respectively) and a low probability of ruin (5%, 1%, and 0.5%, respectively). The value-at-risk is then the capital w such that the probability of ruin $\mathbb{P}(S > w)$ is equal to $1 - \alpha$, i.e., $\mathbb{P}(S > w) = 1 - \alpha$.

Thus, we express as $w = \text{VaR}_\alpha(S)$ the minimum amount of capital that a company must have to cover a potential loss S with a probability of α. Similarly, we can say that the probability of ruin is then equal to $1 - \alpha$. If the available capital w is greater than $\text{VaR}_\alpha(S)$, then the confidence level is greater than α, and the probability of ruin is less than $1 - \alpha$. The graph in figure 3.17 illustrates the value-at-risk of level $\alpha = 95\%$ of a potential loss S associated with a speculative risk exposure and described using the standard normal distribution. The expected value of S is zero. In this example, the value-at-risk is approximately 1.65. The cumulative probability of losses greater than the value-at-risk of level 95% is equal to 5% (gray area).

Two risk exposures can be compared by calculating for each the capital required by the value-at-risk of the same level α. The exposure that requires the least capital is preferred.

Definition 3.28 (*Value-at-risk criterion*)

The **value-at-risk criterion** *is a risk assessment principle that assigns to the random variable S describing the losses associated with a risk exposure its value-at-risk of level α, $\mathrm{VaR}_\alpha(S)$,*

$$S \mapsto \mathrm{VaR}_\alpha(S).$$

Let us now consider the special case of a random variable S that follows a normal distribution with an expected value $\mathbb{E}(S)$ and a standard deviation $\sigma(S)$. In this case, we have

$$\mathbb{P}(S > \mathrm{VaR}_\alpha(S)) = \mathbb{P}\left(\frac{S - \mathbb{E}(S)}{\sigma(S)} > \frac{\mathrm{VaR}_\alpha(S) - \mathbb{E}(S)}{\sigma(S)}\right)$$
$$= \mathbb{P}\left(Z > \frac{\mathrm{VaR}_\alpha(S) - \mathbb{E}(S)}{\sigma(S)}\right),$$

where Z follows a standard normal distribution (see section 3.3). Then

$$\mathbb{P}(S > \mathrm{VaR}_\alpha(S)) = 1 - \alpha \quad \Longleftrightarrow \quad \mathbb{P}\left(Z < \frac{\mathrm{VaR}_\alpha(S) - \mathbb{E}(S)}{\sigma(S)}\right) = \alpha.$$

We deduce that

$$\mathrm{VaR}_\alpha(S) = \mathbb{E}(S) + c_\alpha \cdot \sigma(S),$$

where c_α is the quantile of the standard normal distribution corresponding to α, i.e., c_α is such that $\mathbb{P}(W > c_\alpha) = 1 - \alpha$ for a random variable W with standard normal distribution.

In the case of a normal distribution of the loss S, the risk assessment is given by the expected value, to which we add a margin proportional to its standard deviation. This formula is reminiscent of the result calculated for the risk premium in section 3.4. In that case, the margin was proportional to the variance of S. It should be noted that in the case of a non-specific distribution of the random loss S, the formula for $\mathrm{VaR}_\alpha(S)$—which is valid for a loss with a normal distribution—will be at best a rough approximation.

Two specific criticisms are often made of the value-at-risk concept. First, value-at-risk does not take into account the severity of the excess potential loss $(S - \mathrm{VaR}_\alpha(S))^+$: this is the amount whose potential loss is greater than the value-at-risk. This excess amount can be significant and reach extreme values, and as such, it must be taken into account when assessing a risk.

Second, value-at-risk is not a consistent measure of risk, and combining two portfolios does not necessarily reduce the risk. It is important to note that there are loss distributions S_1 and S_2 resulting from two different risks for which $\mathrm{VaR}_\alpha(S_1 + S_2) > \mathrm{VaR}_\alpha(S_1) + \mathrm{VaR}_\alpha(S_2)$. In this case, looking at the risks separately, the capital required to achieve a given level of safety would be lower. This is particularly inconsistent when a financial institution calculates the regulatory capital required to cover its risks. Value-at-risk produces inconsistent results because the firm would be better off splitting its risks so that its total capital requirement is less than the capital required to cover the entire risk pool.

Therefore, although value-at-risk is one of the preferred measures used today, it is far from perfect. In addition to the problems outlined above, value-at-risk is the minimum loss we can expect over a given period of time for a given probability. In other words, it cannot be used to assess a group of combined risks. A better measure is expected shortfall, or conditional value-at-risk, which is the average loss if things go wrong (Rockinger, 2012).

Expected shortfall criterion We have seen in the previous principles that each assessment principle has its own characteristics and weaknesses. The way we measure risk is critical. Although value-at-risk (see definition 3.27) is currently the preferred measure, it is not perfect. It indicates the minimum loss that can be expected over a given period for a given probability. However, it does not take into account the higher—sometimes extreme—losses that a risk exposure can lead to.

A better, though less popular, measure is expected shortfall, or conditional value-at-risk, which amounts to a measure of the average loss incurred above a certain level. Expected shortfall is a second measure of the capital required to ensure that a random loss does not jeopardize the financial security of a company. It is the recommended measure in the Swiss Solvency Test for insurance companies. Formally, it is defined as follows:

Definition 3.29 (*Expected shortfall*)

The **expected shortfall** *of level α of a potential loss S, represented as $\mathrm{CVaR}_\alpha(S)$, is the conditional expectation of the potential loss S, i.e., the expected value of S under the condition that S is above the value-at-risk of level α, i.e., $\mathrm{VaR}_\alpha(S)$. Formally,*

$$\mathrm{CVaR}_\alpha(S) = \mathbb{E}(S|S > \mathrm{VaR}_\alpha(S)).$$

The concept is essentially a theoretical one. In order to calculate this expected value, one needs to know the exact distribution S of the potential loss, especially the tail of the distribution. This is almost never possible in the real world, as the tail of the distribution corresponds to events that are (extremely) rare and for which there are very few observations. We plot the expected shortfall of level $\alpha = 95\%$ of a potential loss S with a standard normal distribution in figure 3.17. The expected shortfall is the expected value of realizations of losses greater than the value-at-risk (gray area). In this example, it is about 2.33.

We define the expected shortfall criterion as follows:

Definition 3.30 (*Expected shortfall criterion*)

The **expected shortfall criterion** *is a risk assessment principle that assigns to the random variable S describing the losses associated with a risk exposure its expected shortfall of level α,* $\mathrm{CVaR}_\alpha(S)$,

$$S \mapsto \mathrm{CVaR}_\alpha(S).$$

As with value-at-risk, a risk exposure is preferable if the resulting potential loss minimizes the expected shortfall.

Other criteria In risk management, actuarial science, and financial economics, a measure of risk can be defined in various ways, provided that it has a certain set of properties. To clarify the concept, these properties can be studied and described from a theoretical perspective. A common requirement is that the measure of risk be consistent, i.e., that it be monotonic (a set of risk exposures with lower losses than another set is less risky), translation invariant (adding safe capital reduces risk by the same amount), homogeneous (doubling all exposures means doubling risk), and subadditive (two sets of risk exposures considered together must not be riskier than each set considered separately). Theoretically, many measures of risk and assessment criteria can be imagined.

In practice, measures such as possible maximum loss and expected maximum loss—or probable maximum loss—complete the range of measures mentioned above, from which criteria can be developed. We use the following definitions:

Definition 3.31 (*Possible, expected, and probable maximum loss*)

- *The* **possible maximum loss** *is the maximum amount of the potential loss.*
- *The* **expected maximum loss** *or* **probable maximum loss** *is the probable amount of the potential loss.*

For example, consider the various buildings and facilities of a factory located on a company's premises that are exposed to the risk of fire. Assume that the company has implemented a system to reduce the extent of a fire, including leaving space between buildings and installing fire doors inside. In this situation, total destruction of all buildings and facilities is theoretically possible but can be excluded in practice. The possible maximum loss refers to the amount of loss resulting from the total destruction of the site; it is the maximum amount. The expected maximum loss refers to a much lower amount, representing the most likely loss.

Finally, there is also the worst conditional expectation, which can be considered as a practical interpretation of the expected shortfall. The method consists of selecting a certain number of scenarios A that may occur with a probability greater than or equal to a given level α, and assessing the risk by taking the highest expected value of the loss corresponding to each of the selected scenarios.

Definition 3.32 (*Worst conditional expectation*)

The **worst conditional expectation** *of level α of a potential loss S, written as $WCE_\alpha(S)$, is the supremum of the conditional expectations of the potential loss S in the scenarios A. The supremum is based on all scenarios A whose probability of occurrence is greater than or equal to α. Formally,*

$$WCE_\alpha(S) = \sup\{\mathbb{E}(S|A)|\mathbb{P}(A) > \alpha\}.$$

In particular, it is a more formal and precise definition of the expected maximum loss mentioned above. In practice, the risk manager develops several scenarios A_1, ..., A_n, and selects only those whose probability of occurrence is greater than or equal to a predetermined level. For each scenario, they calculate the conditional expectation $\mathbb{E}(S|A_j)$ of the potential loss S. Finally, they select the highest of the values obtained as the worst conditional expectation.

The list of risk assessment criteria can be summarized as follows. First, for risk-averse agents, the assessment of a risk is higher than its expected value. Each concept leads to the consideration of a safety margin. At first glance, this safety margin is proportional to a parameter that measures the variability of the loss, such as the variance or the standard deviation. Then, two specific characteristics of the entity responsible for financing these risks are taken into account in the assessment (see also the end of section 3.4). The first is the entity's *financial capacity*, represented by its capital. The second is its subjective behavior, or *individual attitude*, toward risk; this behavior is quantified using the mathematical models of risk aversion or the tolerated probability of ruin. These two characteristics are used to assess all the risks to which the entity in question is exposed. We conclude that there is no such thing as an objective assessment of a risk but that this assessment depends on subjective factors specific to the entity that must finance it.

CHAPTER 4

Risk management

The purpose of risk management is to limit the occurrence of adverse events and to minimize their impact when they do occur. Negative consequences can be considered at different levels, such as the number of victims or the cost of the losses. It is essential to take into account all values exposed to risk (see section 2.7) in order to correctly estimate these consequences. Risk management cannot prevent all risks. For example, everyone dies sooner or later; in this context, risk management means living a healthy life. It is also possible to insure your loved ones against the financial consequences of your death. Similarly, while it is sometimes impossible to completely prevent a car from being stolen, preventive measures can reduce the occurrence of theft and are an integral part of risk management.

In section 4.1, we will present a definition of the term "risk management." We will also discuss the objectives of a risk management program and define the processes involved. We will then illustrate the various steps in the process: identifying and analyzing risk exposures (section 4.2), studying applicable risk management techniques (section 4.3), selecting the most appropriate techniques (section 4.4), implementing the selected techniques (section 4.5), and monitoring the results (section 4.6). When we present techniques, we will provide details on alternative risk transfer; in the sections dedicated to implementation and monitoring, we will examine the organization, the three lines of defense model, and the risk culture. We will conclude with an application in the context of cyber risk management (section 4.7).

4.1 Definition and objectives of risk management

Activities and definition   The starting point of the concept of risk management is the intention to plan, anticipate, and manage risks relevant to an individual or a company. These agents are subject to uncertainty, such as natural disasters, the stock market, tax reforms, accidents, and diseases. In a company, the risk management framework takes into account the concepts of uncertainty and degree of risk, as well as information, communication, and shareholder value. These factors influence the company's value through its stakeholders. Stakeholders include all entities that may influence the company's activities or be affected by its decisions. They include, for instance, creditors, employees, suppliers, and customers. The price and risk premiums demanded by these parties have a significant impact on a company's values.

Within a company, activities related to risk management include helping to identify risks, implementing programs to prevent and limit losses by avoiding and controlling risks, training on risk management activities, monitoring compliance with regulations, developing various ways to manage, finance, and transfer risks, designing products, and handling claims. Thus, a company may have objectives of various types, such as profit, growth, or public service. To achieve these objectives, the organization must first satisfy a fundamental priority: the ability to survive despite adverse events.

A brief definition of risk management could, therefore, be that it is a management and decision-making process whose purpose is to minimize, at a reasonable cost, the consequences of adverse events that jeopardize the organization's objectives. Risk management has a dual nature: it is both a *management process* and a *decision-making process*. A broader definition of risk management, which includes both the management and decision-making aspects of the process, is as follows:

Definition 4.1 (*Risk management*)

Risk management *is a management and decision-making process that enables an entity to plan, organize, lead, control, and monitor its activities in order to minimize, at a reasonable cost, the adverse consequences of risks to which the entity is exposed.*

Our definition incorporates parts of the definition found in the ISO Guide 73:2009 standard by the International Organization for Standardization (2009, section 2.1), reproduced in the ISO 31000:2018 standard by the International Organization for Standardization (2018, section 3.1), which defines risk management as "coordinated activities to direct and control an organization with regard to risk."

Obviously, such a process is not static and cannot be established once and for all. Rather, it is a dynamic process that must be continually adjusted to reflect changes in risk exposure and the results of risk management, including the results of monitoring the effectiveness of the program. We will take a closer look at the characteristics of the organization and all the processes involved in section 4.5. Before implementing a risk management system in an organization, two questions need to be answered. First, what types of risks should the risk management program address? Second, what exactly is the scope of the company's risk manager? In this context, questions related to the leadership of the risk manager and the integration of risk management methods into the company's activities and culture are examined.

Initially, risk management was intended only for pure accidental losses (see the discussion of enterprise risk management in section 1.3). Today, priority is still given to losses resulting from pure risks (see definition 2.4 in section 2.4). Pure risks generally do not include risks associated with financial investments, economic risks associated with a company's business, such as the commercial failure of a new product, political risks, technological risks, and military risks. Speculative risks, also known as business risks, are often considered only as a second step in a company's risk management process because they are the result of intentional actions whose potential consequences have been analyzed at the time of the initial decision. However, as part of a broader concept of risk that is becoming increasingly common, the techniques and methods developed for risk management are being applied to broader areas. In our view, risk management can encompass both types of risk: pure risk and speculative risk.

In addition to the decision-making aspects, our definition of risk management includes objectives related to administration and management. In fact, risk management involves the implementation of processes designed to plan, organize, manage, and monitor an organization's resources to enable it to achieve its objectives at a reasonable cost. The risk management process, as an administrative process, must, therefore, cover four functions: planning, organizing, managing, and monitoring.

The ISO 31000:2018 standard (International Organization for Standardization, 2018, chapter 4) mentions the principles that define the broad strokes of effective and efficient risk management. While creating and preserving value is at the heart of the objectives of a risk management program, it is important to communicate the intent and value of the program. Among the basic principles are that the program must be integrated into all the company's activities, follow a structured and comprehensive approach, be appropriate and proportionate to the company's context, and be inclusive and relevant to all areas. The program is based on the best available information and takes into account both human aspects and corporate culture. Risk management should be dynamic and subject to continuous improvement.

The risk management cycle In addition to administration and management, risk management requires decision making. In order to implement a risk management program within an organization, a decision-making process must be defined. This iterative process can take many forms, and we present below a decision cycle that includes the following five steps:

1. Identification and analysis of the risk exposure,
2. Study of the applicable risk management techniques,
3. Selection of the most appropriate techniques,
4. Implementation of the selected techniques,
5. Monitoring of the results of the implemented techniques to ensure effectiveness.

Figure 4.1: The five steps of the risk management process.

These five steps of a risk management program will serve as a guide for the remainder of this chapter. We will discuss and illustrate each step in the process, as each one requires a careful approach. The graphical representation as a cycle highlights the fact that this is an iterative process that repeats itself. Iterations are often annual; however, depending on the industry, changes in risk exposures may require more frequent revisions. It is important to note that the five-step model presented here is only an example of the most important steps. Depending on a company's needs, a risk management program may be more or less sophisticated and may follow variations of these steps, depending on the organization's circumstances.

4.2   Risk identification and analysis methods

The first step in risk management is the systematic identification of risks, both before and after they occur, in order to identify and understand what random losses may occur and to assess the consequences of these potential losses. The implementation of a risk management program begins with the mapping of risks, initially on a summary basis and with increasing precision over time. The goal is to identify all risk exposures, which are then evaluated. Risk appreciation (see chapter 3) involves evaluating the consequences of potential losses, in particular, determining the frequency and severity of events, their predictability, and their impact on the organization's ability to achieve its objectives.

To ensure that this step is completed, three conditions must be met. First, a logical classification system must be used to identify loss exposures. Such a system was introduced in chapter 2, and it includes, in particular, a characterization of risks and risk exposures, as well as a classification of the perils and types of values exposed to losses. Second, appropriate methods must be used to identify and analyze each of these exposures. These are discussed in detail in this section. Finally, it is necessary to be able to test the potential negative consequences of each of these risk exposures: to what extent can they prevent the company from achieving its objectives? These factors are part of the risk appreciation we studied in chapter 3.

Risk exposure identification methods A number of standard methodologies have been developed to systematize the identification of risk exposures. However, regardless of these methods, the most important requirements are related to the risk managers themselves: they must have in-depth knowledge of the company, its activities, and its organization. Experience and skills in risk management, as well as critical thinking skills and creativity, are also important. With regard to the methods to be used, the following provides an overview of the wide range of options available:

- *Standardized questionnaires*: These documents are used to identify and analyze risk exposures, allowing the risk manager to create a list of all the company's values that are exposed to losses. Industry or topic questionnaires make it possible to compile checklists of a company's vulnerabilities using standard questions that cover a wide range of issues. The main problem with these types of questionnaires is that they are not necessarily tailored to the specifics of a given company. As a result, they cover an extremely wide range of topics with a large number of questions to cover all potential risk exposures. Many organizations and associations have such questionnaires available.

- *Past losses and loss statistics*: Adverse events that have occurred in the past help to better prepare for the future. In particular, a study of the past makes it possible to avoid or to better manage certain risk exposures. However, this cannot be the only step, as it implicitly assumes that the company and its environment do not change, which is not the case. Loss statistics provide insight into various risk exposures and allow for an initial analysis. In this case, it is important to ensure that the statistics cover a sufficiently large number of samples and that they are not biased. These conditions are generally met for frequent, small events—for example, the number of days absent in a year among a company's employees— but not for more rare or severe events. A company's risk manager can draw on the company's own history and statistics as well as those of the industry in general. This type of comparison provides a broader view of potential adverse events and allows the manager to confirm certain statistics. In particular, any natural or man-made disaster (see section 1.2) causes risk managers to review and update their assessments.

- *Financial, accounting, and audit reports*: Documents such as the company's balance sheet, income statement, list of financial obligations, cash reserves, and budget are necessary to analyze risk exposure. The balance sheet provides an initial look at the company's assets and liabilities. It also makes it possible to calculate various indicators to assess the company's financial strength. The income statement shows which activities generate the company's profits. The detailed statement of losses shows which losses are related to risk exposures. The cash flow statement provides information on the main financial flows, while the notes show off-balance-sheet commitments. Audit reports often indicate which of a company's activities have risks that need attention.

- *Other reports and internal documents*: In principle, any documents about the company that provide insight into its activities and processes can be helpful in better understanding risk exposures.

- *Organizational charts, diagrams, and graphs*: A graphical representation helps visualize the steps in, for example, a production process, a distribution process, or an information flow. It allows the risk manager to identify key activities and individuals, including those who could block the entire process if they were to malfunction.

- *Personal inspections*: Ideally, the risk manager should be in direct contact with the company's activities in order to supplement their information and get a concrete idea of the daily work of the various departments.

- *Internal and external expertise*: Risk managers working within companies are, in principle, generalists who have a broad view of each company's business. Occasionally, they may find it helpful to bring in specialists in certain areas to help them identify risks in more detail. These analyses may also be requested by the company's governing bodies (non-executive and executive management). All major consulting firms offer risk management services.

It should be noted that in order to implement these methodologies, risk managers must understand the risks. They consult with key people from different disciplines and ensure that all perspectives are considered. At the same time, the risk management program includes communication initiatives designed to raise risk awareness and create a sense of involvement among those who are affected by risk exposures on a daily basis. An example of integration is the use of company-wide applications that invite each employee to identify the risks they have observed (Meyer et al., 2021).

Representation of risks   Given the variety of risks that companies may be exposed to, Darsa (2016) proposes the "pyramid approach," a tool that provides a structural and hierarchical representation of the major risk classes. The graph in

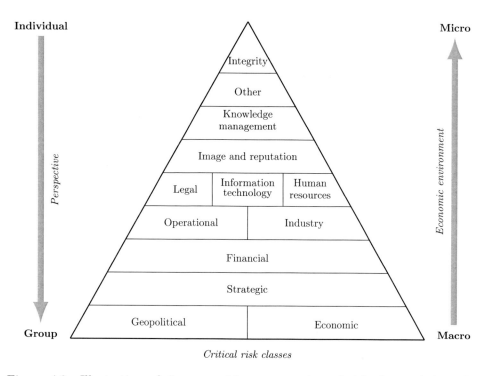

Figure 4.2: Illustration of the pyramid representation of risk classes (adapted from Darsa, 2016, chapter 3).

figure 4.2 illustrates this structure. It has been designed according to three logical approaches:

- *Perspective*: The initial approach starts with the individual and progresses to the group. First, information is gathered about the risks associated with an individual, a unit within the organization, or a customer or supplier. These risks are then aggregated into larger and larger groups: a team, a department, the company itself, and even the broader industry.

- *Economic environment*: The second approach completes the previous bottom-up process by starting with the company's macroeconomic environment, such as the market or geographic areas. It then examines microeconomic units, countries, regions within a country, and finally, the company itself.

- *Critical risk classes*: Finally, from a general perspective, the critical risk classes for an entire company should be considered. The proposed pyramid contains thirteen classes of risk. These are related to geopolitical, economic, strategic, financial, operational, industry, legal, information technology, human resources, image and reputation, knowledge management, integrity, and other risks. We have covered many of these risk classes in chapter 2.

Master risk list At the end of the risk identification process, the company's risk manager has a list of all risk exposures. This master risk list is useful in the risk management process, especially to ensure that no risk is overlooked, and it also serves as a rough map for management. Table 4.1 illustrates this master risk list using the example of a manufacturing company taken from the book by Müller et al. (2019). The list contains fifty major risks grouped into twelve categories: these risks are related to markets, customers, products and services, occupational

Markets	*Human resources*
1. Development of the macroeconomic situation	28. Recruitment, training, skills,
2. Evolution of market share	and expertise
3. Competition	29. Integrity and reliability of employees
4. Legal/political context	30. Motivation
Customers	31. Compensation
5. Customer porfolio	(incl. employee benefits)
6. Loss of customers	32. Union relations
7. Customer satisfaction/	*Commitments*
customer behavior, reputation	33. Contractual obligations/ purchase
Products/services	and delivery commitments
8. Portfolio of products/services	34. Receivables and pledges
9. Product/service life cycle, innovations,	35. Product liability/
replacement	warranty claims
10. Quality of the product/service	36. Ethical obligations/reputation
Occupational safety and accident prevention	37. Moral obligations
11. Technical safety	*Finance*
12. Occupational health, hygiene, and safety	38. Ability to generate cash
13. Prevention of workplace accidents	flows/value creation
Production and distribution	39. Access to financing/interest rates
14. Innovation and product development	40. Payment system
15. Supply and logistics	41. Foreign exchange risks
16. Production (including services)	42. Reliability, punctuality, and availability
17. Sales, price and distribution	of financial information
18. Customer service	*Assets*
19. Trademark and reputation	43. Natural disaster losses
Corporate governance	44. Fixed assets (including valuation)
20. Planning	45. Inventory (including valuation)
21. Organization structure	46. Integrity
22. Communication	47. Availability
23. Reports	*Compliance*
24. Projects	48. Legal compliance
25. Investments (including acquisitions)	49. Compliance with corporate
26. Mergers and cooperations	governance recommendations
27. Risk management	50. Tax laws

Table 4.1: Illustration of the master risk list for a manufacturing company (adapted from Müller et al., 2019, section 4.36).

safety and accident prevention, production and distribution, corporate governance, human resources, commitments, finance, assets, information technology, and compliance. As mentioned above, all the features of risk management must be adapted to the specific context of the company. Thus, we note that while some of these categories are identical to the risk classes illustrated above in figure 4.2, others are specific to this case.

Once these risks have been identified and briefly described, an initial estimate of their probability of occurrence and impact can be made. For example, the probability of occurrence can be qualified as "low," "possible," or "almost certain." The impact can be qualified with adjectives such as "negligible," "moderate," or "catastrophic." These two items are qualitative indicators of frequency and severity and are sufficient to perform an initial risk mapping (see section 3.1 on risk exposure analysis and the illustration in figure 3.2).

Then, for each risk, a strategy is chosen (see sections 4.3 and 4.4), for example, "avoid," "insure," "control," or "accept." Finally, the chosen measures are implemented and monitored (see sections 4.5 and 4.6). This information can be completed in a table next to the identified risks, as illustrated in Müller et al. (2019, section 4.58).

4.3   Study of applicable risk management techniques

For each risk identified and analyzed in the previous step, a risk management technique must be chosen. We will study technique selection in the upcoming section 4.4. But first, let us look at the range of techniques available and applicable. To manage risk, we distinguish two complementary families of risk management techniques: risk control techniques and risk financing techniques.

Risk control techniques include all techniques and measures taken to minimize the frequency and severity of losses or to make the consequences of accidental events more predictable and, therefore, less threatening. This is known as risk control to stop losses or loss control. For most risk exposures, the risk manager will attempt to select a first technique in this family, if possible, to limit the overall exposure to losses. Next is the family of techniques known as risk financing to pay for losses. This second family includes techniques and methods designed to cover the financial consequences of losses that are not averted. Below, we will describe these two families of techniques in detail and provide definitions 4.2 and 4.5. Figure 4.3 provides an overview of the different techniques we will look at.

Risk control techniques   The primary purpose of risk control techniques is to minimize the frequency or probability of occurrence and the severity or magnitude of potential losses. Overall, this makes losses more predictable. Such measures must be implemented before the adverse event occurs and may be activated before, during, or after the event.

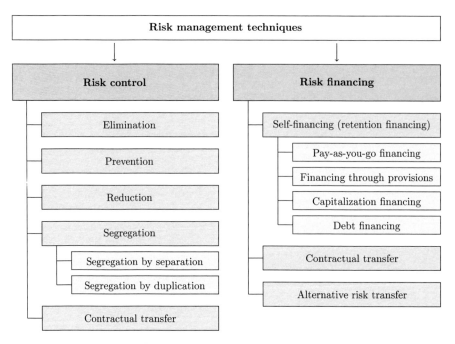

Figure 4.3: Overview of risk management techniques.

Definition 4.2 (*Risk control techniques*)

Risk control techniques *include all risk management techniques and measures that aim to minimize the frequency and severity of potential losses or to make losses more predictable.*

Definition 4.3 (*Categories of risk control techniques*)

- **Elimination** *of a risk exposure consists of not creating or completely eliminating the condition that leads to the exposure.*
- **Prevention** *refers to techniques designed to reduce the frequency of potential losses.*
- **Reduction** *refers to techniques designed to reduce the severity of losses when the adverse event occurs.*
- **Segregation** *refers to techniques designed to reduce the cumulative losses resulting from a single adverse event.*
- **Contractual transfer** *of risk control refers to an agreement by which the control of the risk exposure is transferred to another party.*

We distinguish five categories of measures that belong to the family of risk control techniques (see figure 4.3): elimination of the risk exposure, prevention, reduction, segregation, and (contractual) transfer of risk. The following definitions clarify the purpose of each technique.

The techniques of elimination, prevention, and reduction also appear in the field of insurance economics, particularly in the context of insurance demand. This is because there is a link between the insurance coverage purchased, the price to be paid, and the risk management measures implemented. Thus, terms such as "self-protection" and "self-insurance" (Ehrlich and Becker, 1972) appear in the literature. We will use the following definitions:

Definition 4.4 (*Self-protection and self-insurance*)

- **Self-protection** *refers to a measure intended to reduce the probability of occurrence of a potential loss, i.e., the frequency of potential losses.*
- **Self-insurance** *refers to a measure intended to reduce the negative consequences of a loss, i.e., the severity of a loss, if the adverse event occurs.*

We conclude that self-protection, which reduces the probability of a loss or the frequency of losses, is synonymous with prevention. A self-protection measure affects the probability of a loss. A self-insurance measure that reduces the amount of loss when an adverse event occurs is a reduction measure. It affects the amount of loss. Depending on the context, the terms "self-protection" and "self-insurance" may be used interchangeably with "prevention" and "reduction," respectively.

Below are some observations and examples (gray boxes) of the five risk control techniques we have introduced.

- *Elimination of the risk exposure*: When the risk exposure is eliminated, the probability of a potential loss becomes zero, and no further risk management techniques are required. Elimination can also be interpreted as a prevention technique (where the frequency is reduced to zero) or a reduction technique (where the severity is reduced to zero). In other words, it is both a self-protection and a self-insurance technique.

  - When a person chooses never to drive a vehicle, they eliminate the possibility of being civilly liable for a traffic accident.

  - The systematic introduction of road-rail transport through the Alps is a measure that eliminates the risk of traffic accidents.

  However, there are some limitations. First, this technique can only be used under certain circumstances. Certain risk exposures cannot be eliminated, such as the risk of death. In addition, eliminating one risk exposure may increase another.

> – The decision by some countries not to build nuclear power plants forces them either to rely on other methods of energy production—which may turn out to be riskier or result in other risk exposures—, or to purchase energy produced in other countries where safety standards may be less stringent. In the latter case, it is not really a risk elimination technique but rather a transfer of risk control to another energy producer or another country.

- *Prevention*: This technique must be implemented before the adverse event occurs. It is sometimes called self-protection. Examples of prevention measures can be found in virtually all areas (see also section 1.3).

> – Road safety measures such as driver licensing, speed limits, speed enforcement, and warning signs at dangerous locations are examples of prevention techniques aimed at reducing the frequency of traffic accidents.
>
> – Tobacco and alcohol abuse are the focus of many prevention and education efforts that target exposure to health risks.
>
> – Clinical trials conducted during the development of a new drug ensure that fewer people will experience serious side effects.
>
> – Prevention includes measures taken in the machine and tool industry to reduce the frequency of accidents related to their use.
>
> – The installation of lightning rods and the insulation of flammable materials are preventive measures against the risk of fire.

Observation and analysis of past events can help improve and strengthen prevention techniques.

> – After the September 11, 2001 attacks on the WTC (see section 1.2), security measures at airports around the world were significantly increased.
>
> – Cases of cancer caused by inhaling asbestos dust have led to the use of alternative construction materials.

- *Reduction*: Reduction techniques aim to reduce the severity of the losses and are linked to the concept of self-insurance. These techniques can be split into two groups: measures implemented before the event and measures implemented afterwards. The measures taken upstream of the event often also have an effect on its frequency. These are both prevention and reduction measures.

- Speed limits on roads reduce both the frequency and severity of accidents.

- Providing fire safety training to building occupants helps prevent fires and can also prevent an existing fire from spreading too quickly.

Reduction techniques applied after the adverse event has occurred are often aimed at speeding up rescue efforts and limiting the damage caused.

- The installation of an alarm system, a sprinkler system, fire extinguishers, and fire doors allows firefighters to be alerted quickly and can limit or even reduce the extent of damage caused by a fire.

- In the canton of Vaud, the installation of a single fire call center, which coordinates the activities of the fire brigade, ambulance, and hospital emergency services, is an example of this type of measure.

- *Segregation*: The goal is to organize a company's activities and resources in such a way that an event cannot cause losses across multiple business units. A distinction is generally made between segregation by separation and segregation by duplication.

  - *Segregation by separation* consists of separating the various entities exposed to a risk so that they are not all affected by a single event.

    This can be done, for example, by spreading manufacturing facilities across multiple locations or by ensuring that company executives never travel on the same plane. To reduce the risk of fire in a large warehouse, the inventory should be spread out across multiple locations.

  - *Segregation by duplication* requires the complete reproduction of one of the units of the organization, which is kept as backup. These measures are generally very costly. For this reason, they are much less common than prevention and reduction.

    In practice, in a manufacturing company, segregation by duplication means that two of every machine used in production must be available. Another example of this technique is ensuring that projectors used in university auditoriums always have two lamps so that classes can continue even if one lamp burns out.

- *Contractual transfer of risk control*: The purpose of risk control transfer is to transfer risk management to another party. A contractual transfer is an agreement that transfers control to another organization.

– By leasing a car rather than buying it, the risk exposure associated with property value—and the resulting potential losses—is transferred to the leasing company. For this reason, the leasing company requires the lessee to purchase comprehensive insurance for the car. This requirement is a contractual transfer of risk financing to an insurer, as we will see later.

This transfer to a third party does not mean that the risk exposure is eliminated.

– When a company decides to rent rather than buy a building, it has not eliminated the exposure to loss of property value, such as fire, but has transferred it to the owner. The fire risk exposure remains. The only way to eliminate that exposure would be to abandon all operations in the building.

Companies often transfer the control of speculative risks through outsourcing. A company transfers the business risks associated with an activity or product to another organization for an agreed-upon price. However, this technique can be used in perverse ways to circumvent regulatory safety requirements.

– Oil companies often subcontract the operation of offshore drilling rigs to another company or have their oil transported by a specialized shipping company. The subcontractor and the shipowner may be subject to different regulatory requirements, or they may subcontract the activity themselves. The original company that transferred risk control has little information about the safety requirements of its subcontractors or the condition of the vessels. This increases the risk exposure in terms of image and reputation.

Risk financing techniques   Risk financing techniques complement risk control techniques and are concerned with covering the financial consequences:

Definition 4.5 (*Risk financing techniques*)

Risk financing techniques *include all risk management techniques and measures whose purpose is to cover the financial consequences of losses that could not be avoided.*

The source of the financing may be internal to the company, as in the case of retention financing techniques, or external to the company, as in the case of contractual transfer of risk financing. In practice, rational risk financing is often achieved through a combination of retention and transfer techniques. In figure 4.3, we also mention alternative risk transfer (ART), a hybrid option that combines features of both external and internal financing. These financing techniques do not fit into either of the previous two categories.

Definition 4.6 (*Categories of risk financing techniques*)

- **Retention financing** or **self-financing** *includes all techniques that consist of planning to finance potential losses by building up appropriate reserves.*
- *The* **contractual transfer** *of risk financing refers to insurance policies by which an insurer covers all or part of potential losses.*
- **Alternative risk transfer** *includes financing techniques, which generally have features of both self-financing and contractual transfer.*

- *Retention financing or self-financing*: In the case of self-financing, the funds necessary to compensate for losses in the event of an adverse event are provided by the company itself. Sometimes, the company has no choice but to finance all accidental losses resulting from certain risk exposures if

  - no transfer of financing is possible in the case of exposure to a specific risk,

  - retention financing is less expensive than the transfer of financing.

  Even if a solution is found to transfer financing through an insurance policy, part of the financial consequences of potential losses are often borne by the company itself. This residual amount must be self-financed. This is the case when

  - the insurance policy includes a deductible or a contribution payable by the insured,

  - the insurance policy places a limit on the financial coverage provided by the insurer, and the amount of the loss exceeds that limit,

  - certain losses, such as indirect losses in the case of a property value, are not covered by the insurance policy,

  - the insurer is insolvent and can only partially meet its obligations (credit risk).

  There are four types of self-financing: pay-as-you-go financing, financing through provisions, capitalization financing, and debt financing. Some sources include a fifth method, self-financing through the creation of a captive company; we consider this to be a type of ART, as it shares characteristics with the transfer of financing. The first four categories are discussed in more detail below.

  - *Pay-as-you-go financing*: In this simplest form of self-financing, losses are paid as part of the organization's ordinary expenses and are included in the profit and loss statement of the period in which the loss is paid. The use of this technique is appropriate for low-severity, high-frequency risk exposures as long as the amount of loss does not threaten the ability of the entity to achieve its objectives. A major limitation of this method is that the actual losses must be predicted with sufficient accuracy to ensure that the relevant budget line is not exceeded.

> In simple terms, this is how the Swiss old age and survivors' insurance is financed: pensions are charged to the year in which they are paid, and they are financed by the contributions paid by active members in the same year.

– *Financing through provisions*: This type of financing consists of creating a new liability on the balance sheet that acts as a fund to cover losses that cannot be predicted with sufficient accuracy. The provision is released when the loss is realized. It represents the amount of losses expected to be incurred as a result of a past or future accidental event. Increases in this provision are charged to the period in which the increase occurs, thereby reducing the profit for that period.

> This risk financing technique is consistent with the financing system required by law for non-life insurance companies. They are required to set aside in the form of reserves the total amount of future payments to be made on past claims, which we call "provisions for pending cases." Companies must also set aside an amount equal to future payments to be made for future events covered by an insurance policy, i.e., "provisions for outstanding risks."

Depending on the industry, the creation of such provisions, particularly provisions for future events, may raise challenges with tax authorities and shareholders. They may also be inconsistent with certain accounting standards.

> – Five years ago, a pharmaceutical company launched a new drug on the market. Experience showed that this drug could have significant unexpected side effects, potentially exposing the company to civil liability. Several patients filed lawsuits against the company, and a trial is underway. The company believes that the evidence that the side effects were caused solely by the drug is inconclusive and is awaiting the results of additional analyses. The company also believes that the damages being sought by the victims are excessive. The accidental event, i.e., the failure to recognize the side effects of the drug, occurred several years earlier when the drug was in clinical trials. The final amount of the damages, and therefore the amount of loss to the company, will likely not be known for several years. The company sets aside a provision to fund its future losses resulting from a past event.

> – A company relies on a single supplier for a software application
> that is critical to its production process. Changing the software
> would be very costly because of the adjustments that would need
> to be made to the company's equipment and IT platforms. The
> company has set aside a provision to cover its losses in the event
> of the supplier's failure. In this case, the company's provision is
> intended to fund future losses that may be caused by a future
> event.

– *Capitalization financing*: In the previous case of financing through provisions, the provision was simply a liability added to the balance sheet.
Here, the company creates a true fund, i.e., a portfolio of assets whose
specific purpose is to finance a given risk exposure. This fund is financed
and managed in such a way that its resources can finance expected future losses. In principle, this method only applies to a limited range of
economic activities, such as pension funds or life insurance companies.

– *Debt financing*: An alternative to the previous risk financing method is
self-financing through debt. Instead of using a fund, the company relies
on a loan, usually from a bank. On certain occasions, it may receive
(repayable) support from the government, which is a special type of
loan. This is a risk financing technique that an organization will use
after the event, i.e., after it has realized that its resources do not enable
it to finance the losses incurred. This technique is used as a last resort
when the company has no other choice.

• *Financing by contractual transfer of the risk financing*: This is the field
of insurance companies. Contractual transfer of risk financing is the last
solution that a risk manager comes up with, especially when risk control
measures cannot completely eliminate the risk, prevent its realization, or
reduce its financial consequences to the point where self-financing is possible.

Contractual transfer occurs through a contract in which one party, the insurer, agrees to finance, usually against payment, certain types of losses
resulting from certain risk exposures. In principle, this transfer does not
require the insurer to be an insurance company. The contract could legiti-
mately be between two individuals. We use the term "insurance" only when
the party to whom the financing is transferred is an institution that is offi-
cially authorized by the government to offer this type of contract, and that
is subject to specific prudential regulations for this industry.

In chapter 5 we study the economics of insurance and distinguish between
social and private insurance. In the same chapter, we will look at different
categories of private insurance products.

• *Alternative risk transfer*: When the management of a risk exposure uses
both self-financing and contractual transfer techniques, it is known as ART.
These solutions are tailored to the needs of a specific company in a specific

situation. Risks are compensated over time and are typically underwritten by large (re)insurance companies. ART solutions are generally implemented in large companies, mostly international companies. While the first ART solution was the creation of insurance captives (see below) starting in the late 1960s, more recent solutions aim to transfer risk financing directly to the financial markets (see examples of other solutions below).

ART solutions were developed as a result of the "traditional" insurance industry's preference at the time for a monoline and insular approach to risk (Swiss Re, 1999, 2003). Increasingly complex risks and increasingly technical risk management processes eventually required a more comprehensive approach to enterprise risks. ART solutions were developed to meet these needs and to reduce the cost of risk over time (see "finite risk" contracts discussed below). "Good risks," those that generate little or no loss, subsidize the others and are not always properly valued. Actuarial pricing is often based on statistics that reflect average risk. Due to information asymmetries between insurers and policyholders, risks are not covered at premium rates that reflect individual risk levels, but rather at—higher—market rates. As a result, companies with favorable risk characteristics and a reluctance to subsidize others will prefer self-insurance or alternative financing solutions.

ART products push the boundaries of insurability. Features of self-insurance are introduced into ART solutions by increasing the risk financing component and reducing the risk transfer or by defining triggers that are independent of the policyholders' behavior (see multi-trigger contracts). ART products also make it possible to increase coverage capacity. Certain risks are well-known but considered uninsurable due to their magnitude. Some natural catastrophe scenarios have costs ranging from 50 billion dollars to 100+ billion dollars, depending on the location and intensity of the event. Risk securitization (see below), i.e., the partial transfer of risk to external investors, can increase the capacity of the commercial insurance market by giving it direct access to capital markets. As the risk is spread across many investors, each investor only has to bear a small part of a potential loss. It should be noted that insurability is often limited by a lack of experience with new risks, such as terrorism or cyber risks (see section 4.7).

Captive insurance companies

Historically, the first alternative risk transfer solution was the creation of captive insurance companies beginning in the late 1960s. Today, many existing captives function essentially as vehicles for building a variety of ART solutions.

- *Definition*: A captive is an insurance or reinsurance company that belongs to a company or group of companies and is not active in the insurance market.

- *Operation*: The primary purpose of a captive is to insure the risks associated with the industrial activities of its owners, i.e., its parent companies and other group companies. Captives are, therefore, instruments used by their owners to self-finance their risks. In general, they do not fully finance these risks but transfer them, in whole or in part, to the traditional international reinsurance market or through ART solutions. Figure 4.4 shows the structure of a captive's parent company. The captive finances the financial consequences of the transferred risks and collects insurance premiums in return.

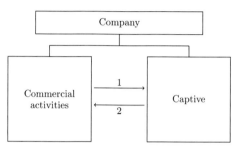

1: Payment of insurance premiums
2: Coverage of risk exposures and compensation

Figure 4.4: Structure of a company owning an insurance captive.

Insurance captives (cont.)

- *Historical motivations for the creation of captives*: The considerations that led to the creation of captives were tax advantages, excessive insurer margins prior to market deregulation, escape from the civil liability crisis in the United States, and the use of these entities as tools to enable ART solutions.

  - *Tax advantages*: In the early days of the captive boom, these advantages were the main reason why captives were formed. Compared to self-financing, setting up an offshore captive meant that premiums were tax deductible and provisions enjoyed favorable tax treatment. For this reason, many captives were registered in either Bermuda or the Cayman Islands. This tax aspect is now less important as most developed countries have responded to the situation by requiring captives to demonstrate the technical relevance of the premiums they collect.

  - *Excessive insurer margins prior to market deregulation*: In continental Europe, the non-life insurance market has long been highly regulated, providing insurers with high margins. In the case of high-frequency, relatively low-severity risks, i.e., risks that result in easily predictable losses for a large company, the creation of a captive could significantly reduce the cost of risk financing compared to traditional insurance. The deregulation of the market in the early 1980s led to a significant reduction in premiums for commercial insurance, so this is no longer a major reason for the use of captives.

- *Escape from the civil liability crisis in the United States*: Captives proliferated in the wake of the civil liability crisis in the United States. The ever-increasing damages awarded by courts led not only to massive premium increases but also to a shortage of coverage in the insurance market as insurance companies refused to insure certain civil liability risks. To address this shortage, in 1986, the federal government allowed businesses to form "purchasing groups," or multi-parent captives, as opposed to traditional single-parent captives.

- *Captives as tools to enable ART solutions*: Originally designed as an alternative to traditional insurance, captives were intended to finance only certain property and civil liability risks. The range of risks ceded to captives has expanded to include risks related to brand image and product warranties. Captives are also the foundation upon which other ART solutions can be built.

- *Current arguments in favor of creating a captive*: A captive offers many benefits to its parent company. These are primarily due to the captive's ability to provide customized and specific services. The parent company of the captive is not subject to the fluctuations of the insurance market, and because a captive is registered as an insurance company, it has access to the global reinsurance market. A captive provides more effective control of risks and claims and is able to cover risks that cannot be insured in the market. A captive is more efficient in terms of risk coverage. Insurance premiums are calculated to cover the current amount of expected claims, the insurer's underwriting costs, overhead, and profits to compensate for the cost of capital provided by investors. The percentage of premiums that is not used to pay claims can range from 30 to 40%. In addition, a captive can allow for better management of the retention required by insurers through the use of customized insurance policies. Finally, a captive can be a source of profit that is returned to the parent company.

Examples of other alternative risk transfer solutions

ART solutions are tailored to the specific needs of a company in a specific situation. In principle, each solution is unique, and the solution chosen is not available to the public. Some of the techniques presented here involve at least a partial transfer of the financing to an insurance or reinsurance company, while others can be implemented without the involvement of an insurer. Below are some of the ideas that emerge from these solutions. These include finite risk coverage, multi-line and multi-year products, multi-trigger contracts, contingent capital, risk securitization, and derivative insurance products. With these

ART solutions, a company can access customized products that meet its specific needs; additionally, it can also partially insulate itself from the pricing cycles of the insurance industry and reduce the amount of equity it needs in order to finance its risk exposures. We will summarize the main features, which are detailed in Swiss Re (1999, 2003) and refer to Swiss Re (2005, 2012) for additional reading.

- *Finite risk policies*: Traditional insurance is based on the assumption that if a large number of companies are exposed to similar risks, only a few will actually be affected by the adverse event over a given period of time. The premiums paid by each company offset the losses incurred by some of them. Finite risk solutions are based on a different assumption, namely that this equilibrium can be achieved for a single company over a long period of time. These solutions involve the transfer of financing with an overall cap for various risks from a captive to a reinsurer. This transfer covers both pure insurance risks and exposure to speculative risks, such as the risk of fluctuations in exchange rates and returns, commercial risk, i.e., the inability of the company to pay its premiums, and risks related to the evolution of premiums. Another characteristic of these products is that the period of coverage extends over several years. The premium paid depends on the evolution of the losses transferred. There are several types of solutions that tend to smooth the captive's results and, therefore, the parent company's results. However, because the funding is capped, these solutions are not suitable for protecting the company against exposures with extremely high severity.

- *Multi-line and multi-year products*: These solutions consist of grouping in a single insurance plan the financing of different risk exposures over periods of several years. They are generally limited to the financing of pure insurance risks, but unlike finite risk policies, they allow the coverage of potential losses of very high amounts, as in traditional insurance. The main advantages of these solutions are that they avoid the risk of over-insurance for a company, reduce its financial transfer costs, and benefit from risk diversification within a single policy. With traditional insurance, the company would have to cover each exposure separately.

- *Multi-trigger policies*: In their simplest form, these products require two types of events to occur during the coverage period before the financing transfer becomes effective. First, a loss related to the insured pure risk exposure. This is the first trigger. Then, the policy requires the occurrence of another uninsured event related to a speculative risk exposure; this is the second trigger. These products are based on the assumption that a company has sufficient financial capacity to self-finance either event, but not both at the same time.

- *Contingent capital*: One retention technique is to borrow the amount needed to finance the losses after the adverse event has occurred. One of the problems with this technique is that a major adverse event will make it much more difficult for the company to secure a loan, as its weaker financial position will increase the cost of the loan or even make it impossible. With contingent capital solutions, the company purchases the right to borrow capital upon the occurrence of a specified adverse event under contractually defined terms.

- *Risk securitization*: In the insurance markets, the financial capacity available to cover very large natural catastrophes is only a fraction of the potential losses. To manage these risks, some insurance and reinsurance companies, as well as some merchant banks, offer securities whose returns are directly linked to the occurrence of a natural catastrophe. This is attractive to investors who can diversify their portfolios, as natural disasters are not generally correlated with events in the financial markets. With this type of security, the coupon amount and even the face value of the security will depend on the disasters that have occurred over the life of the security. Generally, these solutions are implemented through a captive, in this case, a special purpose vehicle. Risk securitization is used both in non-life insurance—where the main securities are cat bonds linked to natural catastrophes—and in life insurance—with mortality bonds linked to mortality risk. In general, these insurance-linked securities have the following structure, which is illustrated in figure 4.5.

  1. The ceding company or sponsor enters into a financial risk transfer contract with an ad hoc structure known as a special purpose vehicle (SPV). It pays a premium to the SPV in exchange for coverage of the risk.

  2. The SPV covers the financial contract by issuing securities to institutional investors on the capital markets. These investors buy the securities by paying their value, the principal amount.

  3. The proceeds (premiums and investments) are invested in high quality, stable value securities held in a collateral trust.

  4. The investment income belongs to the SPV. Depending on the agreement, coupons are paid periodically to investors.

  5. If an event covered by the securities occurs, the losses are covered by the SPV, which compensates the sponsor using funds available in the investment.

  6. At the end of the agreed coverage period, a coupon and the principal amount are repaid to the investors.

Before the 2007 subprime crisis began in the United States in 2007, the structure typically included a swap counterparty that guaranteed the SPV a fixed return using a credit derivative known as a total return swap. Sometimes, this counterparty was Lehmann Brothers, which led to the partial default of some securities when the firm collapsed in September 2008.

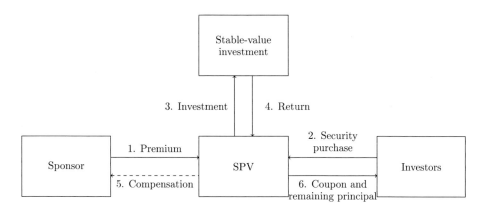

Figure 4.5: Typical structure of insurance-linked securities (based on Swiss Re, 2009).

Examples of other alternative risk transfer solutions (cont.)

- *Derivative insurance products*: Insurance derivatives are similar to stock index options. They are financial instruments whose value is determined by the evolution of an index specific to the risk being financed (e.g., an accident or a weather index). Several such options are traded on the exchange, but their volume remains modest despite the sophistication of the underlying instruments and indexes. The challenge is to define an index that investors will agree is objective.

4.4 Selection of the most appropriate techniques

After studying all the available techniques, the risk manager must select the most appropriate control and financing techniques. This requires two types of activities. First, the techniques must be evaluated, i.e., the impact of each technique on risk exposure must be studied. Second, selection criteria must be defined and applied.

Assessing the techniques To evaluate the available techniques, the risk manager analyzes the impact of each technique on the organization's ability to achieve its objectives. Three different assessments must be made for each risk exposure and each applicable technique:

- the assessment of the frequency and severity of the potential losses,

- the assessment of the technique's impact on the frequency, severity, and predictability of potential losses,

- the assessment of the costs of implementing the technique.

The first step is to estimate the frequency and severity of potential losses. To do this, the risk manager uses the mathematical tools and methods mentioned in chapter 3. Then, using the models they have developed, they assess the impact of each technique on frequency and severity. It is also important to analyze their impact on the predictability of potential losses. Finally, the application of a technique results in additional implementation costs. If statistics are not available, these assessments can be based on expert opinion, professional experience, projections, or simulations.

Definition and application of selection criteria   The risk manager must also define the criteria on which they will base their selection of the technique to be used. There are two categories of selection criteria for measuring the likelihood and consequences of risk exposures:

- purely economic criteria,

- other criteria.

Purely economic criteria include maximizing the expected value of profits or the present value of cash flows. Other criteria focus on stabilizing profits to minimize the likelihood of bankruptcy. Still others seek to maximize utility or efficiency. Depending on the circumstances, one criterion may be much more relevant than another. For example, for the IT system that manages a bank's customer data and accounts, maximum accuracy—that is, avoiding any possibility of error—is much more important than a purely financial criterion. The choice of criteria must take into account the types of exposed values which have an impact on the company's objectives. Particular attention must be paid to the consistent use of measures and the way in which different risk exposures are combined. Finally, the level of risk must be determined, taking into account the company's capacity.

The graph in figure 4.6 provides an overview of risk management techniques that are generally applicable depending on the frequency and severity of the risk exposure. For low frequency and low severity exposures, retention (or self-financing) is generally appropriate: typically, the financial consequences of losses are then paid as normal expenses (pay-as-you-go financing), or a reserve is created (financing through provisions). For high-frequency exposures, there are often many observations that can help understand the risk exposure and learn how to reduce the number of realized losses through prevention measures. This is the first technique to apply as it can reduce the frequency of losses. If the severity is high, the risk manager will try to avoid the risk exposure if possible. As a second step, depending on the severity, a financing technique must be selected. For high-severity but low-frequency exposures, the risk is more difficult to investigate, but the severity may be such that it threatens the achievement of the organization's objectives. In this situation, the preferred financing technique is insurance, i.e., a contractual transfer of risk financing. This can be explained by the fact that insurers often have more data on low-frequency exposures, which enables them to calculate in-

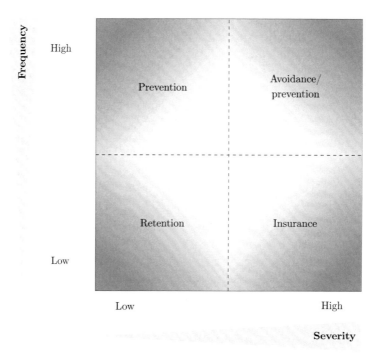

Figure 4.6: Selection of risk management techniques based on frequency and severity.

surance premiums. By pooling similar risks from different clients, they can reduce their overall risk exposure. The above observations are generally more relevant to exposures whose frequency and severity are either clearly low or high. Despite these general observations, each exposure must be analyzed individually.

4.5 Implementation of the techniques chosen

Risk policy and organization Once the appropriate techniques have been selected, the decision needs to be implemented. Successful implementation depends largely on the priority given to risk management in the organization and the hierarchical position of the risk manager. In many companies, risk management is becoming increasingly important. Because the effectiveness of risk management depends on the position of the risk manager, many large companies in all industries have created the position of chief risk officer (CRO) in recent years.

One of the most important factors is, therefore, the risk policy defined by non-executive management. This policy defines the risks to be managed as a matter of priority and ensures that the actions taken by management and the risk manager are followed up. The implementation of the policy requires a clear definition of the

141

roles and responsibilities of non-executive and executive management and the risk manager. Typically, non-executive management delegates the implementation of risk management to executive management with the support of the risk manager. The risk manager reports to the executive management but also provides regular and emergency reports to the non-executive management or one of its committees. The primary purpose of these reports is to communicate the activities and results of risk management. They also provide the information necessary to improve the implementation of the program and to make decisions. Non-executive management has overall responsibility for risk management. We illustrate this organization in figure 4.7, which is adapted from Müller et al. (2019). The risks to be managed are grouped into three categories: strategic, operational, and external (see section 2.3).

Figure 4.7: Risk management organization (adapted from Müller et al., 2019, section 4.39).

According to the ISO 31000:2018 standard (International Organization for Standardization, 2018, chapter 5), the organizational framework must be based on the values of leadership and commitment. The integration of risk management into all activities of an organization is based on a code of conduct that is communicated and understood by all. Authority and accountability can be used to align strategy, objectives, and culture (see also section 4.6). Implementation of the program throughout the organization depends on the responsibility of each party (see the 1st line of defense below). It is essential to consult with and involve operational management in the design, implementation, and evaluation of the program. Experts in the various relevant fields must also be involved in both the initial establishment and the ongoing adaptation and improvement of the risk management program.

The three lines of defense model A commonly used model in risk governance is the three lines of defense model. It is used in most organizations and has been proven successful for years. This model details the roles and responsibilities of the control, risk management, compliance, and internal audit functions within the governance system. A clear division of responsibilities ensures that all risks are identified and managed effectively and efficiently. Non-executive and executive

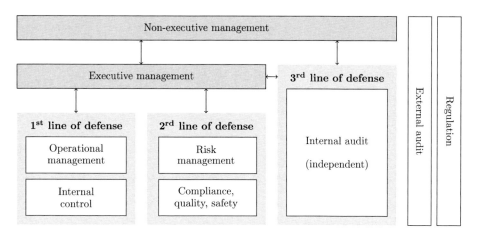

Figure 4.8: The three lines of defense model.

management are the key players in this model, which was originally designed for the internal organization. The Institute of Internal Auditors, an international authority, issues standards, guidelines, and certifications.

The model incorporates three levels of risk control within a company. The first line of defense is provided by the business units and includes internal control mechanisms as well as other controls overseen by executive management. It consists of the management of day-to-day operations. The primary task of the first line is to regularly identify, assess, and manage (new) risks in everyday business. It is also responsible for monitoring the company's risk appetite. Finally, the activities of the first line of defense include identifying and reporting weaknesses in control processes, as well as contributing to and improving policies and procedures.

The second line of defense relates to risk management and compliance. Its main purpose is to establish a risk management framework and a general control structure, followed by a report and assessment of the overall situation with respect to common and emerging risks. This line's responsibilities include monitoring legal compliance, ensuring the adequacy of processes, methods, quality, and safety, and coordinating the preparation of the overall risk situation report. It also provides expertise and support on all risk-related issues. The activities of the first two lines of defense are directed by management.

The third line of defense is internal audit, a regular and independent process for monitoring the adequacy and effectiveness of risk management processes. In this context, governance and the interaction between the three lines are important. Internal audit, like executive management, reports to non-executive management. The process of the three lines of defense is subject to external audit and regulatory control. Figure 4.8 provides a visual illustration of the three lines of defense model.

4.6   Monitoring of the results

The purpose of this final step in risk management is to verify that the expected results are being achieved and, if necessary, to adjust the risk management program to changes that may occur in the exposure to losses. Several monitoring and review activities are required to complete this step:

- define acceptable performance standards,
- compare the results achieved to those standards,
- correct or adjust the program as necessary.

Risk culture   Iterative adjustments to the program are an integral part of the risk management processes. A critical approach and a strong corporate culture are important for proper development. For example, in the event of significant losses, instead of criticizing, we should imagine the losses that would have occurred if no measures had been taken, and fix and improve the system. The idea is to develop best practices and raise standards. We conclude that consistent and mindful implementation of risk management techniques can only occur in the presence of a healthy risk culture. This approach is highly dependent on the culture of the society in which the company operates. Employees, as human beings, must be placed at the center of the processes and taken into account in the operations. The company's governing bodies are responsible for promoting a risk culture within the company through their actions and attitudes (Métayer and Hirsch, 2007).

The term "risk culture" refers to the attitudes and behaviors that an individual, a company, or a society adopts with respect to risk. This risk culture will, therefore, shape the organization, behavior, attitudes, and ethics of the company as individual predispositions to risk are manifested. The risk culture defines, often unconsciously, which rules and standards are perceived as rational and important (Zeier Roeschmann, 2014). The influence of risk culture is threefold. First, it affects the systems, processes, and structures that deal with defining objectives, identifying events, assessing risks, responding to risks, monitoring activities, information and communication, and monitoring within an organization. Second, it affects the values adopted, i.e., the corporate culture that shapes the fundamental way in which risk is perceived and dealt with by employees, including their philosophy of risk management, risk aversion, integrity, and ethical values, and the environment in which they operate. Finally, risk culture affects the underlying assumptions, i.e., the beliefs and values of a group that have been built up over time as decisions involving risk have been made (Schein, 2016).

Costs and benefits   When monitoring risk on a regular basis, two key questions need to be asked: What are the benefits of risk management to the organization? What is the cost of risk management to the organization? This cost-benefit analysis can be done at different scales, because the costs and benefits of exposure to potential losses affect the company itself, other companies in the same industry, and the broader economy.

In regards to costs, we divide them into three categories:

- losses,
- inertia,
- wasted resources.

The category of "losses" includes property, revenue, lives, and other assets that are damaged or destroyed. "Inertia" refers to the dissuasive effects that potential losses have on a company's activities. Certain activities are perceived as too risky and are not undertaken; therefore, the associated benefits are not realized. Finally, "wasted resources" are any resources devoted to managing losses—whether potential or realized— that could instead be devoted to more profitable activities.

These wasted resources are the costs of risk management, while the reduction in losses and inertia are its benefits. The purpose of a risk management program is to minimize the sum of these three cost categories. To properly analyze the costs and benefits of risk management, given the importance of the reference framework (see section 2.2), it is preferable to consider three separate perspectives: the company itself, the community of which it is a part, and the broader economy of all companies and communities.

- *Company perspective*: From a business point of view, the goal is to reduce the costs associated with the risks of day-to-day operations. A company's losses correspond to the payments it must make for self-financed risk exposures, and expenses not covered by insurance or an alternative source. Wasted resources include insurance premiums paid to insurers, as well as interest and repayments to lenders. They also include expenses associated with implementing prevention and reduction measures and administrative overhead. In addition, if a company's marginal tax rate is progressive, additional costs arise from fluctuations in profits over time. The convexity of the tax rate curve means that stable annual profits are preferable to large fluctuations. In fact, dampening earnings volatility is one of the goals of a risk management program. A risk management program will seek to reduce the overall cost of risk while minimizing disruption to the company's everyday operations.

  Fear of potential future losses tends to dampen the entrepreneurial spirit and enthusiasm of business leaders. These concerns make them reluctant to engage in activities they consider too risky. As a result, the net income that could have been generated by these activities is a loss to the company. Good risk management tends to reduce the dissuasive effects of uncertainty associated with potential losses. One way to reduce uncertainty is to reduce the frequency and severity of potential losses while making them more predictable. Lower uncertainty has two tangible benefits. First, once reluctance is overcome, certain projects become more feasible. Second, the company becomes safer and, therefore, more attractive to investors. In summary, an effective risk management program creates additional opportunities for a company, which ultimately benefits the company.

- *Community perspective*: The concerns of the community or industry lie between those of an organization and those of the broader economy. The losses of a single company can have a large impact on a community but only a small impact on the economy as a whole. A company in a small town is likely to have a significant impact on the region's economy—for example, on the local labor market with a potential ripple effect on the local economy— but not on a broader scale. If the community is the industry or sector to which the company belongs, poor risk management that results in bankruptcy, for example, affects the image of all companies in the industry as well as consumer confidence. As a result, the community is concerned with the risk management programs implemented by the companies that are part of it.

- *Economic perspective*: Finally, from the perspective of the broader economy, the view is quite different. The focus is on reducing waste and improving the allocation of productive resources. This is because in a given economy, there is only a limited amount of resources available to produce goods and services. If losses occur, resources are completely wasted. A portion of a nation's resources is devoted to preventing, repairing, or compensating for losses. From this perspective, risk management helps to reduce the amount of wasted resources. In addition, reducing uncertainty for individual companies leads to a better allocation of productive resources for the economy as a whole. Effective risk management means that managers no longer have to worry about the consequences of potential losses. This allows them to pursue more profitable activities without worrying about financing.

4.7   Cyber risk management and insurability

From frequent website hacks to the countless fraudulent "spam" emails that users of major service providers receive every day, and from the various high-profile WikiLeaks revelations to the suspected manipulation of the U.S. presidential election, many events remind us that all actors, large and small, are vulnerable to digital risks. Cyber risks are a technological and societal challenge that can affect the real world as well as the virtual world; more than ever, they are at the heart of global and local concerns. Evidence of this can be found in the World Economic Forum's ranking of cyber risks, which places them just after climate change, on par with natural disasters, and ahead of terrorist attacks, asset bubbles, and structural unemployment (see figure 1.1 in section 1.1).

Organizations of all sizes, in both the public and private sectors, are increasingly dependent on technology and information, as well as on human resources and facilities, to carry out the operational processes that support the delivery of services. Any disruption can have a negative impact on these operational processes, resulting in an inability to deliver services.

Definition of cyber risks Operational cybersecurity risks, or cyber risks, are risks that we define as follows (see also Cebula and Young, 2010):

Definition 4.7 (*Cyber risks*)

> **Cyber risks** are operational risks related to data, information, and technical assets that compromise the confidentiality, availability, or integrity of information or information systems.

Thus, cyber risks threaten both tangible elements, such as digital infrastructure in the broadest sense, and intangible elements, such as data and virtual streams and communication networks. By their very nature, communication networks will continue to pose many challenges in terms of understanding and quantifying the losses associated with them.

Categorization and examples To better understand these operational risks, we present a categorization by peril in table 4.2. We identify and organize sources of operational cybersecurity risk into four classes: actions of people, systems and technology failures, failed internal processes, and external events. Actions of people consist of either human error—whether intentional or unintentional—or inaction by an individual due to a lack of skills, knowledge, or instructions necessary to act in a given situation and prevent a loss from occurring. The second category relates to problems with digital systems, whether caused by hardware, software, or the interaction between the two. Third are failures in internal processes that result from poor design, execution, or support. Finally, events that originate outside the organization include man-made and natural disasters, legal and business issues, and public services and partners on which the organization's operations depend. We note that the concept of cyber risk covers a wide range of events and is not limited to risks associated with cybercrime.

Continuing the categorization of cyber risks, we distinguish two types of causes, depending on whether a criminal element is present. Non-criminal risks include cases of force majeure, i.e., events such as natural disasters that cause damage to physical IT infrastructures. Then there are technical failures, which can affect systems either virtually (software bugs) or physically (short circuits, hard drive problems, computer crashes). Finally, human error includes, among other things, incorrect manipulation. Criminal causes, as studied by Kshetri (2010), imply a violation of applicable laws or regulations. We distinguish between physical

Category	Description	Elements
Actions of people		
Inadvertent	unintentional actions taken without malicious or harmful intent	mistakes, errors, omissions
Deliberate	actions taken intentionally and with the intent to do harm	fraud, sabotage, theft and vandalism
Inaction	lack of action or failure to act in a given situation	lack of appropriate skills, knowledge, guidance and availability of personnel to take action
Systems and technology failures		
Hardware	risks traceable to failures in physical equipment	failure due to capacity, performance, maintenance and obsolescence
Software	risks stemming from software assets of all types, including programs, applications and operating systems	compatibility, configuration management, change control, security settings, coding practices and testing
Systems	failures of integrated systems to perform as expected	design, specifications, integration and complexity
Failed internal processes		
Process design and/or execution	failure of processes to achieve their desired outcomes due to poor process design or execution	process flow, process documentation, roles and responsibilities, notifications and alerts, information flow, escalation of issues, service-level agreements, and task hand-off
Process controls	inadequate controls on the operation of the process	status monitoring, metrics, periodic review and process ownership
Supporting processes	failure of organizational supporting processes to deliver the appropriate resources	staffing, accounting, training and development, and procurement
External events		
Catastrophes	events, both natural and of human origin, over which the organization has no control and that can occur without notice	weather event, fire, flood, earthquake, unrest
Legal issues	risk arising from legal issues	regulatory compliance, legislation and litigation
Business issues	risks arising from changes in the business environment of the organization	supplier failure, market conditions and economic conditions
Service dependencies	risks arising from the organization's dependence on external parties	utilities, emergency services, fuel and transportation

Table 4.2: Categories of cyber risk by peril (based on Cebula and Young, 2010 and Biener et al., 2015b, table 1, reproduced with permission from Springer Nature).

attacks, such as sabotage or theft of (physical) data, and cyberattacks, which affect systems through their virtual components, such as the introduction of malware (virus, spam) or digital data theft. It also includes extortion and all other forms of online threats (e.g., ransomware attacks).

The analysis of technological risks in figure 1.1 (see section 1.1) highlights the fact that the risk of a cyberattack is perceived as high probability and high severity. As cyber risk is still considered an emerging risk, there are few statistics available on the assessment of losses resulting from cyber incidents. Heon and Parsoire (2017) mention that the first U.S. law on the loss of personal data was signed in California in 2002. In the following years, many companies reported the theft of millions of customer records. It was not until 2010 that an insurance market for cyber risks began to develop. In Switzerland, the federal authorities created a reporting and analysis center for information security in 2004 with a view to providing information and prevention. This portal brings together various government partners active in the field of information security and the protection of national infrastructures; it collects documentation on cyber risks and can be used to report cyber breaches. These efforts seem necessary, as cyber risks are often underestimated by companies and individuals alike. In 2020, the National Cyber Security Centre (2020) was created in Switzerland. The Swiss Confederation's competence center for cybersecurity is the first point of contact for companies, public administrations, educational institutions, and the general public for all questions related to cybersecurity.

More recently, cybercrime has raised concerns in the global business community about the vulnerability of power companies, airlines, hospitals, and keyless cars. Data is often unavailable, IT systems and websites are inaccessible, and communications systems are down. Stolen data is sometimes released, and user passwords or identities are used after successful "social phishing" attempts (see below). The organization that suffers a breach of personal or banking data not only faces reputational risk but also litigation.

In general, cyber risks need to be addressed on a global scale. All online systems, such as the internet, rely on a physical infrastructure that spans the globe. From undersea and underground cables that cross oceans, seas, and continents to switches—physical relays that redistribute and share internet traffic on a more local scale—and satellites, this hardware skeleton is a major source of network vulnerability at all scales. Satellites are vulnerable to solar storms, cables and switches can be damaged, and the internet domains that host website content can be targeted by virtual attacks. The structure of these networks is designed to be highly decentralized, but local damage can still have widespread consequences due to the high density and interdependence of data flows. As a result, experts agree that the internet can be paralyzed on a continental scale but not on a global scale—the cost of such an outage, even for a short period of time, could be in the hundreds of billions of dollars.

Table 4.3 provides an overview of the types of exposed values. Recognizing that generalizations are difficult, we essentially list potential losses in the categories of property value or net income and liability. For property or net income, potential losses are related to the recovery or replacement of data and hardware, direct and indirect business interruption losses, and financial and reputational losses. Liability losses result from claims by affected third parties, whether customers or

Category	Elements
Property / net income	• Costs associated with the recovery and replacement of data and systems, including hardware
	• Costs related to business interruption
	• Costs related to misappropriation of assets
	• Extortion payments
	• Costs of crisis management services
	• Loss of reputation
Liability (third-party claims)	• Claims arising from breach of privacy
	• Liability related to network security (claims based on breach of duty resulting in financial loss to a third party)
	• Costs associated with the retrieval of third parties' data
	• Liability for one's own online activities or statements in e-mails (costs incurred as a result of infringement or illegal use of intellectual property)
	• Costs associated with impeding or denying legitimate access to customers

Table 4.3: Overview of the types of values exposed to cyber risk (based on Biener et al., 2015a, table 5).

partners, and from litigation. The claims are diverse in nature. They include claims related to privacy violations, liability for inadvertent online activities, and costs resulting from breaches of contractual relationships.

Phishing and "social phishing"

With the democratization of the internet and email systems, we are faced with the phenomenon of phishing, which consists of sending large numbers of fraudulent emails in an attempt to obtain personal information—usually related to online payments—from as many recipients as possible. For example, the "phishers" may pretend to be a bank and, claiming that the user needs to update their information, send a link to a web page that resembles the bank's website; the user is asked to enter confidential information (e.g., password or credit card number), which the fraudsters then retrieve and use for criminal purposes (in particular, identify theft, online purchases, and wire transfers). In order to prevent such attacks, it is a good practice to check the sender's address, which usually does not look official (suspicious domain name and subject line) in contrast to the appearance of the message; the address of the hyperlink in the email should also be checked. The page where the hackers collect confidential information is usually not encrypted (its address does not start with "https://"), and the domain name is not the correct one for the institution being impersonated. There are also digital solutions (third-party software or built-in features of certain email clients) that automatically perform these checks on all incoming messages.

The term "social phishing" refers to an attempt to steal data using the same method described above, but in the real world, through the actions of one or more people in an everyday situation. For example, a person could enter a company's offices, act like an employee, and log into a computer to steal data or install malware. Preventing this risk means addressing a company's network infrastructure and physical security since the threat comes from a human action on the premises. Major Swiss banks, for example, go as far as installing security gates and retina or fingerprint scanners to restrict access to certain locations or digital devices; many companies simply disable USB ports on their employees' workstations, eliminating part of the risk. Finally, educating employees on security issues is paramount. This includes establishing good digital practices such as locking computers when leaving a desk for even a moment, changing passwords regularly, not opening emails from unknown senders or with content unrelated to the business, and blocking access to non-business sites such as social networks and messaging or data storage platforms.

Cyber risk management Following the risk management concepts presented in this chapter (see figure 4.1 in section 4.1), we divide the cyber risk management process into five main steps, illustrated in figure 4.9. The process begins with defining objectives in terms of the desired level of security, taking into account available resources. During this step, the risk manager uses established cybersecurity frameworks. These take into account, among other things, the level of implementation of risk management practices and the maturity profile of the measures in place within the organization. The risk manager then moves on to identifying and appreciating the risks. In recent years, we have seen the emergence of several books on IT security best practices. At the same time, cyber risk self-assessment tools have been developed to help companies determine their own risk exposure, as it is important to look at obvious risks as well as hidden or suppressed risks. Once risk exposure has been defined and classified within a single matrix that summarizes all risks by frequency and severity, we can decide how important each risk exposure should be within a risk management program. When it comes to techniques, the first step is to control risk exposures by avoiding or reducing them, followed by choosing between retaining or transferring risk financing. The final step is monitoring. This means reviewing results over time, but also monitoring the developments of new cyber risks, an area that is evolving faster than others.

To summarize, let us recall the seven guidelines for good cyber risk management as laid out by Biener et al. (2015a):

- *Accountability*: First, it is important to give cyber risk a proper place in the organization by assigning a person or team to be responsible for it.

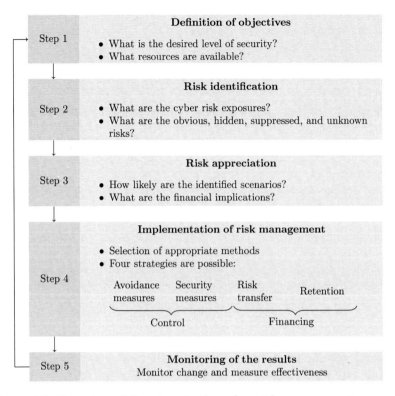

Figure 4.9: Overview of the steps in the cyber risk management process.

Appointing a chief information security officer can reduce the average cost of a cyber incident by 30% (Shackelford, 2012).

- *Crisis management*: Crisis management is a critical aspect of risk management and includes, in particular, the definition of processes corresponding to specific scenarios (e.g., in the event of data loss) and the clear definition of the responsibilities of each person and the actions to be taken.

- *Intra-company dialogue*: Cyber risks are not confined to one department of an organization. As with all risks that can affect an organization's operations, it is important to establish a risk dialogue that includes cyber risks; this must be done at the level of the entire organization, including through employee awareness and training programs.

- *Interactions with partners*: The above dialogue must extend to customers and suppliers to determine their own level of security and the risk management measures they have implemented.

- *Continuous monitoring*: Given the pace of technological development and the emergence of new threats, the risk management process needs to be continuously adapted. This means that a monitoring and control process is essential.

- *Standards and certification*: Certification to recognized IT security standards can send a strong message to customers and suppliers.

- *Insurance*: Finally, risk transfer through an insurance policy, if available, may be an appropriate way to manage risk in certain situations.

Insurability of cyber risks Insuring cyber risks presents many challenges. With increasingly stringent data protection regulations, traditional insurance policies that do not cover IT-related risks, and the high costs associated with an incident (e.g., direct losses, data recovery, business interruption, professional services), insurability is a key factor in the cyber risk discussion.

More recently, specific insurance policies have begun to cover cyber risks, generally providing coverage for out-of-pocket expenses and third-party claims. These policies may cover expenses or civil liability (see section 5.4 and figure 5.7). The former cover, in particular, costs related to business interruption (lost revenue, recovery costs), information recovery (lost data, software resources), crisis management (intervention of external specialists, monitoring of the event, notification of customers and authorities), and extortion in case of ransomware (ransom payment, investigation costs). The latter covers the loss of confidential information, damage to third-party systems (legal costs, analysis, compensation to victims), and damage to a company's reputation associated with an event (for example, defamation). This is a high-growth market, and forecasts for the coming years are optimistic.

Because of the fundamental uncertainty surrounding the insurability of cyber risks, policies currently offered often have relatively low coverage limits or high premiums. This is because the insurability criteria defined by Berliner (1982) are applied to cyber risks. From an actuarial perspective, insurers can only cover events that occur randomly and independently and whose losses can be estimated based on a manageable maximum loss, moderate average severity, and relatively high frequency. It is also important to avoid excessive information asymmetry, especially with regard to adverse selection and moral hazard. Of all these criteria, the maximum size, severity, and frequency of events are the least problematic. This can be explained by the fact that although the frequency of events has increased in recent years as a result of the spread of information and communication technologies, the average severity has decreased as a result of the spread of self-insurance. However, the factors used to determine an insurance premium are not easy to assess or quantify. Estimating the risk of loss and the role of adverse selection and moral hazard is challenging. Market conditions are also difficult. Insurance premiums should remain affordable for acceptable limits of coverage. For risks that are variable and difficult to estimate, coverage limits offered tend to be low, policies exclude many indirect losses, and premiums charged are high. Insurance companies offer only products that are consistent with societal values and legal restrictions. In this context, for example, insurance policies covering ransoms paid to hackers are problematic because some legal systems defend them. Table 4.4 summarizes these aspects.

Insurability criteria		Requirements	Assessment
Actuarial	Randomness of loss occurrence	Independence and predictability of loss exposures	✗
	Maximum possible loss	Manageable	✓
	Average loss per event	Moderate severity	✓
	Average probability of a loss event	Relatively high frequency	✓
	Information asymmetry	Adverse selection and moral hazard not excessive	✗
Market	Insurance premiums	Cover the losses and remain affordable	✓–✗
	Cover limits	Acceptable	✗
Societal	Public policy	Consistent with societal value	✓–✗
	Legal restrictions	Allow the coverage	✓–✗

Note: The assessment symbols identify criteria that are problematic (✗), not problematic (✓), and potentially or slightly problematic (✓–✗).

Table 4.4: Assessment of the insurability of cyber risks (based on Berliner, 1982 and Biener et al., 2015b, table 3, reproduced with permission from Springer Nature).

In short, according to Biener et al. (2015a), the barriers to insurability are the following:

- *Risk of cumulation*: The risks affecting a single customer can cumulate in a single area or across multiple insurance policies. For example, an IT problem can lead to a fire and property loss.

- *Portfolio diversification*: The relatively small size of portfolios covering cyber risks means that insurers do not benefit from the usual advantages of pooling (see the economic justification of insurance in section 5.1) and risk diversification.

- *Data availability*: Lack of data makes pricing more difficult and less accurate.

- *Relevance of historical data*: The rapid pace of technological change means that any model developed may soon become obsolete. Historical cyber risk data is not a good predictor of future losses.

- *Actuarial models*: There are no established actuarial standards for modeling cyber risks. Extreme scenarios and risks (low frequency, high severity) are difficult to estimate.

- *Insurance capacity*: The volume available to insure cyber risk events is limited, so early insurance products are characterized by high deductibles and relatively low coverage.

In order to improve the management of cyber risks and facilitate the development of insurance products, a number of measures could be taken in response to the factors outlined above.   Among other measures, it seems necessary to expand regulations to establish cyber risk management standards, such as an assessment procedure and a duty to notify when a "cyber event" occurs. From an information and awareness-raising perspective, it is also important to make data available, for example, through widely accessible online platforms and databases, in order to encourage and improve sharing. More generally, innovation is a critical factor for risk management and for the development of insurance products; it requires significant investment in terms of skills and financial resources (see also Swiss Re, 2012).

From a financial perspective, it could be useful to develop a public or private insurance pool for cyber risks, similar to the Swiss pool for earthquake losses. Such an initiative could help overcome the reluctance of insurers to enter this market for cost reasons. An alternative or complementary solution would be to strengthen the role of the state, for example, as a manager. Finally, the creation of solutions directly linked to the financial markets could be explored, for example, through the securitization of cyber risks (see section 4.3).

Reflections on a cyber risk scenario

Let us consider a company's dependence on the internet with the following scenario: "The internet is down all over Switzerland for an unknown period of time." What happens to the company? How to manage this event?

First, we look at the relevance of the scenario: What is the true significance and impact of cyber risks? Is the organization aware of the risks? What are the consequences in terms of loss of reputation?

Next, we can look at risk management: How are cyber risks currently managed? Is there a contingency plan in place? Who is accountable for what? What is the IT security strategy, if any? What new risks are created by outsourcing and storing large amounts of data in the cloud?

Finally, we can think about potential improvements. How can cyber risk management be improved? Should companies be required to disclose their losses related to cyber risk? Should insurance play a role in cyber risk management? If so, what role?

These suggested questions are more an invitation to think than an exhaustive list, especially considering that the field of cyber risk is multifaceted and, more importantly, constantly evolving and being redefined.

CHAPTER 5

Insurance economics and insurance market

Insurance is a service that promises that the policyholder, in return for payment of a premium, will receive compensation—typically the financing of certain losses—if a previously agreed-upon risk materializes. We examine the economic sector that encompasses these services, and this chapter is devoted to the economics of insurance and the private insurance market. First, in section 5.1, we will discuss the economic foundations of insurance and ask what justifies insurance: why is it attractive to pool risks in an insurance company? At the end of the section, we provide an overview of how much Swiss households spend on insurance. We find that, on average, a quarter of all money spent goes to insurance premiums.

In section 5.2, we will introduce the distinction between social insurance and private insurance, which have different goals and financing profiles. We will define the branches of social insurance as established by Swiss law, describe how they work and how they are financed, and study their income structure. The data presented will allow us to understand in particular, how the old-age pension system in Switzerland works and why it is a difficult balancing act.

We will then cover the private insurance market in section 5.3. We will present indicators that measure the size of the insurance industry; we will also analyze the distribution of markets around the world, and we will take a closer look at the Swiss market. Premiums paid in Switzerland currently amount to 60 billion francs. We will look at the structure of the market and the allocation of assets. In section 5.4, starting with the definition of a private insurance policy, we will study the basic legal principles of insurance and divide the private insurance offering into categories by industry, type of exposed values, and market segment.

5.1 Economic functions and justification of insurance

Insurance is part of the financial sector of the economy, and its purpose is to manage the risks of companies and individuals. It supports economic agents by providing two services: risk coverage and the recycling of savings generated in the economy. The basis of this activity is the risk aversion of agents, which hinders activity in general and innovative companies in particular. Insurers cover the potential losses associated with these risks by pooling them. This requires each policyholder to pay a regular premium, the amount of which is determined in advance, and to receive compensation if an adverse event occurs. As we saw in section 3.4, policyholders prefer to pay a small amount with certainty rather than face the uncertainty of a larger potential loss. This allows economic agents to better manage the hazards of daily life. By paying a premium, companies can include the cost of risk in their balance sheets. Risk management, and in particular the pricing and monetization of risk, is at the heart of the insurance industry.

Economic functions of insurance   The insurance industry contributes to the efficiency of the economy and supports economic growth in many ways. In particular, insurance enables the development of new profitable businesses while protecting existing wealth. Figure 5.1 illustrates six economic functions of insurance described by Zweifel and Eisen (2012, section 1.4), which we will summarize below.

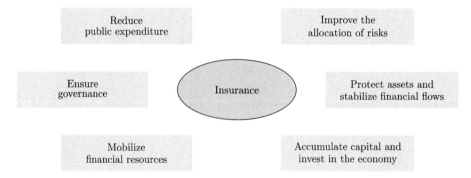

Figure 5.1: Economic functions of insurance (adapted from Zweifel and Eisen, 2012).

- *Improve the allocation of risks*: Efficient risk allocation minimizes transactions costs. Insurers reduce or eliminate potential losses by conducting technical inspections and investigating the causes of losses. They quickly finance the replacement of lost resources and identified defects to prevent further damage. These measures make the economy more efficient, which promotes stability and growth. One might think that moral hazard (see section 2.6) could increase risk-taking in the presence of insurance, but insurers are aware of these effects and charge higher premiums to cover these risks.

In the end, the ability to insure risks always increases the expected return, profit, or utility.

- *Protect assets and stabilize financial flows*: Insurers provide businesses and individuals with a more stable foundation on which to plan. This is often essential for taking entrepreneurial risks. For example, a company may need to insure against product liability risks before launching a new product. This support for entrepreneurship is often seen as the insurance industry's most important contribution to economic prosperity. Insurance also helps to stabilize cash flows. At the individual level, pension funds serve to guarantee income in retirement by deferring part of the income earned during a worker's active life. With a more stable income, consumption is smoothed over a person's lifetime.

- *Accumulate capital and invest in the economy*: Capital accumulates automatically because premiums are paid at the beginning of the policy period, while claims are paid only after losses have occurred. This delay can be very long, even decades, in the case of life insurance. In non-life insurance, for example, insurers set aside reserves for catastrophic events. These funds are invested, and insurers have significant influence over the supply of capital and the credit market. Such investments are regulated and, in Switzerland, consist mainly of Swiss government bonds.

- *Mobilize financial resources*: The premiums paid into life insurance policies and pension funds create a provident fund from which pensions are later paid. Although everyone could save on their own without going through an insurer, the insurance model mobilizes additional capital, especially during the accumulation phase. The provident funds that belong to the 2nd pillar in Switzerland have a total of one trillion francs in capital (see section 5.2).

- *Ensure governance*: Because premiums reflect the level of risk, insurance encourages people to limit excessive risk-taking. Insurers also monitor the management of companies and encourage them to use their resources effectively. This function of insurance is particularly important in the context of environmental risks posed by businesses. For example, insurance can cover these types of losses as part of a corporate liability policy; because premiums are based on the level of pollution risk, companies have the incentive to prevent or reduce potential for losses.

- *Reduce public expenditure*: Insurance results in lower costs for the government and taxpayers. By purchasing insurance, companies and individuals protect themselves against everyday risks that would otherwise be borne by the community through solidarity mechanisms. Examples include health insurance, unemployment insurance, and liability insurance. Nowadays, it is considered preferable to make insurance compulsory rather than to let the community compensate for losses.

Economic justification of insurance We mentioned earlier that insurance is based on the principle of mutuality and shared risk financing. One might even say that the law of large numbers underlies insurance. However, this is not quite true: although the law of large numbers plays an important role in insurance, it is not its economic justification.

Assume that $X_1, X_2, ..., X_n$ are random variables representing potential losses associated with specific risk exposures for n firms and that, for simplicity, these n random variables all have the same distribution, expected value $\mu = \mathbb{E}(X_i)$, and standard deviation $\sigma = \sigma(X_i)$. The sum of the potential losses is $S = \sum_{i=1}^{n} X_i$. Assuming further that these random variables are independent, the law of large numbers tells us that the empirical mean $\frac{1}{n}\sum_{i=1}^{n} X_i$ converges in probability to the expected value μ (see theorem 3.2 in section 3.3),

$$\frac{S}{n} = \frac{1}{n}\sum_{i=1}^{n} X_i \xrightarrow{n \to +\infty} \mu.$$

The law of large numbers provides the insurer with a method for estimating its risk and, more specifically, the expected value of potential losses. However, a number of important points need to be made. First, while the average of the potential losses converges, their sum S, i.e., the total amount to be paid by the insurer, diverges. The variance of S is proportional to n. Second, in practice, in most cases, the risks are not independent but rather positively correlated. For example, changes in price indices, interest rates, and the climate affect each of the n potential losses, creating interdependencies between risks. Even in life insurance, the possibility of a pandemic is an example of a factor that prevents risks from being completely independent.

Regardless of the initial assumptions made, the law of large numbers is a tool that the insurer can use to assess its risks, not an economic justification for insurance per se. The economic justification of insurance can be expressed as follows: *Insurance makes it possible, for a given level of security, to manage the financing of risks while minimizing the capital required and, therefore, the cost of that capital.*

Let us use the same example as above, with n potential losses X_i, and assume for simplicity that each X_i has a normal distribution with mean μ and standard deviation σ. We can use the value-at-risk of level α (see definition 3.27 in section 3.5) to estimate the capital needed to cover the losses X_i.

If each firm decides to self-finance its potential losses, the capital required for each firm can be calculated as follows:

$$\text{VaR}_\alpha(X_i) = \mathbb{E}(X_i) + c_\alpha \cdot \sigma(X_i) = \mu + c_\alpha \cdot \sigma,$$

where c_α is the quantile of the standard normal distribution corresponding to α (see section 3.5).

Thus, the total capital required for all firms is

$$\sum_{i=1}^{n} \text{VaR}_{\alpha}(X_i) = n \cdot \text{VaR}_{\alpha}(X_i) = n \cdot \mu + c_{\alpha} \cdot n \cdot \sigma.$$

However, if all firms pool the financing of their risk by transferring it to an insurer, the total capital requirement, estimated using the value-at-risk with the same level of confidence α, is

$$\text{VaR}_{\alpha}\left(\sum_{i=1}^{n} X_i\right) = \text{VaR}_{\alpha}(S) = \mathbb{E}(S) + c_{\alpha} \cdot \sigma(S) = n \cdot \mu + c_{\alpha} \cdot \sigma(S).$$

If the risks are independent, then the standard deviation $\sigma(S) = \sqrt{n} \cdot \sigma \leq n \cdot \sigma$. Thus, a comparison of the above expressions shows that the total capital required—and therefore the cost of that capital—is lower for the same level of safety when the risks are pooled through an insurer.

In conclusion, insurance minimizes the capital required to cover risk. This result is not related to the law of large numbers; rather, the economic justification of insurance is based on *risk diversification*.

Private household spending on insurance   Before discussing the main areas of insurance, we illustrate how much individual households spend on insurance. The Federal Statistical Office (2020c) regularly publishes statistics on the income and spending of private households in Switzerland. These statistics use the results of the household budget survey and present data for 2018, when the average household had 2.16 people. The average Swiss household earns CHF 10,114 per month. We break down how this money is spent in the graph in figure 5.2.

Consumption spending makes up the largest portion of spending, with 52% of gross income (CHF 5,296). This includes housing, transportation, food, leisure, and all other costs related to goods and services necessary for daily life. The total of all contributions and premiums paid to insurance is CHF 2,335 per month, or 23% of total spending. This amount includes mandatory contributions to social insurance and basic health insurance, as well as all premiums for supplementary health insurance, life insurance, and non-life insurance. Taxes, duties, and other mandatory transfers account for 16% of gross income. Finally, about one thousand francs (9%) is left over for savings.

In table 5.1, we provide a detailed breakdown of the contributions and premiums paid for insurance. The highest monthly expenditures in this area are for social insurance and basic health insurance—which is also a social insurance in Switzerland— with CHF 1,035 and CHF 655, respectively. These are mandatory. Social insurance contributions are particularly high because they include contributions to old age and survivors' insurance (AVS) and the pension fund (occupational

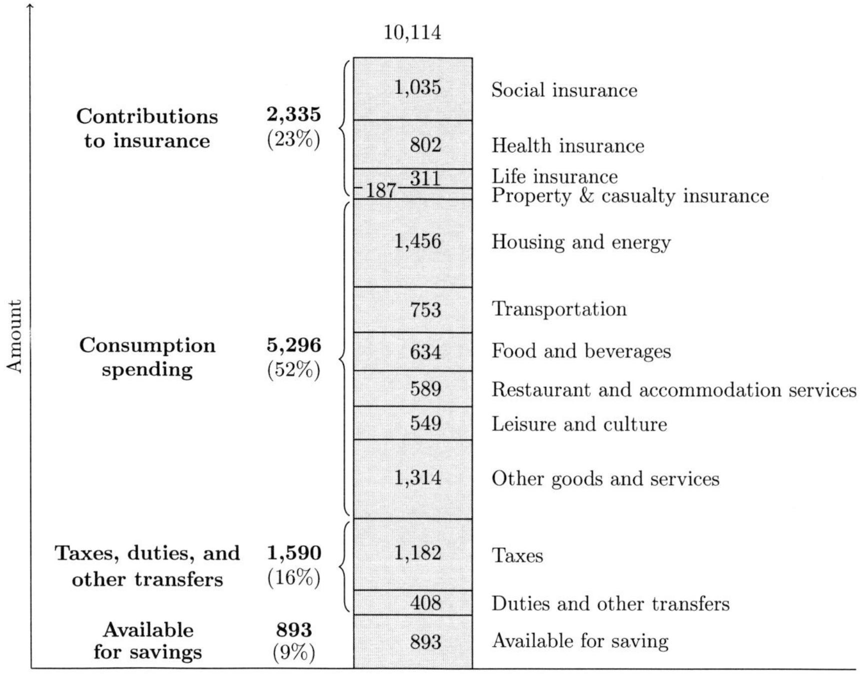

Note: Amounts are in Swiss francs. Health insurance includes basic health insurance and supplementary health insurance. Non-life insurance includes household insurance, civil liability insurance, fire and other building-related insurance, motor insurance, and other private insurance. Table 5.1 presents a breakdown of the contributions and premiums paid for insurance.

Figure 5.2: Breakdown of monthly spending by private households in Switzerland (based on Federal Statistical Office, 2020c).

pensions or LPP). These contributions build up savings for retirement as part of the 1st and 2nd pillars.

The amounts of CHF 147 for supplementary health insurance and the remainder of CHF 498 are premiums paid to private insurance companies. More information about life and health insurance can be found in section 5.4. A total of CHF 311 is paid for 3rd pillar life insurance policies (pillars 3a and 3b), which supplement retirement savings. This is followed by non-life insurance, which includes household insurance and liability insurance. Table 5.1 provides separate data for household insurance, third-party liability insurance, fire and other building-related insurance, motor insurance, and other private insurance. We note that the premiums paid for these policies are rather low compared to the premiums for social insurance and life insurance. Nevertheless, some of these policies are very important to private individuals as they protect their property and assets.

Category	Amount
Social insurance: contributions	1,035
Contributions for AVS, AI, and loss of income	406
Unemployment insurance (AC): contributions	73
Non-occupational accident insurance (AANP): contributions	79
Pension fund (LPP): contributions	474
Other social insurance: contributions	3
Basic health insurance: premiums	655
Basic health insurance: premiums	644
Accident insurance (excluding occupational accidents): premiums	11
Supplementary health insurance: premiums	147
Supplementary hospital insurance: premiums	83
Other supplementary insurance: premiums	64
Household, liability, fire, and other building-related insurance: premiums	60
Household insurance: premiums	14
Private third-party liability insurance: premiums	5
Household and third-party liability insurance: total premiums	19
Fire and other building-related insurance: premiums	22
Vehicle insurance: premiums	107
Motor vehicles: premiums	107
Non-motorized vehicles: premiums	0
Other private insurance: premiums	20
Legal protection insurance: premiums	7
Associations that include insurance cover (REGA, ETI, etc.): contributions	8
Travel insurance: premiums	3
Other private insurance: premiums	2
Life insurance: premiums	311
Pillar 3a (tax-qualified life insurance): premiums	285
Pillar 3b (non-tax-qualified life insurance): premiums	26
Total	2,335

Note: Amounts are in Swiss francs.

Table 5.1: Monthly spending for insurance by private households in Switzerland (based on Federal Statistical Office, 2020c).

On the importance of non-life insurance for private customers

The primary purpose of life insurance, health insurance, and other types of social insurance is to ensure that a person receives a retirement pension and that their health problems are covered. These policies also cover accidents, invalidity, loss of income, and unemployment. Obviously, such coverage is important. Since the financial consequences in these situations can be existential, these insurance policies are part of the mandatory social insurance in Switzerland.

The purpose of non-life insurance is to protect the policyholder's property and assets. Certain policies, such as motor third-party liability insurance and fire insurance, are mandatory, while others are not. With regard to optional insurance, it is important to be aware of the extent of potential losses.

Among the most significant potential losses for individuals are situations in which they are civilly liable for damages. Civil liability as a driver of a motor vehicle, as well as personal civil liability, can result in losses in the millions of Swiss francs, threatening a person's financial viability. Serious cases include, for example, being forced to pay a life annuity to an injured party.

In real estate, losses can quickly run into hundreds of thousands of francs or even more than a million francs if a building is completely destroyed. Property protection is included in insurance policies that cover fire and other damage to a building. Similarly, a (partial) comprehensive insurance policy covers events such as theft or damage to a car.

At the lower end of the spectrum are small or even minor losses, such as losing luggage while traveling, car breakdowns, broken windows, or the theft of a bicycle or pair of skis. Private insurance companies offer products that cover these losses (luggage insurance, roadside assistance, glass breakage insurance, bicycle or ski insurance), often for modest annual premiums, less than CHF 100. It is important to check which of these policies are really useful.

5.2 Social insurance in Switzerland

There are two main areas of insurance:

- social insurance,
- private insurance.

In this section, we look at social insurance in Switzerland and refer the reader to sections 5.3 and 5.4 for more information on the private insurance market and the products offered.

The purpose of social insurance is to enable individuals and families to transfer the financing of pure risks to personal values. These are pure risks that cannot be eliminated. They include, for example, old age and illness. In particular, social insurance covers risk exposures whose financial consequences can be existential for the individual or the family.

Branches of social insurance Each country has its own interpretation of the notion of social insurance and social security. The only precise definition may be the following: a country's social insurance is what that country's law defines as such.

Insurance	Law and date of entry into force
AVS	Federal law of 20 December 1946 on old age and survivors' insurance (LAVS) ⧉ www.admin.ch/opc/fr/classified-compilation/19460217/index.html
AI	Federal law of 19 June 1959 on invalidity insurance (LAI) ⧉ www.admin.ch/opc/fr/classified-compilation/19590131/index.html
PC	Federal law of 6 October 2006 on supplementary benefits on top of AVS and AI (LPC) ⧉ www.admin.ch/opc/fr/classified-compilation/20051695/index.html
PP	Federal law of 25 June 1982 on occupational pensions, survivors, and invalidity (LPP) ⧉ www.admin.ch/opc/fr/classified-compilation/19820152/index.html
AMal	Federal law of 18 March 1994 on health insurance (LAMal) ⧉ www.admin.ch/opc/fr/classified-compilation/19940073/index.html
AA	Federal law of 20 March 1981 on accident insurance (LAA) ⧉ www.admin.ch/opc/fr/classified-compilation/19810038/index.html
APG	Federal law of 25 September 1952 on loss of earnings compensation (LAPG) ⧉ www.admin.ch/opc/fr/classified-compilation/19520192/index.html
AC	Federal law of 25 June 1982 on mandatory unemployment insurance and compensation in case of insolvency (LACI) ⧉ www.admin.ch/opc/fr/classified-compilation/19820159/index.html
AF	Federal law of 24 March 2006 on family benefits and financial assistance to family organizations (LAFam) ⧉ https://fedlex.data.admin.ch/eli/cc/2008/51

Table 5.2: Swiss social insurance laws and date of entry into force.

Swiss federal social insurance is a fundamental element of the social welfare system. The Federal Social Insurance Office (2014) provides a historical overview of the development of social security in Switzerland (see also section 1.4). The benefits provided by social insurance protect households and individuals by covering many risks whose financial consequences they could not bear on their own. There are nine main social insurance branches in Switzerland:

- old age and survivors' insurance (AVS),
- invalidity insurance (AI),
- supplementary benefits (PC) to AVS and AI,
- occupational pensions (PP),
- health insurance (AMal),
- accident insurance (AA),
- loss of earnings compensation (APG),
- unemployment insurance (AC),
- family benefits (AF).

Table 5.2 provides information about federal laws and when they went into effect. Federal Council (2020) has a complete list of laws, ordinances, and regulations.

The components of social security in Switzerland can be grouped into five areas: old age, survivors, and invalidity pensions (AVS, AI, PC, PP), health and accident insurance (AMal, AA), compensation for loss of earnings during military or civil service or maternity (APG), unemployment insurance (AC), and family benefits (AF). These cover social risks by providing financial benefits (such as pensions, compensation for loss of earnings, or family allowances) or by covering costs related to illness or accidents (Federal Social Insurance Office, 2020a).

Occupational pensions play an important role in the Swiss pension system for old age, survivors, and invalidity, which is based on three pillars. The 1st pillar is the state pension scheme, including the AVS and AI. The pensions provided by these two insurance schemes cover the vital needs of the insured. The PP constitute the 2nd pillar and complement AVS/AI. The 3rd pillar is made up of individual provisions. For a long time, Switzerland's three-pillar pension system was well-balanced and considered a success worldwide. For this to continue and for the pensions to remain sustainable, a number of challenges must be addressed, including increased life expectancy and low interest rates in the financial markets.

It should be noted that in the case of social insurance, the insurer is not necessarily the government or a government-controlled public entity. In Switzerland, for example, pension funds are foundations, and health insurance funds are non-profit public or private legal entities whose main function is to manage social health insurance. Compulsory accident insurance, such as occupational and non-occupational accident insurance for employees, may be taken out with a private insurer, depending on the industry.

The nine main social insurance branches in Switzerland
(adapted from Federal Social Insurance Office, 2020b, Federal Office of Public Health, 2020, and Federal Statistical Office, 2020d)

- *Old age and survivors' insurance (AVS)*: The AVS is the main pillar of the Swiss social pension system and is intended to provide a minimum standard of living in the event of loss of income due to old age or death. Its benefits are paid to the elderly as an old-age pension or to their survivors as a widow(er)'s or orphan's pension. Benefits depend on the amount of income previously earned and the length of time the person contributed. In general, everyone who lives or works in Switzerland must be affiliated with the AVS.

  The AVS is financed by contributions from both members and the state, according to a specific distribution system (see also section 4.3). The contributions received during a given period directly finance the benefits paid during the same period, which corresponds to the pay-as-you-go system. Thus, the active generation finances the pensions of the elderly, and no capital is accumulated (see table 5.4). This system works perfectly as long as roughly the same amount of money is paid out each year as comes in.

  However, with life expectancy becoming higher than what was anticipated when the system was set up, this balance is in danger. In 1948, the

CHF 581 million coming into the system easily covered the CHF 127 million paid out. But since 2014, the balance has been negative. As a capital of CHF 45 billion has been saved since the beginning of the AVS, the product of this capital influences the operating result of the system. In 2018, the income of CHF 41.9 billion did not cover the expenses of CHF 44.1 billion; in 2020, a year in which the financial markets gave good results, the income of CHF 47.9 billion was higher than the expenses of CHF 46.0 billion (Federal Statistical Office, 2020b).

- *Invalidity insurance (AI)*: The AI is a compulsory insurance for everyone. Its aim is to enable people who have become invalid as a result of a deterioration in their physical, psychological, or mental health to meet all or part of their needs by providing rehabilitation. The same objective can be achieved by granting a full or partial pension or allowances when (re)integration is not possible or only partially possible. These benefits may be in cash or in kind and are intended to ensure subsistence. All rehabilitation options must be explored before a pension is granted. AI is financed by contributions from both members and the state, mainly at the federal level.

- *Supplementary benefits (PC) to AVS and AI*: Supplementary benefits are paid on the basis of a person's financial needs. They are granted to recipients of an AVS or AI pension who live in Switzerland and whose total income is below the subsistence level. These benefits are based on the principle of purpose and are distinct from social insurance benefits, which are based on the principle of causality and are paid regardless of need. Supplementary benefits are paid before economic social assistance. They are financed (in part) by federal, cantonal, and municipal taxes. No contributions are made from salaries.

- *Occupational pensions (PP)*: Occupational pensions, also known as the 2nd pillar, are financed equally by employers and employees. They are paid in addition to the AVS and AI in case of old age, invalidity, or death. Together with the benefits paid by the AVS and AI, the PP enable insured persons to maintain a reasonable standard of living in the event of old age, death, or invalidity. It aims to cover about 60% of the income earned during a person's active life. As of 2021, all active persons who receive a salary of more than 21,510 francs from a single employer must be insured under the PP program. This threshold will be adjusted periodically. The PP law defines a mandatory minimum level of benefits. The approximately 1,500 pension funds and private insurers that manage assets can go beyond this legal minimum and offer extended pension programs. It should be noted that only pension funds are included in the social insurance statistics. The activities of private insurers that fall under the 2nd pillar are reported to the Swiss Financial Market Supervisory Authority (FINMA).

Unlike the AVS, the PP are based on the accumulation of capital. The conversion rate is a percentage that allows the conversion of retirement assets into an annual pension. This ratio, which applies to the standard retirement age for the AVS, i.e., 65 for men and 64 for women, is 6.8% in 2021. The conversion ratio means that each tranche of 100,000 francs in mandatory retirement assets grants an annual pension of 6,800 francs. Given current life expectancy, this ratio is too high: pension funds need to earn annual returns of more than 4.5% to break even, which is much higher than the returns on fixed-income investments. As with the AVS, a reform is needed to ensure the sustainability of the PP.

- *Health insurance (AMal)*: Social health insurance, also known as basic health insurance or compulsory health insurance, guarantees access to medical care in the event of an illness or accident that is not covered by accident insurance. Since 1996, when the AMal law was introduced, all residents of Switzerland are required to be insured. Approximately 50 non-profit insurers recognized by the Swiss Confederation offer AMal, and each insured person is free to choose their provider. Adults and children are insured individually. The AMal program is largely funded by individual premiums, a unique feature among social insurance schemes in Switzerland and abroad.

The AMal covers health care expenses related to illness, maternity, and accidents, offering the same benefits to everyone. Insurers must treat all policyholders equally, without distinction, based on health status or indications thereof. This applies in particular to enrolment, the choice of type of insurance, and the reimbursement of care provided. The AMal is financed by individual contributions (premiums), contributions to health care costs (deductible, percentage, contribution to hospital fees), and federal and cantonal subsidies (premium reduction). The premiums charged by the insurers are calculated to cover the total costs incurred. Premiums are not based on income and depend on the insurer, the policyholder's place of residence, and the type of insurance chosen (deductible, limits on eligible health care providers). Policyholders of modest means, children, and young adults in education often benefit from lower premiums. The cantons determine who is eligible for lower premiums. It should be noted that only the basic AMal is social and compulsory. Supplementary health insurance, on the other hand, is private and optional.

- *Accident insurance (AA)*: The compulsory AA is an insurance that covers the economic consequences of occupational accidents, non-occupational accidents, and occupational diseases. Its purpose is to compensate for damage to policyholders' health and earning capacity in the event of an accident or occupational disease. Compulsory insurance premiums for occupational accidents and diseases are paid by the employer, while compulsory premiums for non-occupational accidents are paid by the employee. It should be noted that people who work for an employer for less than eight hours a week are not compulsorily insured against non-occupational accidents. These people can apply for accident insurance from their health insurance company.

- *Loss of earnings compensation (APG)*: The APG scheme compensates for part of the loss of earnings incurred by people in military, civilian, or civil protection service. The allowance is 80% of the salary for the year preceding the service (up to 196 francs per day). Since 2005, this insurance also covers loss of earnings due to maternity (maternity allowance) and, from 2021, loss of earnings due to paternity leave. The APG is compulsory, and all persons who contribute to the AVS and AI also contribute to the APG. Contributions are shared equally between employers and employees and are collected by compensation funds together with those for AVS and AI.

- *Unemployment insurance (AC)*: The purpose of the law on unemployment insurance is to compensate insured persons for loss of income due to unemployment, reduced working hours (partial unemployment), weather conditions (suspension of work), and employer insolvency. Its aim is to promote integration into the labor market by financing reintegration measures. The AC is financed by equal contributions from employees and employers and by federal and cantonal authorities.

- *Family benefits (AF)*: According to the federal law on family benefits, all cantons must pay a minimum monthly child allowance of 200 francs per child and a minimum monthly vocational training allowance of 250 francs per child between the ages of 16 and 25. Higher allowances are paid in many cantons and are financed exclusively by employers in all cantons except Valais. Family benefits are both social security and family policy. They are intended to partially offset the costs of caring for one or more children. In addition to child and educational allowances, they include birth and adoption allowances.

Financing and income structure Contributions to the AVS, AI, APG, and AC are paid equally by employers and employees. Table 5.3 shows the contribution rates as of January 1, 2021. For the AVS, the total contribution rate (employee and employer) is 8.7% of salary in 2021. The contribution rates for the AI and APG are 1.4% and 0.5% respectively. Total contributions to the AC are 2.2% of salary. For self-employed, contributions are calculated based on the total income earned during the year. For self-employed earning more than CHF 57,400, the rates are similar to those for employees. For those earning less, contributions are calculated on a sliding scale. People who are not gainfully employed also pay contributions. Non-working persons contribute according to their status, and the amount depends on their assets and/or the pensions they receive. As a reminder, the PC are financed (in part) by federal, cantonal, and municipal taxes. No contributions are made from salaries.

Insurance	Employees (% of salary)			Self-employed (% of income)	Non-working persons (CHF per year)
	Employees	Employers	Total		
AVS	4.35	4.35	8.70	8.10	413 to 20,650
AI	0.70	0.70	1.40	1.40	66 to 3,300
APG	0.25	0.25	0.50	0.50	24 to 1,200
AC	1.10	1.10	2.20	–	–
AF	–	0.70 to 3.50	0.70 to 3.50	0.30 to 3.30	–

Note: The table shows contributions in 2021. For the self-employed, the AVS/AI/APG/AC contribution rate is reduced on a sliding scale for income below CHF 57,400. For the AC, the rate of 2.2% applies to the portion of salary up to CHF 148,200; a rate of 1% is levied on the portion in excess of CHF 148,200. The contribution of non-working persons is set according to their social status. For the AF, the rates shown apply outside agriculture, and employees pay contributions of 0.3% of salary in Valais.

Table 5.3: Social insurance contribution rates in Switzerland (based on Federal Social Insurance Office, 2021).

In the PP, contribution rates vary from one pension fund to another and also depend on the financing method chosen. Contributions are paid by both the employer and the employee. The total contributions paid by the employer must be at least equal to the total contributions paid by its employees. According to the PP law, the contribution to the old-age pension is expressed as a percentage of the "coordinated salary," i.e., the tranche of the annual salary between CHF 25,095 and CHF 86,040 (values in 2021). This rate depends on age. For employees aged between 25 and 34, it is 7%; between 35 and 44, 10%; between 45 and 54, 15%; and between 55 and retirement age—65 for men and 64 for women—18%.

The AA premiums for occupational accident and disease coverage are paid by the employer. For this purpose, companies are divided into categories and levels that determine the premiums. These categories take into account the nature of each company and its specific conditions, including the risk of accidents and the level of prevention measures. General information on net premium rates cannot be provided because each insurer sets its own rates. For non-occupational accidents, premiums are generally paid by the employee and also depend on the insurer chosen by the employer. Contributions for the AF are fully paid by the employer, except in the canton of Valais. Finally, AMal premiums depend on the insurer, the policyholder's place of residence, and the type of insurance chosen. They vary, among other things, according to the deductible and the insurance model (limits on eligible health care providers).

The statistics on social insurance provided by the Federal Social Insurance Office (2020c) give an overview of the development of the various branches of social insurance. The 2020 report presents information for the year 2018. Contributions by employers and insured persons constitute by far the largest source of income, except for supplementary benefits, which are financed exclusively by tax revenue.

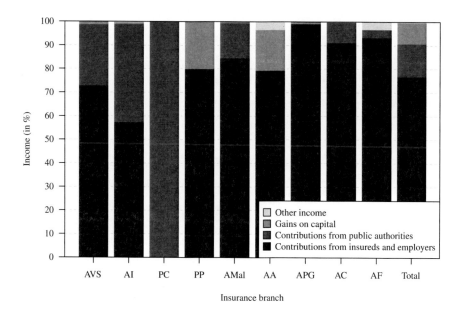

Note: The chart shows the income structure in 2018.

Figure 5.3: Income structure of social insurance branches in Switzerland (adapted from Federal Social Insurance Office, 2020c, figure CGAS 17A).

For loss of earnings compensation, family benefits, and unemployment insurance, contributions account for more than 90% of income. Overall, in 2018, 76.7% of income originated from contributions by employers and insured persons. Such contributions have accounted for at least 75% of revenue since 2013. The graph in figure 5.3 illustrates the breakdown of income between contributions from insureds and employers, contributions from public authorities, gains on capital, and other income for the various branches of social insurance. It can be seen that investment income makes up a large part of the revenue for occupational pension schemes, acting as a 3rd contributor alongside employers and insured persons. Until the 2000s, returns on capital accounted for a third of income. In 2018, this share was only 20%. This decline in recent years can be explained by lower returns in the financial markets.

Total social insurance accounts   One section of the statistics published by the Federal Social Insurance Office (2020c) presents the total social insurance accounts. It provides detailed information on the finances of social security, showing their evolution over the years and allowing comparisons between different branches. These total accounts are summarized in table 5.4.

	AVS	AI	PC	PP	AMal	AA	APG	AC	AF	Total
Income	43.6	9.3	5.1	71.0	31.5	8.0	1.7	7.9	6.3	183.5
– from insureds/employers	31.7	5.3	–	56.7	26.7	6.4	1.7	7.2	5.9	140.8
– from public authorities	11.3	3.8	5.1	–	4.7	–	–	0.7	0.2	25.8
– from gains on capital	0.6	0.1	–	14.2	0.2	1.4	0.0	0.0	−0.0	16.4
Expenses	44.1	9.3	5.1	55.0	30.0	7.0	1.7	6.7	6.3	164.4
Result	−0.5	0.0	–	15.9	1.5	1.0	0.0	1.2	−0.1	19.1
Capital	43.5	−5.5	–	865.2	14.6	62.1	1.0	0.2	2.7	983.8

Note: The table shows data as of 2018. Amounts are expressed in billions of Swiss francs and rounded to one decimal place under each heading. The total income includes other income items not shown in the table.

Table 5.4: Excerpt of the total social insurance accounts in Switzerland (adapted from Federal Social Insurance Office, 2020c, p. 2).

The comparison between the total benefits paid and the gross domestic product (GDP) shows the share of total economic production that could be bought with these benefits. In 2018, the various branches of social insurance paid out a total of CHF 143.9 billion in benefits, i.e., a rate of 20%.

5.3   The private insurance market

Private insurance companies play an important role as a complement to social insurance. They allow individuals and companies to transfer the financing of risks to a private institution (see section 4.3). The risk coverage offered by private insurers complements social insurance, with life and health insurance (see the insurance products in section 5.4) whose benefits go beyond those of social insurance. Examples include capital life insurance, annuities, and invalidity insurance. Private insurers also offer non-life insurance, including property insurance, liability insurance, and supplementary health insurance (see also section 5.4).

From a legal point of view, a private insurance policy is a contract that transfers the financing of risk: one of the parties, the insurer, undertakes, in return for the payment of premiums, to pay all or part of the losses, as defined in the contract, that the other party, the policyholder, may suffer under the conditions laid down in the contract. In principle, only pure risk exposures, i.e., accidental events in the strict sense, can be insured.

In the area of non-life insurance, social insurance branches provide only health and accident insurance. Private insurance companies provide additional coverage. In the area of life insurance, private institutions partly play a complementary role to social insurance. The importance of life insurance depends on the level of development of social insurance.

Measuring the importance of the insurance sector Private insurance is strongly entrenched in developed countries, known as "advanced markets," while "emerging markets" are smaller by comparison. We measure the size of the market by the volume of insurance premiums, typically separating life premiums from non-life premiums.

> **Definition 5.1 (*Insurance premium*)**
>
> The **insurance premium** *is the amount of money charged by an insurer for a given insurance coverage.*

The evolution of the industry can be studied from the perspective of premium income, looking at historical data. It should be noted that in addition to life and non-life premiums, there are reinsurance premiums collected by reinsurers, i.e., the "insurers' insurers."

Two other measures can be used to compare the private insurance markets in different countries. The first is insurance density, which relates the premium income to the number of inhabitants.

> **Definition 5.2 (*Insurance density*)**
>
> **Insurance density** *is calculated by dividing the total volume of insurance premiums by the total population.*

Insurance density, expressed in monetary units per inhabitant, measures the revenue potential of a market. It shows how much each inhabitant spends on insurance. The second measure is insurance penetration, which is the ratio of premium income to gross domestic product (GDP). As a reminder, GDP measures the value of all goods and services produced in a given period.

> **Definition 5.3 (*Insurance penetration*)**
>
> **Insurance penetration** *is calculated by dividing the total volume of insurance premiums by the gross domestic product.*

Insurance penetration is therefore expressed as a percentage of GDP. It measures the level of development of a market and the size of the insurance industry in the economy. These concepts are illustrated below (see figure 5.4 and table 5.5).

The private insurance industry is also measured by its volume, for example, the number of insurance companies and the number of employees. Many other indicators available in the annual reports published by the companies can be used. The evolution of these indicators is then used to analyze the development of the industry. Finally, the value created by insurance is also measured by the industry's contribution to GDP.

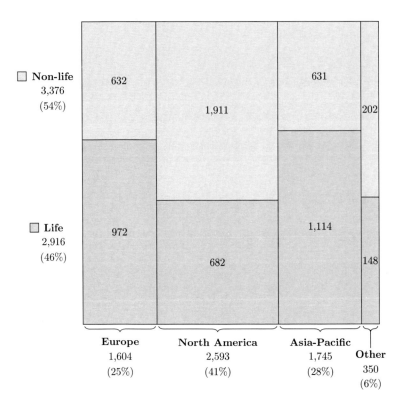

Note: The chart shows 2019 figures. Premiums are expressed in billions of dollars. North America consists of the United States and Canada. Europe includes the State of Israel. Asia-Pacific includes Asia and Oceania. "Other" includes premiums from emerging markets in Europe, the Middle East, Latin America, the Caribbean, and Africa.

Figure 5.4: Overview of life and non-life insurance premiums worldwide (based on Swiss Re, 2020b, table I).

Overview of the worldwide market The Swiss Re (2020a) database tracks the evolution of life and non-life insurance premiums in all countries of the world since 1980. Global insurance premiums amounted to 6,293 billion dollars in 2019, which is 7.2% of world GDP (Swiss Re, 2020b). The annual report on world insurance (Swiss Re, 2019b) is entitled "The great pivot east continues." Indeed, in the longer term, emerging markets are expected to account for a progressively larger share of insurance premiums. However, given their size, developed markets will continue to account for nearly half of the growth in premium volume over the next decade despite growing at a slower rate. The Asia-Pacific region, which includes China, other emerging markets, and the advanced markets in the region, will account for 42% of global insurance premiums by 2029.

The graph in figure 5.4 shows the volume and distribution of life and non-life insurance in the world's regions in 2019. The volume of premiums in Europe accounts

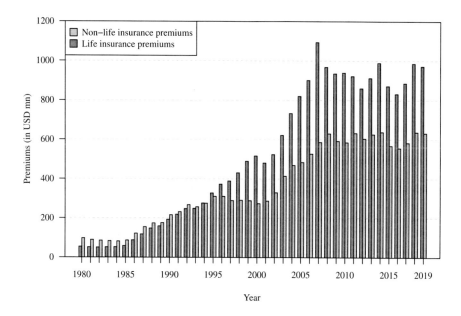

Note: The "Advanced EMEA" region includes the advanced countries in Europe, the Middle East, and Africa.

Figure 5.5: Development of life and non-life insurance premiums in the advanced EMEA region (adapted from Swiss Re, 2020a).

for a quarter of the world total. North America accounts for 41% and Asia-Pacific for 28%. Total premiums in Asia-Pacific have grown significantly over the past two decades. Countries in other regions account for less than 10% of premiums. We note that life and non-life insurance premiums are not evenly distributed. In Europe and Asia-Pacific, life premiums account for a higher proportion of the total. In North America, however, non-life premiums are higher than life premiums.

The "Advanced EMEA" region, as defined by Swiss Re (2020a), includes advanced countries in Europe, the Middle East and Africa. The largest insurance markets in terms of premium income are the United Kingdom, France, Italy, Germany, Ireland, Spain, Switzerland, and Luxembourg. The graph in figure 5.5 shows the evolution of premium income from 1980 to 2019. We can see a significant increase in life insurance premiums, which overtook non-life insurance premiums from the mid-1990s. In the last decade, both insurance branches seem to have stagnated.

Table 5.5 shows the volume of premiums as well as the density and penetration of insurance for selected countries. In absolute terms, the largest insurance markets are the United States, China, and Japan, followed by the United Kingdom, France, and Germany. Switzerland, with 59 billion dollars in premiums, accounts for 0.94% of the world market. In terms of insurance density, the United States and

Pays	Premiums (Bn USD)	Density (USD per capita)	Penetration (% of GDP)
Switzerland	59	6,835	8.4
United Kingdom	366	4,362	10.3
France	262	3,719	9.2
Germany	244	2,934	6.3
Italy	168	2,764	8.3
Luxembourg	45	5,165	4.5
Austria	20	2,219	4.4
United States	2,460	7,495	11.4
China	617	430	4.3
Japan	459	3,621	9.0
South Korea	175	3,366	10.8
Canada	133	3,548	7.7
Taiwan	117	4,993	20.0
World	6,293	818	7.2

Note: The table shows data as of 2019.

Table 5.5: Comparison of insurance premiums, density, and penetration in selected countries (based on Swiss Re, 2020b, tables III, VIII, IX).

Switzerland are at the top of the ranking. According to these statistics, per capita premiums in Switzerland amount to USD 6,835. The highest insurance penetration is recorded in Taiwan. In Switzerland, it accounts for 8.4% of GDP. The insurance industry plays an important role in the economy. It should be noted that a deeper interpretation of these comparisons is difficult. Just as social insurance systems vary from country to country, so too do private insurance systems. In Switzerland, for example, old-age pensions and health insurance are social insurance schemes and are therefore not included in these statistics. In other countries, however, they may be provided by private insurers and, therefore, appear in the statistics.

Indicators on the Swiss market   The contribution of Swiss private insurance companies to GDP is practically equal to that of banks, i.e., 30.5 billion francs in 2018 (Swiss Insurance Association, 2019). Insurance companies contribute to about 5% of the value added to the Swiss economy as a whole. In 2019, the Swiss Financial Market Supervisory Authority (2020) counted 19 life insurance companies, 118 non-life insurance companies—18 of which offer supplementary health insurance—, 11 health insurers offering supplementary health insurance, and 50 reinsurance companies, for a total of 198 companies. Private insurance companies employed nearly 46,000 people in Switzerland in 2019, including about 14,500 insurance advisors (Swiss Insurance Association, 2020).

In the 2019 financial year, insurance companies in Switzerland collected CHF 32.02 billion in life insurance premiums and CHF 28.58 billion in non-life

Insurance branch	Premiums CHF bn	Share (%)
Life insurance		
Group life occupational pension schemes	22.05	(68.9)
Classical individual capital insurance	4.68	(14.6)
Classical individual annuity insurance	0.52	(1.6)
Unit-linked life insurance	1.81	(5.7)
Life insurance linked to internal investment portfolios	0.41	(1.3)
Capitalization and tontines	0.23	(0.7)
Other life insurance segments	0.22	(0.6)
Foreign branches	1.72	(5.4)
Reinsurance accepted	0.38	(1.2)
Total life insurance	32.02	(100.0)
Non-life insurance		
Illness	11.19	(39.2)
Fire, property damage	4.15	(14.5)
Accident	3.18	(11.1)
Motor vehicle (comprehensive)	3.37	(11.8)
Motor vehicle (liability)	2.60	(9.1)
Liability	2.00	(7.0)
Marine, aviation, transport	0.32	(1.1)
Legal protection	0.64	(2.3)
Financial losses	0.51	(1.8)
Credit, surety	0.38	(1.3)
Tourist assistance	0.24	(0.8)
Total non-life insurance	28.58	(100.0)

Note: The table shows data as of 2019.

Table 5.6: Total life and non-life insurance premiums in Switzerland (based on Swiss Financial Market Supervisory Authority, 2020, pages 13 and 29).

insurance premiums (including private health insurance). The collected premiums come from several branches of life and non-life insurance (see 5.4, where we look at these branches). Table 5.6 shows the premiums collected in the different branches. In life insurance, the premiums collected can be divided into regular premiums and single premiums. With interest rates still low, the classical business of individual life insurance, i.e., individual annuity insurance, is less attractive. As a result, the volume of premiums for life insurance policies linked to shares in funds (unit-linked life insurance policies), which require less capital in terms of solvency regulations, is increasing. Occupational pensions dominate the Swiss life insurance market, accounting for 68.9% of the total. General insurance in Switzerland (see the bottom half of the table), including private health insurance, is stable. The motor insurance industry is experiencing fierce price competition. Due to the economic slowdown, the decline in sales, the volume of salaries, the decline in the active and employed population, and the weakening of the overall situation due to the Covid-19 pandemic, almost all branches of the insurance industry have collected less in premiums. At the same time, the increased demand for extended

	Company	Premiums CHF bn	Market share (%)
Life insurance	Swiss Life SA	13.05	(43.6)
	Helvetia Compagnie Suisse d'Assurances sur la Vie SA	3.64	(12.2)
	Bâloise Vie SA	3.58	(11.9)
	AXA Vie SA	3.18	(10.6)
	Allianz Suisse Société d'Assurances SA	1.87	(6.3)
	Zurich Compagnie d'Assurances SA	1.54	(5.2)
	Six largest life insurance companies	26.86	(89.8)
P&C insurance	AXA Assurances SA	3.43	(18.6)
	Mobilière Suisse Société d'assurances SA	2.98	(16.2)
	Zurich Compagnie d'Assurances SA	2.49	(13.5)
	Allianz Suisse Société d'Assurances SA	1.89	(10.3)
	Helvetia Compagnie Suisse d'Assurances SA	1.56	(8.5)
	Bâloise Assurance SA	1.31	(7.1)
	Vaudoise Générale, Compagnie d'Assurances SA	0.93	(5.0)
	Generali Assurances Générales SA	0.76	(4.1)
	Eight largest property and casualty insurance companies	15.36	(83.3)

Note: The table shows data as of 2019. "Property and casualty insurance" (P&C insurance) refers to non-life insurance, excluding health insurance.

Table 5.7: Direct business in Switzerland for the major life and property and casualty insurance companies (based on Swiss Financial Market Supervisory Authority, 2020, pages 14 and 30).

risk coverage and the emergence of new needs (e.g., cyber risks) should stimulate the market.

Table 5.7 shows the volume of direct business in Switzerland for the six largest life insurance companies and the eight largest non-life insurance companies. These six life insurers and eight non-life insurers account for 89.8% and 83.3% of premiums, respectively, indicating that the insurance market is concentrated. The Swiss insurance market is currently stable, but it is saturated, and growth is difficult. The graph in figure 5.6 illustrates the market shares of direct business in Switzerland for the nine main companies active in life and non-life insurance. It should be noted that life and non-life insurance are offered by separate legal entities. We identify Swiss Life as an insurer that offers only life insurance. AXA is one of the large multi-branch companies, as the group offers both life and non-life insurance. AXA's position in terms of market share is skewed towards non-life insurance. The companies operating under the Mobilière, Zurich, Allianz, Helvetia, and Bâloise brands offer both life and non-life insurance. The next largest are Generali and Vaudoise, with the latter offering mainly non-life insurance products.

Table 5.8 provides information on the distribution of assets of life and non-life insurance companies. At the end of 2019, life insurance companies had total assets of

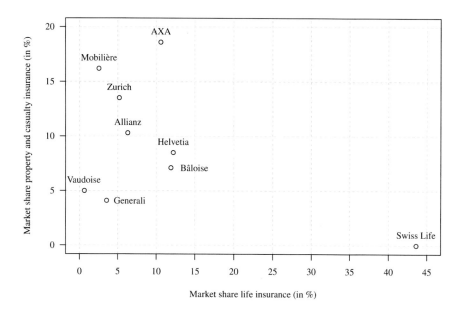

Note: The graph shows data as of 2019. "Property and casualty insurance" refers to non-life insurance, excluding health insurance.

Figure 5.6: Market shares of the direct business in Switzerland for the major life and property and casualty insurance companies (based on Swiss Financial Market Supervisory Authority, 2020, pages 14 and 30, and the relevant companies' annual reports).

CHF 307.8 billion, while non-life insurance companies had assets of CHF 142.3 billion. Asset allocation has been relatively stable over the years. Investments in fixed-income securities are by far the most important investment category, accounting for 50% of life insurance assets and 35% of non-life insurance assets. These investments can be divided into corporate bonds and government bonds. Investments in real estate and mortgages account for 25% of life insurance assets, while these categories are underrepresented in non-life insurance at only 9%.

5.4 Private insurance lines and products

Insurance solutions are the most commonly used methods of risk transfer (see section 4.3). In this section, we look at the types of insurance lines in the private market, what types of insurance products are available, and how they work.

	Life		Non-life	
Asset category	CHF bn	(%)	CHF bn	(%)
Fixed-interest securities	154.9	(50)	50.7	(35)
Loans	9.1	(3)	7.0	(5)
Real estate and land	39.5	(13)	7.6	(5)
Mortgages	33.2	(11)	5.4	(4)
Equities	14.7	(5)	7.7	(5)
Collective investments	16.1	(5)	9.8	(7)
Alternative investments	10.7	(3)	5.2	(4)
Other investments	2.7	(1)	8.2	(6)
Participations	5.8	(2)	40.7	(29)
Investments from unit-linked life insurance	21.3	(7)	–	(–)
Total investments	307.8	(100)	142.3	(100)

Note: The table shows data as of 2019. The "real estate and land" item includes real estate, buildings under construction, and building land.

Table 5.8: Distribution of assets of life and non-life insurance companies in Switzerland (based on Swiss Financial Market Supervisory Authority, 2020, pages 11 and 27).

Insurance policy and insurers   Private insurance coverage and the obligations of the parties involved are defined in an insurance policy:

Definition 5.4 (*Insurance policy*)

> An **insurance policy** is a contract between a natural or legal person, the policyholder, and an institution, the insurer. Through this contract, the insurer agrees to pay for certain potential losses caused by accidental events to which the policyholder is exposed.

Article 3 of the law on insurance contracts (LCA; Federal Council, 2011) stipulates in its first paragraph that the insurer, before signing the insurance contract, must provide the future policyholder with clear information regarding the insurer's identity and the main terms of the insurance contract. In particular, the following information must be provided,

- the risks insured,
- the scope of the insurance cover,
- the premiums to be paid and the other obligations of the policyholder,
- the duration and termination of the insurance policy.

Article 19 of the LCA provides that premiums are due at the beginning of each insurance period.

Historically (see also section 1.4), the development of private insurance in Europe and North America began in the second half of the 19th century, in parallel with the development of industrialization. As a result, the insurance industry is more established in industrialized countries. States quickly recognized the need to strictly regulate this economic activity in order to avoid the various scandals that had plagued its early years. This regulation allows insurance to perform an economic function by contributing to society's overall risk management.

An insurance company is an institution that is subject to specific laws on insurance supervision. It has a license to conduct this type of business, and an insurance policy must correspond to a legally recognized insurance product. Private insurance companies must apply to the Swiss Financial Market Supervisory Authority (FINMA) for authorization to conduct business. Insurance companies covering fire and natural hazards in the various Swiss cantons (see section 1.3) are supervised by the cantons. In particular, the supervisory authorities check that insurers have the financial capacity to meet all the contractual obligations they have entered into. To this end, insurers must report their results to the authorities, providing a specific breakdown of the information.

Below, we look at which risks can be transferred to a private insurer, and under what conditions.

Basic legal principles Four basic principles underlie insurance law. They are the principles of indemnity, insurable interest, subrogation, and good faith, which are described below.

- *Principle of indemnity*: The policyholder shall not receive a sum of money in excess of the loss caused by a peril.

  > A policyholder cannot insure the same object with several insurance companies and receive compensation from each of them if the object is destroyed.

- *Principle of insurable interest*: The policyholder may be compensated only if they prove that they have suffered a personal loss.

  > An individual cannot take out an insurance policy on the life of a complete stranger and receive a lump sum when that person dies.

- *Principle of subrogation (or substitution)*: The insurer who has compensated a policyholder for a loss may recover the same amount from a third party if that party is responsible.

- *Principle of good faith*: The degree of good faith expected of the parties to an insurance contract is higher than in ordinary commercial contracts. This good faith applies, in particular, to the statements made in the contract.

Classification of insurance policies   Because the various branches of the insurance industry emerged independently, their historical development does not suggest a logical structure. Even the names of the branches and types of policies do not help much. Sometimes, the name of the insured risk is used, for example, "fire insurance," and sometimes, the insured object, for example, "car insurance." Definitions may also refer to the purpose of the insurance ("adult-child" insurance), the community of policyholders ("members" insurance), the opposite of the insured situation ("life" insurance provides coverage in the event of death), the location of the risk ("marine" insurance), and so on (Koch, 2012).

We suggest several criteria that can differentiate between types of insurance:

- *Regulation* — distinction between private and social insurance,

- *Branch* — distinction between life and non-life insurance,

- *Type of exposed values (or object)* — distinction between insurance of persons, property and liability,

- *Market (or customer) segment* — distinction between insurance for individuals and insurance for companies,

- *Benefits* — distinction between damage insurance (reimbursement of losses incurred) and capital insurance (payment of a predetermined sum, stated benefit),

- *Obligation* — distinction between compulsory insurance (e.g., basic health insurance) and optional insurance (e.g., supplementary health insurance),

- *Balance sheet effect* — distinction between asset insurance (protecting assets and property) and liability insurance (protecting obligations and civil liability),

- *Financial effect* — distinction between income insurance (protecting income flows) and wealth insurance (protecting assets),

- *Number of insureds* — distinction between individual insurance (e.g., 3rd pillar pension savings insurance) and group insurance (e.g., occupational accident insurance).

Example of an insurance contract classification

On the basis of the above criteria, we can show how a private motor third-party liability insurance policy would be classified. First, it is a private non-life insurance. More specifically, it covers liability for an individual policyholder. The policy compensates for damages and is compulsory. It is a liability insurance that protects wealth. It is an individual insurance.

As for the regulation criterion, we have studied social insurance in section 5.2. These insurance schemes are defined in the country's law, and the list we have provided is exhaustive. Except for the insurance institutions governed by cantonal law—most of which are cantonal institutions for fire and natural hazards insurance, as well as public institutions such as Retraites Populaires— all insurance institutions that are not social insurance are private insurance companies.

Insurance is divided into the branches of life and non-life insurance. Life insurance comes in three main forms: insurance that pays a lump sum if the policyholder dies, insurance that pays a lump sum if the policyholder survives a certain number of years and insurance that pays an annuity if the policyholder survives a certain number of years. A combination of these can exist in the same life insurance contract. A mixed policy, for example, pays a lump sum if the policyholder dies or survives. Strictly speaking, any other form of insurance is non-life insurance. Life insurance may require a very long-term commitment on the part of the insurer and includes not only a risk-financing transfer element but also a savings element. By law, a private insurance company must specialize in either life insurance or non-life insurance. Therefore, insurance groups create a separate legal entity for each branch, which reports separately to the supervisory authority. However, life insurance companies sometimes offer individual coverages such as accident insurance and private health insurance.

Another way to distinguish between different types of insurance is to look at the type of loss covered, i.e., the exposed values that we defined in section 2.7. Based on the type of exposed value, we divide insurance policies into four groups. First is personal insurance, which covers individuals against bodily injury, illness, invalidity, or death. Personal insurance covers life insurance, as well as accident insurance and private health insurance, which are formally counted as non-life insurance. Then, property insurance covers objects and real estate against damages they may suffer (e.g., fire, theft, water damage, glass breakage). Liability insurance includes civil liability insurance and covers liability-related damage. Finally, there are other types of insurance that do not fit into any of the previous three groups. Insurance that is not life or health insurance is called property and casualty (or general) insurance. In other words, property and casualty insurance is non-life insurance, with the exception of accident insurance and private health insurance.

This classification may vary from country to country and also depends on the perspective chosen. It should be noted that a single insurance policy may cover several lines of business. For example, a motor vehicle insurance policy may include liability insurance, comprehensive insurance for the vehicle itself, passenger accident insurance, roadside assistance insurance to cover repatriation and cancellation costs in the event of an accident, and, in certain cases, legal protection insurance. We also note that insurance companies that cover net income, as opposed to pure risk exposure, do not constitute a separate group. They are generally considered to be property insurers. An example is insurance that covers operating losses due to business interruption following a fire or weather event. "Other" types of insurance include certain specific policies, such as transportation or credit insurance. These policies are often classified as property or liability insurance. Figure 5.7 gives an overview of this traditional division of the insurance industry into branches.

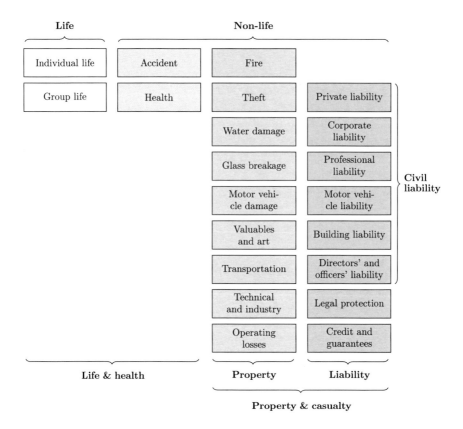

Note: This illustration is for illustrative purposes and shows only a selection of insurance products.

Figure 5.7: Traditional classification of private insurance lines.

In terms of its internal organization, an insurance company is often structured according to market or customer segments. A distinction is made between insurance companies that cover individuals and those that cover businesses. The latter are usually classified according to size, with a distinction being made between small and medium-sized enterprises and large (international) corporations. Insurance for individuals covers situations and risk exposures for customers who are mainly looking for protection in their personal or family environment. The products offered to them are partially standardized but remain flexible. Competition is mostly local, and the relationship between customer and insurer is personal, with both rational and emotional factors. The position of the sales force, which is tied to the company, is important.

Insurance companies for small and medium-sized enterprises (SMEs) cover risk exposures with loss potentials that are in part comparable to those of large corporations. However, the purchasing power of SMEs remains significantly lower than that of international corporations, and complex solutions are often rejected by management. The need for insurance coverage and risk management support exists at the level of the business, its owner, and its employees. Typically, these companies have an urgent need to reduce their administrative costs, not only in terms of insurance. For this reason, they prefer partially standardized solutions. Competition between insurers is usually national or regional, and insurance companies often insure each other. The relationship between customer and insurer is split between emotion and professionalism.

Insurers who cover large, often international, corporations must take into account the complexity and specificity of the risks involved. These companies require risk management and risk engineering services. Insurance coverage is designed on a client-by-client basis. International corporations often use alternative risk transfer instruments (see section 4.3), which offer a high degree of flexibility. Coverage for a predetermined profit level is one of the priorities, and administrative processes must be handled in a professional manner. These companies are often advised by a broker, and competition between insurers is international.

CHAPTER 6

Pricing risk in insurance

In chapter 3, we saw that when we appreciate risk, we assign a value to each risk. When the financing of risk (see section 4.3) is transferred to an insurer, the insurer's role is to put a "price tag" on risk exposures in order to provide coverage. In this chapter, we discuss risk pricing methods. We begin with risk pricing in life insurance, looking at premiums and benefits for the most common types of insurance. In each case, we use the principle of actuarial equivalence (see definition 6.1 in section 6.1) as the basis for the calculations. In life insurance, the most important parameters are the risk of death or the probability of survival. We study these in section 6.2 and illustrate what a mortality table is.

In section 6.3 we discuss the pricing of non-life insurance products. First, we introduce actuarial terminology and notations. The latter are special notations used by actuaries to simplify the writing of certain formulas. We study the characteristics of life insurance premiums and benefits. These elements help us calculate the premiums of insurance products. We will illustrate this calculation with some numerical examples. Continuing with life insurance, we then study the concept of mathematical reserves in section 6.4 and show how these reserves are calculated. Finally, we look at the pricing of non-life insurance products in section 6.5.

The content of this chapter provides an overview of what an actuary does. However, the role of the modern actuary is that of an "insurance engineer," and it would be very simplistic to think that they only do insurance pricing. Specialists in statistics and probability calculations applied to insurance, forecasting, and amortization problems, actuaries also apply their expertise to all matters relating to risk modeling and decision making in an uncertain environment. In fact, actuaries are present at all hierarchical levels of companies operating in the insurance world and beyond.

6.1 Introduction to life insurance pricing

As we mentioned when discussing the history of insurance (see section 1.4), life insurance has been around for a long time—the first contracts covering death appeared in the 17th century—and has evolved significantly over the years. Today, private life insurance products have become an important complement to social insurance (see section 5.4). Of all the types of insurance that exist, life insurance is one of the easiest to understand. Life insurance helps families cope with the financial consequences of the death or invalidity of a person. It also enables entrepreneurs to continue their business under better conditions in the event of the death of a key person, for example, by providing the liquidity needed to buy back the deceased partner's share of the business. Finally, annuity insurance allows the policyholder to receive a pension, for example, after their active life.

One of the main characteristics of life insurance is that it is usually a long-term contract with a strictly defined benefit, usually a fixed amount. This is because many policyholders purchase life insurance around the age of 30, while the events covered, such as annuity or death benefits, occur on average 35 and 50 years later, respectively. Many life insurance products include a significant savings component in addition to covering the risks associated with the policyholder's life. As savings products, many policies are offered for retirement and, as such, fall under the 3rd pillar of the Swiss pension system.

Life insurance and annuity contracts There are literally thousands of different types of life insurance policies. Focusing on the form of benefits, we can distinguish between lump-sum and annuity insurance:

- *Lump-sum insurance*: This insurance pays a lump sum upon the death of the policyholder or a lump sum if the policyholder survives after a certain period of time.

- *Annuity insurance*: This insurance pays an amount specified in the contract at regular intervals for as long as the policyholder is alive. If this annuity is paid until the death of the policyholder, it is referred to as a life annuity; otherwise, it is referred to as a temporary annuity. There are more complex forms of contracts on the market, such as annuity policies for (married) couples: these pay the annuity as long as one of the two insured persons is alive. This is an example of a last survivor annuity: two spouses co-sign a life insurance policy and become joint policyholders. This means that the surviving spouse keeps the policy when their spouse dies.

Certain insurance policies include both types of benefits; these are called mixed life policies and are very common in the Swiss market. They pay a lump sum in the event of death during the term of the policy and guarantee an annuity from a predetermined age. There is another type of mixed life insurance, called endowment insurance, which combines a "death" component and a "savings" component. The death benefit component exists throughout the term of the policy, while the savings component is paid only if the policyholder is alive at the end of the term. We discuss examples of this in section 6.3.

Another distinction is between term (temporary) and whole (permanent) life insurance. A term life policy covers only a specific period of time, while a whole life policy covers the policyholder's entire remaining life. The person who buys an insurance policy is the policyholder, also called the payer. In most cases, the policyholder is also the beneficiary of the policy, but in some cases, the policyholder and beneficiary are different people, such as when a parent takes out a policy for their child. In these cases, the beneficiary of the policy is not the policyholder. The policyholder is the person who can exercise all the rights related to the policy and with whom the insurer deals, especially with regard to the payment of premiums. The policyholder designates a person, the beneficiary, who will receive the insurance payments.

Insurance companies decide whether to issue a policy on the basis of an application, which is usually submitted to them by an insurance intermediary, who, in most cases, is an insurance adviser or broker. The application includes information on insurability to determine whether the beneficiary meets the relevant requirements. In addition to determining the health status of the proposed policyholder, the underwriter wants to ensure that the amount of insurance requested is commensurate with the economic loss that the beneficiary would suffer in the event of the policyholder's death. One of the insurer's main concerns is detecting adverse selection and preventing the creation of moral hazard. Sometimes, the underwriting department will require additional physical examination results, laboratory tests, or other information before making a decision.

Generally, insurance benefits are provided in exchange for the payment of a premium, which may be periodic or single. In order for the policy to become and remain active, premiums must be paid at the beginning of the contract or insurance period.

Equivalence principle Life insurance pricing is one of the actuary's specialties. It consists of determining premiums and benefits according to the principle of actuarial equivalence, which plays a key role in the pricing of insurance policies. This is an extension of the principle of equivalence that we have seen in the context of risk assessment (see definition 3.25 in section 3.5), with an equilibrium between the present values of premiums and future benefits, valued using the expected value. Thus, the principle of actuarial equivalence is based on the idea of a financial equilibrium between the present value of the premium paid by a policyholder and the present value of the future benefits they will receive. This leads to the following definition:

Definition 6.1 (*(Actuarial) equivalence principle*)

The **(actuarial) equivalence principle** *requires a financial equilibrium between the present value of premiums and the present value of future benefits.*

This principle applies to all insurance policies and all possible variations of insurance premiums and benefits. The equivalence principle relates to two main aspects: uncertainty about the present value of the payments received by the insurer—the premiums—, and the present value of the payments made by the insurer to the policyholder—the benefits. These payments to be made or received occur only if the conditions specified in the contract are met. In general, the formulas used take into account the sequence of future payments at times t depending on the mortality or survival of the policyholder and the discount factor $1/(1 + i)$ linked to the interest rate i, leading to an expression such as

$$\mathbb{E}\left(\sum_t \frac{\text{payment at } t}{(1 + i)^t}\right).$$

With the discount rate written as $v = 1/(1 + i)$ and knowing that the expected value of a sum is equal to the sum of the expected values, we can simplify this expression as follows:

$$\sum_t \mathbb{E}(\text{payment at } t) \cdot v^t.$$

The random variable "payment at t" takes the value P_t, which depends on the probability $\mathbb{P}(\text{payment at } t)$ that this payment will occur. We have

$$\sum_t P_t \cdot v^t \cdot \mathbb{P}(\text{payment at } t).$$

In life insurance, the probability $\mathbb{P}(\text{payment at } t)$ is most often linked to the probability of survival or death of the policyholder or portfolio of policyholders.

One-year term life insurance

Let us assume that a person aged x wishes to take out an insurance policy of CHF 100,000 that will pay out if they die during the following year. This is a *term* life insurance (for one year) with a *death benefit*. Let us assume that the insurer's investments yield a rate of return i equal to 3% and that the probability of death of a person aged x of the same sex as the policyholder in the following year is 0.003. According to the equivalence principle, what "pure" premium should the insurer charge this policyholder?

We begin this study with a few observations:
- The "pure" premium here is the premium that covers only the amount of losses or benefits paid. This means that administrative, acquisition, and other costs are not included.
- The probability of death between ages x and $x+1$ for a person aged x can be interpreted as the fact that out of 1,000 people aged x, on average, three will die by the end of the following year. For simplicity, in a deterministic model where the number of deaths is assumed to be known, we assume

that there are exactly three deaths for 1,000 similar policyholders. In reality, the number of deaths is a random variable.

- The insurer uses the basic principles of financial mathematics and considers the value of money over time since these contracts typically cover long periods of time. To calculate the discount factor, we make the simplified assumption that the insurer uses an interest rate equal to the return rate i. Thus, the value of "CHF 1 in one year" is $1/(1+i)$.

If the insurer covers 1,000 people aged x, each pays a one-time premium of A today; at the end of the year, the insurer must make three payments of CHF 100,000 (for three deaths). Pricing or risk appreciation follows the principle of actuarial equivalence, and the single premium A must satisfy the equation

$$1,000 \cdot A = \frac{3 \cdot 100,000}{1+i} \quad \text{where} \quad i = 0.03.$$

Alternatively, instead of posing the equation in the present, we can consider the situation at the end of the year. In this case, we assume that the insurer places the 1,000 premiums, each worth A, in a fund that earns an annual rate of i and that the insurer pays out three times CHF 100,000 from this fund at the end of the year. The single premium A is then the solution of the equation

$$1,000 \cdot A \cdot (1 + 0.03) = 3 \cdot 100,000.$$

In both cases, we get the same result, $A = 291.26$. Thus, for each of the 1,000 insurance policies, the insurer receives 291.26 francs in return for a possible payment of CHF 100,000. Financial equilibrium is guaranteed: 997 policyholders do not die, and their premiums, added to those of the deceased, pay for the benefits paid for the death of the three people from the original 1,000.

In general, if we write the lump sum benefit as C, the probability of dying between ages x and $x+1$ for a person aged x as q_x, and the discount factor as $v = 1/(1+i)$, then the single premium is

$$A = C \cdot v \cdot q_x.$$

The premium is, therefore, equal to the expected value of the benefits to be paid out at the end of the year, $C \cdot q_x$. In section 6.3, we introduce the notations used by actuaries. In addition to the notation q_x, a special notation is used for premiums. Without loss of generality, let us assume that the paid-out benefit is $C = 1$. In this case, the formula used to calculate the single premium per unit of the death benefit, denoted by $A^1_{x:\overline{1}|}$, is

$$A^1_{x:\overline{1}|} = v \cdot q_x.$$

6.2 Risk of death and mortality tables

Mortality tables Lump sum or annuity payments from life insurance products are closely linked to the survival or death of the person covered by the contract. In order to price these products, one must be able to quantify mortality. In this process, it is particularly important to take into account the fact that the mortality of policyholders is different from that of the population in general (for international general statistics, see The Human Mortality Database by Shkolnikov et al., 2021). This is due to a selection process: individual life insurance policies are only offered to people in (relatively) good health. In addition, a medical examination must be passed before a policy with a large amount of cover is taken out. This means that insurers must estimate the probability of death based on data about policyholders. If the company has a large number of policyholders, it can use its own data collected over a period of three, five, or ten years. Smaller companies may pool their data with others in order to have larger volumes to analyze. This is sometimes referred to as "common statistics." In all cases, the process consists of obtaining gross mortality rates $\hat{q}_x$ at ages x such that

$$\hat{q}_x = \frac{\text{number of deaths between ages } x \text{ and } x+1}{\text{number of persons alive aged } x}.$$

The resulting series of gross mortality rates for ages x will generally not be very smooth; this is because the amount of data available is limited. Random fluctuations are normal. For practical reasons, and because of a strong belief that the function describing mortality rates q_x is a regular function of age x, the actuary performs a "graduation" of the gross mortality rates to obtain what is considered a better estimate of the probabilities of death. Graduation consists of smoothing the mortality rates while incorporating into the "graduated" rates properties that seem desirable. These characteristics include, in particular, a probability that increases with age at almost all ages, a good fit with the data, and a smooth curve. This process produces the final probabilities of death q_x.

The probability of death depends on the sex of the person. The process described above is, therefore, performed twice: once for women and once for men. In Switzerland, actuaries distinguish between the sexes by referring to the age of men as x and the age of women as y. However, this convention is not recognized internationally.

A mortality table is a model that allows the actuary to study the number of deaths, probabilities of death or survival, and life expectancy within a population, depending on sex and age. These tables can be used to track the evolution of a population or group of individuals. They are an essential tool for quantifying mortality and, therefore, for pricing life insurance products. All of the notations presented below are commonly used.

In principle, a mortality table starts at age zero and analyzes the mortality of a population up to age ω. This parameter is the maximum age a person can reach, plus one year. In other words, ω is the age that no one reaches. This ensures that mortality tables have a finite length.

Periodic and generational mortality tables

We distinguish between "periodic" and "generational" mortality tables. Periodic tables are based on observed mortality rates. For example, the mortality table for the year 2020 shows the probabilities of death for people aged 0 to 110 in 2020. Periodic tables implicitly assume that life expectancy will not increase: they measure longevity without regard to increases in life expectancy.

In contrast, a generational mortality table follows a generation or cohort. For example, the 1980 table follows the generation born in 1980. Thus, the mortality probabilities are defined not only for each sex and age but also for each year of birth. These generational tables are based on the assumption that life expectancy is increasing, and they use mathematical models of the expected increase in life expectancy based on the year of birth.

Often, an insurance company can choose which table to use (Arnold et al., 2019). There is always uncertainty in determining the exact actuarial bases, but in the context of life expectancy, it is important to consider the choice of tables when calculating total reserves. Nowadays, many institutions are switching from periodic tables to generational tables. It should be noted that in some countries, regulations limit the choice of tables, including requiring that the table used be at least as conservative as a given reference table.

Biometric functions   The values in a mortality table show the evolution of the population between periods x and $x + 1$, for any $x \in \{0, 1, 2, \ldots, \omega - 1\}$. Here, x refers to the age of an individual in general.

We introduce the following notations:

- *Number of persons alive aged x*: The parameter l_x refers to the number of persons alive aged x in the population. In a mortality table, the initial number of individuals is, therefore, l_0.

- *Number of deaths between the ages of x and $x+1$*: We use d_x to represent the number of persons in the population who die between the ages of x and $x+1$. To determine d_x, we can look at the variation in the number of persons alive at age x and at age $x + 1$. The formal calculation is straightforward:

$$d_x = l_x - l_{x+1}.$$

- *Probability of death between ages x and $x + 1$*: The parameter q_x indicates the probability of death between the age of x and the age of $x + 1$ for a person aged x. We can determine this probability by calculating the ratio between the number of persons who die between the ages of x and $x + 1$, i.e., d_x, and the number of persons alive aged x, i.e., l_x:

$$q_x = \frac{d_x}{l_x} = \frac{l_x - l_{x+1}}{l_x}.$$

193

We call these probabilities of death "mortality rates" (see the box below). It is common practice to round the number of deaths d_x and the number of persons alive l_x at each step in the process. As a result of this rounding, the values calculated for q_x do not exactly match the original probabilities of death. In most cases, the difference is negligible. We can determine l_{x+1}, i.e., the number of persons alive aged $x + 1$, as follows:

$$l_{x+1} = l_x - d_x = l_x \cdot (1 - q_x).$$

- *Probability of survival between ages x and $x + 1$:* We use p_x to represent the probability that a person at age x will survive to age $x + 1$. This probability is complementary to the probability of death q_x, and we have

$$p_x = 1 - q_x.$$

By replacing the above expression for the probability of death q_x, the probability of survival p_x can be written as

$$p_x = \frac{l_{x+1}}{l_x}.$$

The probability that persons aged x will survive to age $x + 1$ is the ratio of the number of persons alive aged $x + 1$ to the number of persons alive aged x.

Application of the law of large numbers

From a technical perspective, life insurance is made possible by the application of the law of large numbers and the central limit theorem. Mortality is a key parameter in life insurance, and it has evolved over time. For example, human life expectancy, or the number of years we live on average, has doubled over the past few centuries. However, this has been a relatively gradual increase, with no sudden jumps. In a way, we can say that it is a stable development. This means that life insurers can predict the value of their commitments quite accurately, provided their portfolio is large enough.

We estimate the probability of death q_x of a person between ages x and $x + 1$ based on the gross mortality rate $\hat{q}_x$. If n_x is the number of people aged exactly x at the beginning of the year, the law of large numbers (see theorem 3.2) states that

$$\hat{q}_x = \frac{\text{number of deaths among the } n_x \text{ people}}{n_x} \longrightarrow q_x \quad \text{when} \quad n_x \to +\infty.$$

In other words, the law of large numbers states that when the number of people aged x is very large, the estimate of the gross mortality rate $\hat{q}_x$ converges to the probability of death q_x. According to an alternative formulation of the law, the probability that the absolute difference between the gross mortality rate $\hat{q}_x$ and the probability of death q_x is greater than a very small value ϵ tends toward 0 when the number of people n_x is very large. Formally, we have

$$\mathbb{P}\left(\left|\hat{q}_x - q_x\right| \geq \epsilon\right) \longrightarrow 0 \quad \text{when} \quad n_x \to +\infty \quad \text{for all } \epsilon > 0.$$

We conclude that if a sample of n_x people is sufficiently large, the probability of death can be estimated with good accuracy.

Let us now look at the notations related to the evolution of the population between ages x and $x + n$. The following notations generalize those seen above.

- *Number of deaths between the ages of x and $x + n$*: We use $_nd_x$ to represent the number of persons who die between the ages of x and $x + n$. This is the sum of the number of persons who die at each age from x to $x + n$. It is a sum that covers n years. We calculate $_nd_x$ as follows:

$$_nd_x = d_x + d_{x+1} + \ldots + d_{x+n-1} = \sum_{t=0}^{n-1} d_{x+t}.$$

  By replacing each number of deaths d_{x+t} in the above equation with the formula $d_x = l_x - l_{x+1}$ seen earlier, we determine that the number of deaths between ages x and $x + n$ is written as

$$\begin{aligned}
_nd_x &= (l_x - l_{x+1}) + (l_{x+1} - l_{x+2}) + \ldots + (l_{x+n-1} - l_{x+n}) \\
&= l_x - l_{x+n}.
\end{aligned}$$

- *Probability of death between ages x and $x + n$*: Let $_nq_x$ be the probability that a person dies between ages x and $x + n$. We get this probability by dividing the number of deaths between ages x and $x+n$, i.e., $_nd_x$, by l_x, the number of persons alive aged x:

$$_nq_x = \frac{_nd_x}{l_x} = \frac{l_x - l_{x+n}}{l_x}.$$

- *Probability of survival between ages x and $x + n$*: The parameter $_np_x$ represents the probability that a person aged x will survive to age $x + n$. This probability is complementary to the probability of death, $_nq_x$, introduced above. As a result,

$$_np_x = 1 - {_nq_x} = \frac{l_{x+n}}{l_x}.$$

  This relationship can be demonstrated in another way. If survival at age x, represented by L_x, is independent from year to year, then we can use the properties of independent random variables. Thus, the probability that a person survives from age x to age $x + n$, i.e., $_np_x$, is written as

$$_np_x = \mathbb{P}\left(\bigcap_{t=0}^{n-1} L_{x+t}\right) = \prod_{t=0}^{n-1} \mathbb{P}(L_{x+t}).$$

Now $\mathbb{P}(L_{x+t})$ is nothing other than p_{x+t}, which leads us to the following relationship using the definition of p_{x+t}:

$$_np_x = \prod_{t=0}^{n-1} p_{x+t} = \prod_{t=0}^{n-1} \frac{l_{x+t+1}}{l_{x+t}} = \frac{l_{x+1}}{l_x} \cdot \frac{l_{x+2}}{l_{x+1}} \cdot \ldots \cdot \frac{l_{x+n}}{l_{x+n-1}} = \frac{l_{x+n}}{l_x}.$$

The functions d, q, and l are called biometric functions. Conceptually, these are continuous functions. However, we only have good estimates of these functions at a finite number of points, generally equidistant, especially for each age. This is because mortality tables only contain values for whole ages. To obtain continuous functions, assumptions must be made. For example, actuaries often assume that there is a *uniform distribution of deaths* for non-integer ages. As a result, for durations t that are less than one year, i.e., for $0 < t < 1$, the following formula is used:

$$l_{x+t} = (1 - t) \cdot l_x + t \cdot l_{x+1} = l_x - t \cdot d_x, \quad \text{for } 0 < t < 1.$$

In other words, assuming a uniform distribution of deaths for non-integer ages, the number of survivors is a linear interpolation between the integer ages that bound the non-integer age under study.

Finally, we conclude the presentation of notations with life expectancy, which is another biometric function.

- *Life expectancy at age x:* We call e_x the life expectancy at age x. Expressed in years, it indicates the average life span and is calculated by adding the future probabilities of survival. Formally, we express life expectancy e_x using the following expression:

$$e_x = \sum_{t=1}^{+\infty} {}_tp_x = \frac{1}{l_x} \sum_{t=1}^{+\infty} l_{x+t}.$$

  The second sum can be interpreted as the sum of all future full years lived by l_x persons aged x. By dividing this sum by the initial number of persons l_x, we get the expected number of future years to be lived by people aged x. If we assume that people die, on average, in the middle of the year—which is the case under the assumption of a uniform distribution of deaths—, we get an approximation for the full life expectancy $\mathring{e}_x$ such that

$$\mathring{e}_x = \frac{1}{l_x} \int_{t=1}^{+\infty} l_{x+t} \, \mathrm{d}t \approx \frac{1}{l_x} \sum_{t=1}^{+\infty} l_{x+t} + \frac{1}{2} = e_x + \frac{1}{2}.$$

Technical bases If we add an interest rate assumption to the biometric functions, we get what are called technical bases. In fact, this is all the information needed to calculate the (basic) present values associated with life insurance and annuity products. With the assumption of an effective annual interest rate of i, we can introduce the discount factor v, which allows us to discount the economic flows. The discount factor is given by

$$v = \frac{1}{1+i} = (1+i)^{-1}.$$

In practice, the technical bases used to calculate pure premiums, i.e., the premiums on which the market premiums paid by policyholders are based, are different from those used to assess mathematical reserves, i.e., the amount the insurer must have available to meet its financial obligations (see section 6.4). This is because market premiums, i.e., premiums to which administrative and acquisition costs are added, need to be competitive; on the other hand, in order to ensure the solvency of the insurer, its reserves need to be conservative. Therefore, in practice, a distinction is made between 1st-order and 2nd-order technical bases. Finally, it should be noted that technical bases do not necessarily start at age zero.

Table 6.1 shows an excerpt from the technical bases, including an example of a mortality table and discount factor. We use this table to illustrate the calculation of premiums and reserves in the rest of this chapter. We also add the values for the discount factor v^n, which are helpful in the examples. Mortality tables, however, never include this information. For illustration purposes, we assume that the interest rate i is 3%.

Time n	Age	l_x	d_x	q_x	$_nd_x$	$_nq_x$	$_np_x$	v^n
				Biometric functions				
0	x	1,000	3	0.003	0	0.000	1.000	1.000
1	$x+1$	997	4	0.004	3	0.003	0.997	0.9709
2	$x+2$	993	6	0.006	7	0.007	0.993	0.9426
3	$x+3$	987	9	0.009	13	0.013	0.987	0.9151
4	$x+4$	978	14	0.014	22	0.022	0.978	0.8885
5	$x+5$	964	20	0.021	36	0.036	0.964	0.8626
6	$x+6$	944	28	0.030	56	0.056	0.944	0.8375
7	$x+7$	916	38	0.041	84	0.084	0.916	0.8131

The values for the number of deaths d_x are chosen for illustrative purposes. Interest rate $i = 3\%$ and discount factor $v = 1/(1+i)$.

Table 6.1: Illustration of a mortality table and the discount factor.

In this chapter, we present classical actuarial mathematics with its technical bases and elements of life insurance pricing (see section 6.3). From a risk management perspective, these pricing formulas, which use a fixed mortality table and a deterministic interest rate, ignore certain risks. Both mortality and interest rates are subject to fluctuations that can be significant, especially when one considers the long duration of the contracts involved. The assessment and management of biometric risks (longevity and mortality) and financial risks (returns) are at the heart of the life insurance business. Actuaries develop specific mathematical models for each insurance product. Analysis of a company's balance sheet, risk management, and strategic leadership are integral to asset and liability management.

Importance of the central limit theorem in insurance

When considering the parameters related to pricing, and in particular when determining the technical bases using the insurance portfolio, it is relevant to return to the question of the basis of insurance, the place of the law of large numbers, and the central limit theorem (see theorems 3.2 and 3.3 in section 3.3). In section 5.1, we considered the economic justification of insurance. We concluded that the economic justification of insurance is the diversification of risk, which allows the insurer to minimize the capital required to cover a portfolio of risks. Nevertheless, the law of large numbers is a tool that allows the insurer to price risks.

So, does having a large number of policyholders allow the insurer to balance the different risks it covers? The answer is usually no. Rather, it is a consequence of the central limit theorem because safety and profit margins, for example, must be taken into account for insurance to work. As a reminder, the central limit theorem states that the distribution of a sequence of independent random variables with the same distribution converges to the normal distribution. This is helpful in insurance because, in the presence of many contracts, this theorem allows the insurer to determine an overall estimate of the amounts to be paid out.

To explore this point further, consider the following illustration. Let l_x be the number of policyholders aged x covered by a one-year term life insurance policy with a payout of C, and let q_x be the probability of death as defined above (see also the illustration of a one-year term life insurance at the end of section 6.1).

According to the principle of actuarial equivalence and as seen above, the pure premium A for one-year term insurance with a payout of C is

$$A = C \cdot v \cdot q_x.$$

For simplicity, we assume that the interest rate i is zero. Therefore, $A = C \cdot q_x$.

We use P to represent the market premium, which includes the margin $\theta > 0$ that is proportional to the pure premium A. The market premium P is then expressed as

$$P = (1 + \theta) \cdot A.$$

With the expression of A, we have

$$P = (1 + \theta) \cdot C \cdot q_x.$$

If the number of deaths among l_x people during the year is d_x, then the total amount to be paid out is $S = d_x \cdot C$. Intuitively, the random variable describing the number of deaths d_x follows a binomial distribution with parameters (n, p), where $n = l_x$ and $p = q_x$ (see the notations in section 3.3). Given this distribution, the expected value $\mathbb{E}(S)$ of the random variable S is given by

$$\mathbb{E}(S) = \mathbb{E}(d_x \cdot C) = C \cdot \mathbb{E}(d_x) = C \cdot l_x \cdot q_x,$$

and the variance $\mathrm{Var}(S)$ of the random variable S is

$$\mathrm{Var}(S) = \mathrm{Var}(d_x \cdot C) = C^2 \cdot \mathrm{Var}(d_x) = C^2 \cdot l_x \cdot q_x \cdot (1 - q_x).$$

Now consider $w > 0$, the total wealth of the insurer managing this portfolio. The insurer is bankrupt at the end of the year if the total amount of claims S is greater than its assets w plus the premiums collected $(l_x \cdot P)$. Thus, the probability of ruin at the end of the year is given by

$$\mathbb{P}(S > w + l_x \cdot P) = \mathbb{P}(S > w + l_x \cdot (1 + \theta) \cdot C \cdot q_x).$$

We now transform this expression to use the central limit theorem to obtain information about this probability of ruin for a very large portfolio. To do this, we first center and reduce the random variable. To center, we subtract the expected value $\mathbb{E}(S)$ from both sides of the inequality; to reduce, we divide both sides by the standard deviation of S, i.e., by $\sqrt{\mathrm{Var}(S)}$. The expression describing the insurer's probability of ruin then becomes

$$\mathbb{P}\left(\frac{S - \mathbb{E}(S)}{\sqrt{\mathrm{Var}(S)}} > \frac{w + l_x \cdot (1 + \theta) \cdot C \cdot q_x - l_x \cdot C \cdot q_x}{C \cdot \sqrt{l_x \cdot q_x \cdot (1 - q_x)}} \right),$$

and after simplification, we get

$$\mathbb{P}\left(\frac{S - \mathbb{E}(S)}{\sqrt{\mathrm{Var}(S)}} > \frac{w + l_x \cdot \theta \cdot C \cdot q_x}{C \cdot \sqrt{l_x \cdot q_x \cdot (1 - q_x)}} \right).$$

Finally, we introduce the random variable $Z = \frac{S - \mathbb{E}(S)}{\sqrt{\mathrm{Var}(S)}}$ and note $z = \frac{w + l_x \cdot \theta \cdot C \cdot q_x}{C \cdot \sqrt{l_x \cdot q_x \cdot (1 - q_x)}}$. In this context, the application of the central limit theorem indicates that if the size of the portfolio, l_x, tends to infinity, then the distribution of Z tends to the standard normal distribution. If $\Phi(x)$ is the standard normal distribution, then we have

$$\lim_{l_x \to +\infty} \mathbb{P}(Z \le z) = \Phi(z) \quad \Longleftrightarrow \quad \lim_{l_x \to +\infty} \mathbb{P}(Z > z) = 1 - \Phi(z).$$

Now, when $l_x \to +\infty$, $z \to +\infty$ and $\Phi(z) \to 1$. So we have

$$\lim_{l_x \to +\infty} \mathbb{P}(Z > z) = 0,$$

and we conclude that the insurer's probability of ruin tends to zero when l_x is very large. The fact that the pooling of risk allows the insurer to have a low probability of ruin and predictable results is thus explained by the central limit theorem.

We conclude the discussion with a few notes:

- Throughout the above expressions, we note that if the insurer's wealth is zero, i.e., $w = 0$, then the probability of ruin is

$$1 - \Phi \left(\theta \cdot \sqrt{\frac{l_x \cdot q_x}{1 - q_x}} \right).$$

  We find that for $\theta > 0$, the probability of ruin always tends to zero as the number of policyholders l_x tends to infinity. However, this conclusion is only true in the limited context of our model.

- We note that if the insurer does not include a margin in its premiums, i.e., if $\theta = 0$, then $l_x \to +\infty$ implies $z \to 0$, i.e., $1 - \Phi(z) \to 1/2$, and the probability of ruin is 50% for a large portfolio.

- An insurer cannot have an infinitely large portfolio. Thus, the central limit theorem provides an approximation of the probability of ruin when the portfolio size is finite but large. Under the conditions described above, there is a certain portfolio size with a number of policyholders l_x that makes the insurer's probability of ruin very small.

- An additional consequence of the central limit theorem is that the probability distribution of the total amount of claims S becomes increasingly symmetric as the portfolio size increases. This probability distribution becomes closer and closer to a normal distribution as the number of policyholders l_x increases.

- The law of large numbers and the central limit theorem apply under similar conditions, i.e., when the number of independent random variables to be added is very large. Note that both theorems apply to random variables that are independent, which is not always the case in practice.

6.3 Basics of life insurance pricing

Vocabulary and actuarial notation This section introduces some principles of actuarial notation for payment streams, whether premiums or benefits, in an insurance policy. Actuarial notation takes into account the periodicity of the payments, the payment's term, the fact that payments are deferred, and the duration of the policy in the case of term life insurance:

- *Policyholder age*: In life insurance, premiums and benefits depend on the policyholder's mortality and survival. These parameters depend on the age of the policyholder, which means that the age at which the policy is purchased plays an important role. This age, usually denoted as x, is given in subscripts after the variable referring to the value of the payments.

- *Single payment or series of payments*: A distinction is made between a one-time payment, such as a single premium or lump sum, and a series of payments, such as recurring premiums or annuities. In general, the present value of a single payment is represented by an uppercase letter, typically "A." The present value of a series of payments is represented by a lowercase letter, usually "a," which refers to an *annuity*.

- *Payment terms*: Actuarial notations also include the term of payment(s). Payments may be made at the beginning of the period, or "due," which is indicated by the addition of two dots above the payment notation. For example, the present value of a series of payments due is indicated by two dots (double dot) above the annuity, $\ddot{a}$. If the payments are made at the end of the period, they are called "immediate;" in this case, the present value is simply noted a. In practice, premiums are typically due, i.e., paid at the beginning of the period, while benefits are immediate, i.e., paid at the end of the period.

- *Deferred payments*: The payment(s) may begin as soon as the policy becomes active or may not be due for a number of years. If the first payment is due at a time other than the first period (whether at the beginning or the end), it is called a deferred payment. This time is indicated by placing the number of periods in subscripts to the left of the payment notation. Thus, the notation $_{s|}a$ indicates an annuity immediate deferred for s periods.

- *Whole or term (temporary) life insurance*: A whole life insurance implies a contractual relationship that lasts until the death of the policyholder, before the age ω. If payments are made over a finite number of periods, as is the case with term insurance policies, the duration is given as a subscript after age. Thus, the notation $a_{x:\overline{n}|}$ indicates payments over n years for a policyholder aged x when the contract is concluded.

In short, the notation $_{s|}\ddot{a}_{x:\overline{n}|}$, for a policyholder aged x at the beginning of the contract, indicates a series of payments due (double dot), i.e., made at the beginning of the period, for n periods, and deferred by s periods.

From the above, we use the following definitions, which apply to both the payment of premiums by policyholders and the payment of benefits by insurers:

Definition 6.2 (*Payment due and payment immediate*)

*A payment **due** is typically made at the beginning of the period considered. By contrast, a payment **immediate** is made later, typically at the end of a period.*

Definition 6.3 (*Deferred and non-deferred payment*)

A **non-deferred** *payment is made starting in the first period considered. By contrast, a* **deferred** *payment is made after a delay of several periods.*

It is often useful to draw a timeline to represent the various payments. Figure 6.1 shows an example of a series of payments of the same amount P due over n periods. In these graphs, we show the premium amount P at the value of the payment date, which is not necessarily equal to P units of currency, taking into account the discount factor and the probability of survival. The present value takes into account a discount factor for each payment, as well as the policyholder's probability of survival at the time of the payment.

Figure 6.1: Timeline for payments of amount P due over n years.

Life insurance premiums over several years   In most cases, the duration of a life insurance policy is longer than one year. As an example, consider a one-year term life insurance policy that pays a death benefit C and has a guaranteed annual renewal, i.e., the policyholder can decide each year whether to renew the policy. From the illustration in section 6.1, the base price or pure premium varies with age x and satisfies the following equation:

$$\text{premium at age } x \text{ for one year} = C \cdot v \cdot q_x.$$

In this equation, C is the amount paid out if the policy is triggered, v is the discount factor, and q_x is the probability of death between ages x and $x+1$ for a person aged x. As a reminder, a "pure premium" is a premium equal to the expected value of future payments, excluding other elements such as the insurer's margin and costs.

Such an annual approach creates several problems. First, the premium changes every year, making it difficult for the policyholder to predict and estimate costs. In particular, the premium is very high at older ages because the probability of death is higher. As a result, premiums become unaffordable, and it is impossible to obtain life insurance coverage for one's entire life. In addition, various margins for costs, profit, and taxes must be added each year.

The solution is to use level premiums, which are constant over time and based on single premiums. Thus, a life insurance premium is defined as the total amount that the policyholder must pay to the insurer in order to be covered. We distinguish between "single premiums," where the policyholder pays only one premium, usually at the beginning of the contract, and "level premiums," which are paid at regular intervals throughout the contract.

- *Single premium policies*: In the case of a single premium policy, the policy-holder aged x pays the insurer a one-time amount, the pure premium noted A, at the beginning of the contract. Conceptually, the present value of premiums can be written as

$$\sum_t P_t \cdot v^t \cdot \mathbb{P}(\text{payment at } t) \quad = \quad A \cdot v^0 \cdot \mathbb{P}(\text{payment at } t = 0)$$

$$= \quad A.$$

In the above expression, there is no sum because there is only one payment. This payment is due at the beginning of the first year of the contract, at $t = 0$. Therefore, the discount factor is $v^0 = 1$. For a payment to occur, the policyholder must be alive. The probability of payment at t is, therefore, similar to the probability of survival to t for a policyholder aged x, i.e., $_t p_x$. In our case, this probability is $_0 p_x = 1$: if the policy is purchased at $t = 0$, the policyholder is necessarily alive. This means that the single premium is A, which is a deterministic amount. The timeline shown in figure 6.2 illustrates the policyholder's payment.

Figure 6.2: Timeline for a policy with a single premium of A paid at the beginning of the policy.

- *Level premium policies*: Because insurance policies often cover a long period of time, a single premium is a relatively large sum. In this case, policyholders often choose to pay periodic premiums, called level premiums. Assuming the premium amount P is constant, the present value of the premiums is

$$\sum_t P_t \cdot v^t \cdot \mathbb{P}(\text{payment at } t) \quad = \quad \sum_t P \cdot v^t \cdot \mathbb{P}(\text{payment at } t)$$

$$= \quad P \cdot \sum_t v^t \cdot {}_t p_x.$$

The latter equality is obtained by considering, for the single premium, that the probability of payment at t is equal to the probability of survival of the policyholder until t, i.e., $_t p_x$. This emphasizes the fact that, unlike a single premium that is paid in full at the beginning of the policy, level premiums are paid only if the policyholder survives.

In the following, we will examine the features of the premiums that affect the calculation of the present value. We will focus on the expression $\sum_t v^t \cdot {}_t p_x$, which is the present value of a payment of one *currency unit*.

Finally, we use the following definitions:

Definition 6.4 (*Single premium and level premiums*)

A **single** premium is paid all at once, usually at the beginning of the contract. By contrast, **level** premiums are constant or identical amounts paid periodically throughout the contract.

Characteristics of life insurance premiums   Various characteristics affect the present value of premiums. The most important of these is the payment term—due or immediate—, which determines whether the premiums are paid at the beginning or end of the period. Another parameter is the potential deferral of premiums, i.e., whether they are paid immediately upon inception of the contract or after a period of time.

Since single premiums are essentially defined by the discounting of benefits, we will focus on level premiums in this section. Level premiums are paid at regular intervals, which leads us to the concept of an annuity as used in actuarial science. In other words, we are looking for the present value of the premiums, taking into account mortality and the discounting of amounts paid at regular intervals.

In practice, the term "annuity" refers only to benefits, i.e., amounts paid at regular intervals. However, level premiums also fit the definition of "amounts paid at regular intervals," so we introduce actuarial annuities to apply the concept to the calculation of premiums. Therefore, the same notations are used for level premiums and annuity benefits (see below and table 6.2). For simplicity, we assume that the periods considered are full years. Once one is familiar with the theory of annuities, it is easy to change the period to, say, months if necessary.

We consider the following situations:

- *Non-deferred annual premiums due*: Non-deferred annual premiums due are paid at the beginning of the year ("due"), starting in the first year of the contract ("non-deferred"). The present value of these premiums is identical to that of a non-deferred annuity due. This value is called $\ddot{a}_{x:\overline{n}|}$ in the case of a contract with level premiums paid over n years at the beginning of each year for a person aged x at the beginning of the contract. The mathematical expression for this term is

$$\ddot{a}_{x:\overline{n}|} = \sum_{t=0}^{n-1} v^t \cdot {}_t p_x = \frac{1}{l_x} \sum_{t=0}^{n-1} v^t \cdot l_{x+t}.$$

In the timeline in figure 6.3, we illustrate the stream of level premiums of P resulting from the "due" and "non-deferred" characteristics. The n payments are made between times 0 and $n-1$. The actual payment of the value P at the indicated times is conditional on the survival of the policyholder. To know the level premium P, one must also determine the present value of the expected benefits (see below).

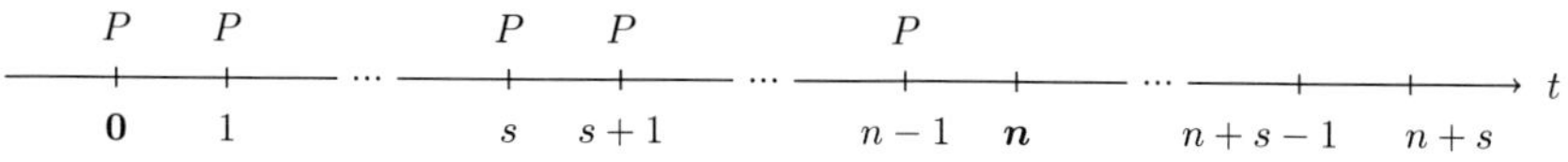

The premium payments P depend on the survival of the policyholder (probability $_tp_x$ at time t).

Figure 6.3: Timeline for non-deferred level premiums due of amount P over n years.

Non-deferred annual premiums due

As a numerical application, we propose to calculate the present value of level premiums over five years, paid at the beginning of the year for a person aged x at the beginning of the contract. Using the technical bases of table 6.1, we have:

$$
\begin{aligned}
\ddot{a}_{x:\overline{5}|} &= \sum_{t=0}^{4} v^t \cdot {}_tp_x \\
&= v^0 \cdot {}_0p_x + v^1 \cdot {}_1p_x + v^2 \cdot {}_2p_x + v^3 \cdot {}_3p_x + v^4 \cdot {}_4p_x \\
&= 1 \cdot 1 + 0.9709 \cdot 0.997 + 0.9426 \cdot 0.993 \\
&\quad + 0.9151 \cdot 0.987 + 0.8885 \cdot 0.978 \\
&= 4.676
\end{aligned}
$$

Thus, the present value of premiums is $\ddot{a}_{x:\overline{5}|} = 4.676$.

- *Non-deferred annual premiums immediate*: In the case of non-deferred premiums immediate, they are paid at the end of the period ("immediate") beginning in the first period ("non-deferred"). The present value of such level premiums is noted $a_{x:\overline{n}|}$, and it represents a contract with premiums paid over n years, payable at the end of the year, for a person aged x at the beginning of the contract. Formally, we have the following expression:

$$
a_{x:\overline{n}|} = \sum_{t=1}^{n} v^t \cdot {}_tp_x = \frac{1}{l_x} \sum_{t=1}^{n} v^t \cdot l_{x+t}.
$$

We can describe the present value of this contract with premiums immediate, $a_{x:\overline{n}|}$, using the present value of a contract with premiums due (and non-deferred) $\ddot{a}_{x:\overline{n}|}$:

$$
a_{x:\overline{n}|} = \ddot{a}_{x:\overline{n}|} - 1 + v^n \cdot {}_np_x.
$$

This is because the term "-1" is related to the term $v^0 \cdot {}_0p_x$ contained in $\ddot{a}_{x:\overline{n}|}$, and the term "$v^n \cdot {}_np_x$" contained in $a_{x:\overline{n}|}$ is not contained in $\ddot{a}_{x:\overline{n}|}$. This gives an idea of the relationships that exist between the different actuarial notations, and underscores the importance of understanding the formulas rather than simply memorizing them.

A person who understands what the formulas mean and how discounting works does not need to memorize anything because the expressions are intuitive. This is why we insist on the graphical representation using timelines. In figure 6.4, we illustrate the stream of non-deferred level premiums immediate of amount P.

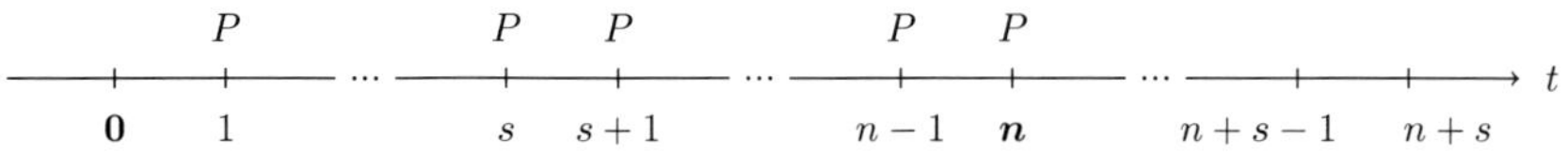

The premium payments P depend on the survival of the policyholder (probability $_tp_x$ at time t).

Figure 6.4: Timeline for non-deferred level premiums immediate of amount P over n years.

Non-deferred annual premiums immediate

Below is a numerical example where we calculate the present value of five-year level premiums paid at the end of the year for a person aged x at the start of the contract. The value $a_{x:\overline{5}|}$ using the parameters in table 6.1 is calculated as follows:

$$
\begin{aligned}
a_{x:\overline{5}|} &= \sum_{t=1}^{5} v^t \cdot {}_tp_x \\
&= v^1 \cdot {}_1p_x + v^2 \cdot {}_2p_x + v^3 \cdot {}_3p_x + v^4 \cdot {}_4p_x + v^5 \cdot {}_5p_x \\
&= 0.9709 \cdot 0.997 + 0.9426 \cdot 0.993 + 0.9151 \cdot 0.987 \\
&\quad + 0.8885 \cdot 0.978 + 0.8626 \cdot 0.964 \\
&= 4.508
\end{aligned}
$$

The value of this annuity is $a_{x:\overline{5}|} = 4.508$. Comparing this result with the present value of a non-deferred annuity due $\ddot{a}_{x:\overline{5}|} = 4.676$ (see above), we see that the annuity immediate has a lower value, i.e., $a_{x:\overline{5}|} < \ddot{a}_{x:\overline{5}|}$. The difference can be explained by the additional discount factor v and the difference in mortality between a payment at $t = 0$ for $\ddot{a}_{x:\overline{5}|}$ and at $t = 5$ for $a_{x:\overline{5}|}$.

- *Deferred annual premiums due*: Deferred premiums due in life insurance policies are paid at the beginning of the year ("due") after a specified period ("deferred") rather than when the policy is issued. The present value of deferred level premiums due is written in actuarial notation as $_{s|}\ddot{a}_{x:\overline{n}|}$ for a contract with n level premiums paid at the beginning of the year beginning in year s for a person aged x when the policy is issued. Formally, we have

$$_{s|}\ddot{a}_{x:\overline{n}|} = \sum_{t=s}^{n+s-1} v^t \cdot {}_t p_x = \frac{1}{l_x} \sum_{t=s}^{n+s-1} v^t \cdot l_{x+t}.$$

In figure 6.5, we illustrate the stream of level premiums due of amount P deferred by s periods.

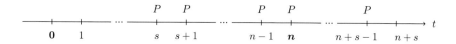

The premium payments P depend on the survival of the policyholder (probability $_t p_x$ at time t).

Figure 6.5: Timeline for level premiums due of amount P deferred by s years over n years.

Deferred annual premiums due

Let us calculate the present value of level premiums over five years, paid at the beginning of the year and deferred by two years, for a person aged x at the beginning of the contract. Using the values in table 6.1 as parameters, we get the following result:

$$
\begin{aligned}
_{2|}\ddot{a}_{x:\overline{5}|} &= \sum_{t=2}^{6} v^t \cdot {}_t p_x \\
&= v^2 \cdot {}_2 p_x + v^3 \cdot {}_3 p_x + v^4 \cdot {}_4 p_x + v^5 \cdot {}_5 p_x + v^6 \cdot {}_6 p_x \\
&= 0.9426 \cdot 0.993 + 0.9151 \cdot 0.987 + 0.8885 \cdot 0.978 \\
&\quad + 0.8626 \cdot 0.964 + 0.8375 \cdot 0.944 \\
&= 4.330
\end{aligned}
$$

Thus, the present value we are looking for, $_{2|}\ddot{a}_{x:\overline{5}|}$, is 4.330. If we compare this to the value calculated for the same individual when the premium was due but not deferred, i.e., $\ddot{a}_{x:\overline{5}|} = 4.676$, we see that deferral reduces the expected present value. Formally, we have $_{2|}\ddot{a}_{x:\overline{5}|} < \ddot{a}_{x:\overline{5}|}$). Even without discussing mortality or survival during the two years of deferral, this result is expected because the payment period for the deferred premium is shifted into the future, which means a higher discount factor must be applied.

- *Deferred annual premiums immediate*: Deferred annual premiums immediate are paid at the end of the year ("immediate") but only after a specified amount of time ("deferred"). The present value of this series of payments is written as $_{s|}a_{x:\overline{n}|}$ and corresponds to a contract with n level premiums paid at the end of the year, starting in year s, for a person aged x when the policy is purchased. The mathematical formulation of this annuity is given by the following expression:

$$_{s|}a_{x:\overline{n}|} = \sum_{t=s+1}^{n+s} v^t \cdot {}_tp_x = \frac{1}{l_x} \sum_{t=s+1}^{n+s} v^t \cdot l_{x+t}.$$

In figure 6.6, we illustrate the stream of level premiums of amount P for this annuity.

The premium payments P depend on the survival of the policyholder (probability $_tp_x$ at time t).

Figure 6.6: Timeline for level premiums immediate of amount P deferred by s years over n years.

Deferred annual premiums immediate

In this example, we calculate the expected present value of an annuity immediate, that is, an annuity with premiums paid at the end of the year, with a duration of five years and a deferral of two years for a person aged x when the policy is purchased. Using the values in table 6.1, the annuity $_{2|}a_{x:\overline{5}|}$ is:

$$\begin{aligned}
_{2|}a_{x:\overline{5}|} &= \sum_{t=3}^{7} v^t \cdot {}_tp_x \\
&= v^3 \cdot {}_3p_x + v^4 \cdot {}_4p_x + v^5 \cdot {}_5p_x + v^6 \cdot {}_6p_x + v^7 \cdot {}_7p_x \\
&= 0.9151 \cdot 0.987 + 0.8885 \cdot 0.978 + 0.8626 \cdot 0.964 \\
&\quad + 0.8375 \cdot 0.944 + 0.8131 \cdot 0.916 \\
&= 4.139
\end{aligned}$$

Therefore, we have $_{2|}a_{x:\overline{5}|} = 4.139$.

The name used for the different types of premiums provides at least three important pieces of information. These are the frequency of payments (annual), whether payments are made at the beginning or end of the period (due or immediate), and whether payments start at the beginning of the contract or after a certain period of time (non-deferred and deferred premiums). It remains clear that the indication of the payment frequency means that these are level premiums. In the case of a single premium, there is no point in specifying the frequency of payments because, by definition, a single premium is paid only once. Although this is not done in practice, there is nothing to prevent a policy from having a single premium paid at the beginning or end of the year or with a deferred period.

Characteristics of lump-sum insurance benefits   Life insurance benefits are obligations or promises of payment made by insurers to their policyholders when an insured event occurs. In life insurance, the insured event is death or survival. In the context of death, insurance policies typically pay a lump sum upon the death of the policyholder. The main distinction is between whole life insurance and term life insurance. There are also lump-sum policies that cover survivorship. Mixed (or endowment) insurance policies provide benefits in the event of both death and survival. In addition to lump-sum policies, there are annuity policies that pay benefits at regular intervals for as long as the policyholder lives.

In the case of lump-sum insurance, we consider four types of insurance that provide different benefits: whole life insurance, term life insurance, pure endowment insurance, and endowment insurance. It should be noted that other types of insurance may fall under the category of lump-sum insurance. In the following examples, unless otherwise indicated, we assume that the lump sum is always paid at the end of the year (and not at the beginning of the year) following death or survival.

- *Whole life insurance*: A whole life insurance policy pays a lump sum upon the death of the policyholder. This means that upon death, the insurer will pay an amount C defined in the policy. Formally, the present value of the benefits corresponds to the discounting of this lump-sum payment at a time t that is not known in advance because it depends on the policyholder's death. The benefits paid by these policies are therefore described by an expression whose form is as follows:

$$C \cdot \sum_t v^{t+1} \cdot \mathbb{P}(\text{payment at } t + 1).$$

Thus, since the death benefit is paid at the end of the year, we write as $\mathbb{P}(\text{payment at } t + 1)$ the probability that it will be paid at $t + 1$. This event requires the policyholder to survive until t, formally denoted $_t p_x$, and to die sometime between t and $t + 1$, formally denoted q_{x+t}. Assuming that both events are independent, we express the probability that the policyholder will survive to t and die between t and $t + 1$ as follows:

$$\mathbb{P}(\text{payment at } t + 1) = {}_t p_x \cdot q_{x+t}.$$

Taking into account the expression of this probability, we now write the present value of the future benefits paid by this contract as

$$C \cdot \sum_t v^{t+1} \cdot {}_t p_x \cdot q_{x+t}.$$

There is an actuarial notation that indicates the expected present value of a death benefit of $C = 1$ (paid at the end of the year of death) for the entire remaining life of the policyholder currently aged x. This actuarial notation is A_x, and the value is determined by the following relationship:

$$A_x = \sum_{t=0}^{(\omega-1)-x} v^{t+1} \cdot {}_tp_x \cdot q_{x+t} = \sum_{t=0}^{(\omega-1)-x} v^{t+1} \cdot \frac{l_{x+t}}{l_x} \cdot \frac{d_{x+t}}{l_{x+t}}$$

$$= \frac{1}{l_x} \sum_{t=0}^{(\omega-1)-x} v^{t+1} \cdot d_{x+t}$$

$$= \frac{1}{l_x} \left(v \cdot d_x + v^2 \cdot d_{x+1} + v^3 \cdot d_{x+2} + \ldots + v^{\omega-x} \cdot d_{\omega-1} \right),$$

where, as a reminder, $\omega - 1$ is the oldest age in the mortality table (ω is the age no one reaches). The last line in the above expression can be interpreted as the sum of the present values of deaths at all ages starting at age x relative to the initial population aged x. In fact, each death triggers a payment of the lump sum $C = 1$.

- *Term life insurance*: Term life insurance follows the same logic as whole life insurance. This is because its benefits are also paid in a lump sum upon the death of the policyholder. However, unlike whole life insurance, the contract covers only a predetermined period of n years instead of the policyholder's entire remaining life after the policy is purchased. The present value of a term life insurance is lower than that of a whole life insurance. The present value of a lump sum $C = 1$ paid by a n-year term life insurance policy purchased by a policyholder aged x is equal to:

$$A^1_{x:\overline{n}|} = \sum_{t=0}^{n-1} v^{t+1} \cdot {}_tp_x \cdot q_{x+t} = \frac{1}{l_x} \sum_{t=0}^{n-1} v^{t+1} \cdot d_{x+t}$$

$$= \frac{1}{l_x} \left(v \cdot d_x + v^2 \cdot d_{x+1} + v^3 \cdot d_{x+2} + \ldots + v^n \cdot d_{x+n-1} \right).$$

Note that in the case of a term life policy, unlike a whole life policy, we add a superscript "1" to the notation. In figure 6.7, we illustrate the stream resulting from the death benefit paid by a term life insurance policy. Note that the payment of C, made on one of the dates on the timeline, is subject to the discount factor and the death of the policyholder in the preceding period. In order to manage its cash, an insurer must be aware that the lump sum C could be owed at any time between $t = 1$ and $t = n$ if the policyholder dies during that interval.

Finally, we note that the formulas for whole life insurance seen above can be found by using $n = \omega - x$ or by letting n tend to infinity since biometric functions are, by definition, zero above age ω.

The payment of the lump sum C depends on the death of the policyholder (probability $_{t-1}p_x \cdot q_{x+t-1} = d_{x+t-1}/l_x$ at time t).

Figure 6.7: Timeline for the payment of a lump sum C of an n-year term life insurance.

Term life insurance benefits

The following numerical example illustrates the benefits paid by this type of contract. Using the parameters in table 6.1, we calculate the present value of a death benefit of $C = 1$ paid by a term life insurance policy with a term of $n = 5$ years for a policyholder aged x at inception as follows:

$$
\begin{aligned}
A^1_{x:\overline{5}|} &= \sum_{t=0}^{4} v^{t+1} \cdot {_t}p_x \cdot q_{x+t} \\
&= v \cdot {_0}p_x \cdot q_x + v^2 \cdot {_1}p_x \cdot q_{x+1} + v^3 \cdot {_2}p_x \cdot q_{x+2} \\
&\quad + v^4 \cdot {_3}p_x \cdot q_{x+3} + v^5 \cdot {_4}p_x \cdot q_{x+4} \\
&= 0.9709 \cdot 1 \cdot 0.003 + 0.9426 \cdot 0.997 \cdot 0.004 + 0.9151 \cdot 0.993 \cdot 0.006 \\
&\quad + 0.8885 \cdot 0.987 \cdot 0.009 + 0.8626 \cdot 0.978 \cdot 0.014 \\
&= 0.032
\end{aligned}
$$

The present value of the death benefit $C = 1$ is $A^1_{x:\overline{5}|} = 0.032$ for this policyholder. The following alternative expression obviously produces the same result:

$$
\begin{aligned}
A^1_{x:\overline{5}|} &= \frac{1}{l_x} \sum_{t=0}^{4} v^{t+1} \cdot d_{x+t} \\
&= \frac{1}{l_x} \left(v \cdot d_x + v^2 \cdot d_{x+1} + v^3 \cdot d_{x+2} + v^4 \cdot d_{x+3} + v^5 \cdot d_{x+4} \right) \\
&= (0.9709 \cdot 3 + 0.9426 \cdot 4 + 0.9151 \cdot 6 + 0.8885 \cdot 9 \\
&\quad + 0.8626 \cdot 14)/1{,}000 \\
&= 0.032
\end{aligned}
$$

For example, for a death benefit of $C = 100{,}000$, it can be multiplied by the present value obtained to get the present value of the benefit:

$$
C \cdot A^1_{x:\overline{5}|} = 100{,}000 \cdot 0.032 = 3{,}200.
$$

- *Pure endowment insurance on survival*: Unlike whole life and term life insurance policies, this is a policy that pays out if the policyholder survives for a period of time that is determined when the policy is purchased. More specifically, if the policyholder aged x is still alive after n years, the insurer agrees to pay them C. The probability that this payment will be made is, therefore, the probability that the policyholder, aged x when the policy is purchased, will survive to time n, i.e., $_np_x$. The present value can be expressed as

$$C \cdot v^n \cdot {}_np_x.$$

The actuarial notation of the present value of a pure endowment insurance for an amount of $C = 1$ to be paid if the policyholder aged x is still alive after n years is the following:

$$_nE_x = v^n \cdot {}_np_x = v^n \cdot \frac{l_{x+n}}{l_x}.$$

This is called the *survival discount factor*. It is the amount needed today to pay, in n years, one unit of currency to each of the l_{x+n} survivors of a group of people whose initial number was l_x. It is the product of two factors: the first includes the discount associated with interest (v^n), and the other includes the discount associated with survival (l_{x+n}/l_x).

We illustrate the flow resulting from the lump sum paid out on survival in figure 6.8.

Figure 6.8: Timeline for the payment of a lump sum C of an n-year pure endowment insurance.

Pure endowment insurance benefits

Using the technical bases in table 6.1, we estimate the present value of a lump sum $C = 1$ paid out if a policyholder aged x survives $n = 5$ years, using the following formula:

$$_5E_x = v^5 \cdot {}_5p_x = 0.8626 \cdot 0.964 = 0.832.$$

We find that the present value of this lump sum paid out on survival is $_5E_x = 0.832$.

- *Endowment insurance*: Endowment insurance can be described as a combination of term life insurance and pure endowment insurance. This type of insurance pays a death benefit if the policyholder dies during the period specified in the contract and also pays a lump sum if the policyholder is alive at the end of the period. For a term of n years with a death benefit of $C = 1$ and a survival benefit of $S = 1$, the present value of the benefits is determined by the following expression:

$$
\begin{aligned}
A_{x:\overline{n}|} &= A_{x:\overline{n}|}^1 + {}_nE_x = \frac{1}{l_x} \sum_{t=0}^{n-1} v^{t+1} \cdot d_{x+t} + v^n \cdot \frac{l_{x+n}}{l_x} \\
&= \frac{1}{l_x} \left(v \cdot d_x + v^2 \cdot d_{x+1} + v^3 \cdot d_{x+2} + \ldots + v^n \cdot d_{x+n-1} + v^n \cdot l_{x+n} \right).
\end{aligned}
$$

Note that the present value of the endowment insurance $A_{x:\overline{n}|}$ is equal to the sum of the present values of the term life insurance $A_{x:\overline{n}|}^1$ and the pure endowment insurance ${}_nE_x$.

Note that if the values of C and S are not a unit, C and S multiply only the relevant term, i.e., in general, we have

$$
A_{x:\overline{n}|} = C \cdot A_{x:\overline{n}|}^1 + S \cdot {}_nE_x,
$$

that is

$$
\begin{aligned}
A_{x:\overline{n}|} &= \frac{1}{l_x} \left(C \cdot v \cdot d_x + C \cdot v^2 \cdot d_{x+1} + C \cdot v^3 \cdot d_{x+2} + \ldots \right. \\
&\qquad \left. + C \cdot v^n \cdot d_{x+n-1} + S \cdot v^n \cdot l_{x+n} \right).
\end{aligned}
$$

Often, the duration of this type of policy is chosen to end when the policyholder reaches retirement age: the probability of receiving the lump sum if the policyholder survives is high, and most of the premium goes to the policyholder's savings. Thus, in the formula above, the single term with the largest value is $v^n \cdot l_{x+n}$ for reasonable values of x and n in practice. Note also that in all cases, whether the policyholder dies or survives, they receive a lump sum. This means that the premium is higher than for the other types of insurance we looked at.

The benefits paid by an endowment insurance policy are illustrated in figure 6.9.

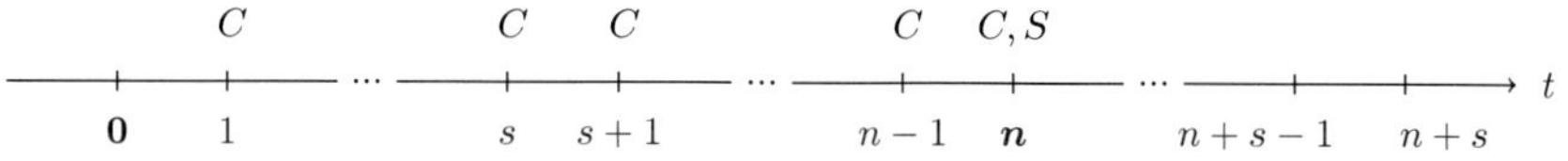

The payment of the lump sum C depends on the death of the policyholder (probability ${}_{t-1}p_x \cdot q_{x+t-1} = d_{x+t-1}/l_x$ at time t). The payment of the lump sum S depends on the survival of the policyholder (probability ${}_np_x = l_{x+n}/l_x$ at time n).

Figure 6.9: Timeline for death benefits C and survival benefits S of an n-year endowment insurance.

Endowment insurance benefits

Using the parameters in table 6.1 or the values obtained in the numerical examples above, we obtain the present value of a $n = 5$-year endowment insurance policy paying a death benefit of $C = 1$ and a survival benefit of $S = 1$ for a policyholder aged x, using the formula

$$A_{x:\overline{5}|} = A^1_{x:\overline{5}|} + {}_5E_x = 0.032 + 0.832 = 0.864.$$

The present value of the benefits paid by this policy is $A_{x:\overline{5}|} = 0.864$.

For a death benefit of $C = 100{,}000$ and a survival benefit of $S = 50{,}000$, the present value of the benefits is

$$C \cdot A^1_{x:\overline{5}|} + S \cdot {}_5E_x = 100{,}000 \cdot A^1_{x:\overline{5}|} + 50{,}000 \cdot {}_5E_x = 44{,}800.$$

Characteristics of annuity insurance benefits In the context of annuities, we distinguish between life annuities and temporary annuities. An annuity is a payment that the insurer makes to the policyholder at regular intervals until the policyholder's death or for a period of time specified in the contract. In the former case, it is called a life annuity, and in the latter case, it is called a temporary annuity. The frequency of payments can be annual, monthly, or even weekly. In Europe, payments are usually made on a monthly basis. For the sake of simplicity, we will assume that payments are made annually, hence the name "annuity." In the following, we will discuss life annuities and temporary annuities, both non-deferred and deferred, always assuming that payments are made at the beginning of the period, i.e., due. At the end of this section, we will also provide the formulas for the same annuities when they are immediate.

- *Non-deferred life annuities due or immediate*: A non-deferred life annuity due consists of the payment of a specified amount at the beginning of each year, beginning in the first year of the contract and continuing for the entire remaining life of the policyholder. Formally, the present value of such an annuity, which pays one unit for a policyholder aged x when the policy is purchased, is equal to

$$\ddot{a}_x = \sum_{t=0}^{(\omega-1)-x} v^t \cdot {}_tp_x = \frac{1}{l_x} \sum_{t=0}^{(\omega-1)-x} v^t \cdot l_{x+t}$$

$$= 1 + \sum_{t=1}^{(\omega-1)-x} v^t \cdot {}_tp_x = 1 + \frac{1}{l_x} \sum_{t=1}^{(\omega-1)-x} v^t \cdot l_{x+t}.$$

The first payment is made at time $t = 0$, when the contract is signed, at a time when the policyholder is alive (${}_0p_x = 1$), hence the "1" as the first term of the sum. Since ω refers to the age that no one ever reaches, the last term of the sum, at $t = \omega - 1 - x$, includes the factor $l_{\omega-1}$. This is because the factor $l_\omega = 0$.

If the same life annuity is immediate, with payments made at the end of the period, the value is

$$a_x = \sum_{t=1}^{(\omega-1)-x} v^t \cdot {}_t p_x = \frac{1}{l_x} \sum_{t=1}^{(\omega-1)-x} v^t \cdot l_{x+t}.$$

Thus, we observe that $\ddot{a}_x = 1 + a_x$.

- *Deferred life annuities due or immediate*: A deferred life annuity due consists of the payment of a specified amount at the beginning of each year for the entire remaining life of the policyholder. However, the first payment is not made until some time has elapsed (hence the term "deferred"). The expression for the present value of a life annuity due deferred by s years for a policyholder aged x is written as follows:

$$_{s|}\ddot{a}_x = \sum_{t=s}^{(\omega-1)-x} v^t \cdot {}_t p_x = \frac{1}{l_x} \sum_{t=s}^{(\omega-1)-x} v^t \cdot l_{x+t}.$$

Similarly, the same annuity immediate has a present value of

$$_{s|}a_x = \sum_{t=s+1}^{(\omega-1)-x} v^t \cdot {}_t p_x = \frac{1}{l_x} \sum_{t=s+1}^{(\omega-1)-x} v^t \cdot l_{x+t}.$$

- *Non-deferred temporary annuities due or immediate*: The formulas used to calculate the present value of temporary annuities are identical to those used for level premiums above. This is because a temporary annuity consists of the payment of a certain amount at regular intervals for a predetermined period of time. With a non-deferred temporary annuity due, the amount is paid at the beginning of each year, starting with the first year (see figure 6.3). The present value of a non-deferred temporary annuity due that pays a benefit of $C = 1$ each year for n years to a policyholder aged x at inception is written as $\ddot{a}_{x:\overline{n|}}$. This notation, and of course, the value itself, is identical to the present value of the non-deferred annual premiums due. We have

$$\ddot{a}_{x:\overline{n|}} = \sum_{t=0}^{n-1} v^t \cdot {}_t p_x = \frac{1}{l_x} \sum_{t=0}^{n-1} v^t \cdot l_{x+t}.$$

If the same non-deferred annuity is immediate (see figure 6.4), we have an expression that is identical to that for non-deferred annual premiums immediate:

$$a_{x:\overline{n|}} = \sum_{t=1}^{n} v^t \cdot {}_t p_x = \frac{1}{l_x} \sum_{t=1}^{n} v^t \cdot l_{x+t}.$$

- *Deferred temporary annuities due or immediate*: A deferred temporary annuity due consists of an amount paid periodically for a predetermined period of time, beginning after a latency period. Here, we assume that a payment is made at the beginning of each year after a certain amount of time has elapsed (see figure 6.5). The formula for the present value of this annuity is identical to the formula for the present value of the deferred annual premiums due. For an individual aged x when the policy is purchased and who receives these annuities for n years after a latency period of s years, the present value is written as:

$$_{s|}\ddot{a}_{x:\overline{n}|} = \sum_{t=s}^{n+s-1} v^t \cdot {_t}p_x = \frac{1}{l_x} \sum_{t=s}^{n+s-1} v^t \cdot l_{x+t}.$$

If the same annuity is immediate (see figure 6.6), its value is calculated as follows:

$$_{s|}a_{x:\overline{n}|} = \sum_{t=s+1}^{n+s} v^t \cdot {_t}p_x = \frac{1}{l_x} \sum_{t=s+1}^{n+s} v^t \cdot l_{x+t}.$$

The expressions for premiums, lump-sum benefits, and annuity benefits are convenient when it comes to calculating these premiums or benefits in the context of life insurance. These expressions, multiplied by the amount of the premium—typically A for a single premium and P for level premiums—or the amount of the lump-sum or annuity benefit—typically C—can be used to establish the equation corresponding to the point of equilibrium between premiums and benefits, according to the principle of actuarial equivalence. Table 6.2 summarizes the various expressions introduced in this chapter.

Examples of premium calculations   In the following section, we first present some numerical applications with concrete examples of insurance policies that combine premium calculations depending on the benefits offered. We use three applications: a single-premium term insurance policy, a level-premium endowment insurance policy, and a single-premium temporary annuity immediate. These examples were chosen for illustrative purposes, but it should be noted that they represent only a small portion of the many combinations of premiums and benefits that exist.

Term insurance with a single premium

An insurer offers $l_x = 1,000$ potential customers, all aged x, a term life insurance policy for $n = 5$ years with a death benefit of $C = 10,000$ francs. Our goal is to determine the single premium A that each policyholder should pay using the technical bases in table 6.1. We illustrate the flows associated with this insurance in figure 6.10.

6.3. Basics of life insurance pricing

Characteristics of life insurance premiums

- Single premium (at the beginning of the contract): 1
- Non-deferred annual premiums due (n payments, at the beginning of each year)

$$\ddot{a}_{x:\overline{n}|} = \sum_{t=0}^{n-1} v^t \cdot {}_t p_x = \frac{1}{l_x} \sum_{t=0}^{n-1} v^t \cdot l_{x+t}$$

- Non-deferred annual premiums immediate (n payments, at the end of each year)

$$a_{x:\overline{n}|} = \sum_{t=1}^{n} v^t \cdot {}_t p_x = \frac{1}{l_x} \sum_{t=1}^{n} v^t \cdot l_{x+t}$$

- Deferred annual premiums due (n payments, at the beginning of each year, after s years)

$$_{s|}\ddot{a}_{x:\overline{n}|} = \sum_{t=s}^{n+s-1} v^t \cdot {}_t p_x = \frac{1}{l_x} \sum_{t=s}^{n+s-1} v^t \cdot l_{x+t}$$

- Deferred annual premiums immediate (n payments, at the end of each year, after s years)

$$_{s|}a_{x:\overline{n}|} = \sum_{t=s+1}^{n+s} v^t \cdot {}_t p_x = \frac{1}{l_x} \sum_{t=s+1}^{n+s} v^t \cdot l_{x+t}$$

Characteristics of lump-sum insurance benefits

- Whole life insurance (benefit paid at the end of the year in the event of death)

$$A_x = \sum_{t=0}^{\omega-1-x} v^{t+1} \cdot {}_t p_x \cdot q_{x+t} = \frac{1}{l_x} \sum_{t=0}^{\omega-1-x} v^{t+1} \cdot d_{x+t}$$

- Term life insurance (benefit paid at the end of the year in the event of death)

$$A^1_{x:\overline{n}|} = \sum_{t=0}^{n-1} v^{t+1} \cdot {}_t p_x \cdot q_{x+t} = \frac{1}{l_x} \sum_{t=0}^{n-1} v^{t+1} \cdot d_{x+t}$$

- Pure endowment insurance (benefit paid at the end of the nth year on survival)

$$_n E_x = v^n \cdot {}_n p_x = v^n \cdot \frac{l_{x+n}}{l_x}$$

Characteristics of annuity insurance benefits

- Non-deferred life annuity due (payments at the beginning of each year)

$$\ddot{a}_x = \sum_{t=0}^{\omega-1-x} v^t \cdot {}_t p_x = \frac{1}{l_x} \sum_{t=0}^{\omega-1-x} v^t \cdot l_{x+t}$$

- Non-deferred life annuity immediate (payments at the end of each year)

$$a_x = \sum_{t=1}^{\omega-1-x} v^t \cdot {}_t p_x = \frac{1}{l_x} \sum_{t=1}^{\omega-1-x} v^t \cdot l_{x+t}$$

- Deferred life annuity due (payments at the beginning of each year, after s years)

$$_{s|}\ddot{a}_x = \sum_{t=s}^{\omega-1-x} v^t \cdot {}_t p_x = \frac{1}{l_x} \sum_{t=s}^{\omega-1-x} v^t \cdot l_{x+t}$$

- Deferred life annuity immediate (payments at the end of each year, after s years)

$$_{s|}a_x = \sum_{t=s+1}^{\omega-1-x} v^t \cdot {}_t p_x = \frac{1}{l_x} \sum_{t=s+1}^{\omega-1-x} v^t \cdot l_{x+t}$$

- Temporary annuities: same expressions as annual premiums

Table 6.2: Summary of the expressions that represent life insurance premiums and lump-sum and annuity insurance benefits per payment unit.

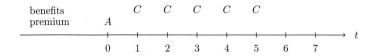

The payment of the lump sum C depends on the death of the policyholder (probability $_{t-1}p_x \cdot q_{x+t-1} = d_{x+t-1}/l_x$ at time t).

Figure 6.10: Timeline for a term insurance policy with a single premium A and death benefit C.

To calculate the single premium A that each policyholder should pay, we seek financial equilibrium according to the equivalence principle. This means that the premiums paid by the l_x policyholders must be equal to their expected benefits:

$$l_x \cdot A = C \cdot \left(v \cdot d_x + v^2 \cdot d_{x+1} + v^3 \cdot d_{x+2} + v^4 \cdot d_{x+3} + v^5 \cdot d_{x+4} \right).$$

Remembering the notations introduced earlier, we also have the following equivalent equation:

$$l_x \cdot A = l_x \cdot C \cdot A^1_{x:\overline{5}|},$$

where $A^1_{x:\overline{5}|}$ refers to the present value of the lump-sum benefit paid by 5-year term life insurance policy purchased by a policyholder at age x. By rearranging the equation, we isolate the term that refers to the single premium, which yields

$$A = C \cdot A^1_{x:\overline{5}|}.$$

By substituting the numerical values of C and $A^1_{x:\overline{5}|}$, we find the single premium A that the insurer must receive in order to achieve financial equilibrium:

$$A = 10{,}000 \cdot 0.03225 = 322.5.$$

The premium $A = 322.5$ francs is the pure premium. In practice, the insurer will then add margins to this premium, resulting in the market premium offered to customers. Finally, we can check whether the sum of the premiums collected at time $t = 0$ exactly covers the benefits paid. To do this, we look at the fund initially available ($l_x \cdot A = 1{,}000 \cdot 322.5$), to which we add interest each year at a rate of $i = 3\%$ (see table 6.1), and from which we subtract death benefits each year. These operations are illustrated in table 6.3. For example, during the first year, the fund of 322,500 francs earns 9,700 francs in interest and pays out benefits totaling 30,000 francs. Thus, at the end of year $t = 1$, the remaining balance in the fund is 302,200 francs. After five years, we see that the balance of the fund is zero.

Time t	Age	Interest	Deaths	Benefits	Fund
0	x				322,500
1	$x+1$	9,700	3	30,000	302,200
2	$x+2$	9,100	4	40,000	271,200
3	$x+3$	8,100	6	60,000	219,400
4	$x+4$	6,600	9	90,000	136,000
5	$x+5$	4,100	14	140,000	0

Interest, benefit, and fund values are based on a single premium of 322.5 francs and are reported rounded to the nearest hundred (retaining the unrounded value for calculations).

Table 6.3: Illustration of the equilibrium between premiums collected and benefits paid for a term insurance policy with a single premium.

Endowment insurance with level premiums

An insurer offers $l_x = 1,000$ potential customers, all aged x, a $n = 5$-year endowment insurance policy with a death and survival benefit of $C = S = 10,000$ francs. The level premiums of P are due and not deferred. The technical bases are those of table 6.1. The flows associated with this policy are shown in figure 6.11.

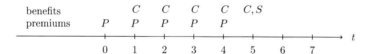

The premium payments P depend on the survival of the policyholder (probability $_tp_x$ at time t). The payment of the lump sum C depends on the death of the policyholder (probability $_{t-1}p_x \cdot q_{x+t-1} = d_{x+t-1}/l_x$ at time t). The payment of the lump sum S depends on the survival of the policyholder (probability $_np_x = l_{x+n}/l_x$ at time n).

Figure 6.11: Timeline for an endowment insurance policy with level premiums P, death benefit C, and survival benefit S.

To determine the value P of the level premiums, the insurer follows the equivalence principle. Therefore, we have

$$l_x \cdot P \cdot \left(1 + v \cdot {}_1p_x + v^2 \cdot {}_2p_x + v^3 \cdot {}_3p_x + v^4 \cdot {}_4p_x\right)$$
$$= C \cdot \left(v \cdot d_x + v^2 \cdot d_{x+1} + v^3 \cdot d_{x+2} + +v^4 \cdot d_{x+3} + v^5 \cdot d_{x+4}\right) + S \cdot v^n \cdot l_{x+n}.$$

Using the actuarial notation introduced earlier, we have

$$l_x \cdot P \cdot \ddot{a}_{x:\overline{5}|} = l_x \cdot \left(C \cdot A^1_{x:\overline{5}|} + S \cdot {}_5E_x\right),$$

and since we know that $S = C$, we can write

$$l_x \cdot P \cdot \ddot{a}_{x:\overline{5}|} = l_x \cdot C \cdot A_{x:\overline{5}|}.$$

By isolating the level premium P in the equation, we get the following expression:

$$P \cdot \ddot{a}_{x:\overline{5}|} = C \cdot A_{x:\overline{5}|} \qquad \Longleftrightarrow \qquad P = \frac{C \cdot A_{x:\overline{5}|}}{\ddot{a}_{x:\overline{5}|}}.$$

After introducing the numerical values, we find

$$P = \frac{C \cdot A_{x:\overline{5}|}}{\ddot{a}_{x:\overline{5}|}} = \frac{10{,}000 \cdot 0.864}{4.676} = 1{,}848.$$

The pure level premium P is, therefore, 1,848 francs.

Non-deferred temporary annuity with a single premium

An insurer offers $l_x = 1{,}000$ potential clients, all aged x, a non-deferred temporary annuity for $n = 5$ years, with annuities of $C = 10{,}000$ francs paid at the end of each year. Using the technical bases in table 6.1, we determine the required single premium A. The flows associated with this contract are shown in figure 6.12.

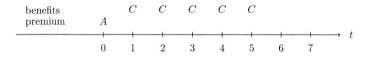

The annuity payments C depend on the survival of the policyholder (probability $_tp_x = l_{x+t}/l_x$ at time t).

Figure 6.12: Timeline for a non-deferred temporary annuity with a single premium A and annuities C.

According to the principle of actuarial equivalence, the single premium A charged by the insurer must satisfy the following equation:

$$l_x \cdot A = C \cdot \left(v \cdot l_{x+1} + v^2 \cdot l_{x+2} + v^3 \cdot l_{x+3} + v^4 \cdot l_{x+4} + v^5 \cdot l_{x+5} \right),$$

or, in other terms:

$$l_x \cdot A = l_x \cdot C \cdot a_{x:\overline{5}|}.$$

We solve this equation for A and introduce the numerical values, which gives

$$A = C \cdot a_{x:\overline{5}|} = 10{,}000 \cdot 4.508 = 45{,}080.$$

Therefore, the pure single premium is $A = 45{,}080$ francs.

Finally, we discuss two types of products that we will study without numerical applications. These are a non-deferred life annuity with a single premium and a deferred life annuity with level premiums.

- *Life annuity due with a single premium*: A life annuity due pays out an amount C at the beginning of each year for the remainder of the policy-holder's life. A single premium A is paid at the beginning of the contract. This type of policy is used, for example, by people who want to enjoy their wealth in the form of a guaranteed annuity or who want to convert a lottery win into a life annuity. The flows associated with this insurance are shown in figure 6.13.

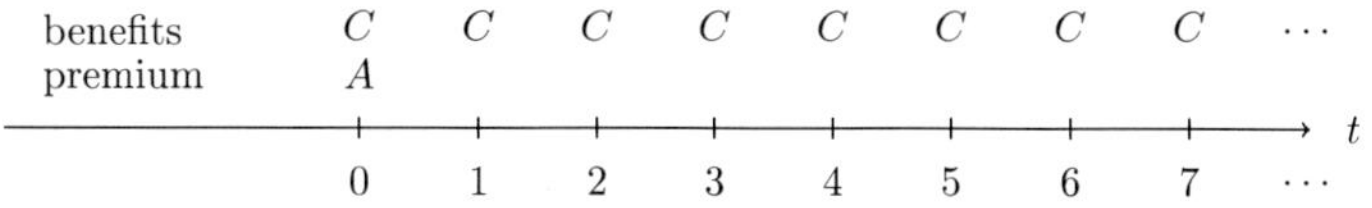

| benefits | | C | C | C | C | C | C | C | C | $\cdots$ |
| premium | | A | | | | | | | | |

$$
\begin{array}{ccccccccc}
0 & 1 & 2 & 3 & 4 & 5 & 6 & 7 & \cdots
\end{array} \quad t
$$

The annuity payments C depend on the survival of the policyholder (probability $_tp_x = l_{x+t}/l_x$ at time t).

Figure 6.13: Timeline for a life annuity due with a single premium A and annuities C.

The relationship between the single premium A and the annuity C is as follows:

$$
\begin{aligned}
A &= C \cdot \left(1 + v \cdot {}_1p_x + v^2 \cdot {}_2p_x + v^3 \cdot {}_3p_x + \ldots \right) \\
&= C \cdot \ddot{a}_x = C \cdot \sum_{t=0}^{(\omega-1)-x} v^t \cdot {}_tp_x.
\end{aligned}
$$

- *Deferred life annuity with level premiums*: Old-age pension insurance policies typically include a period during the policyholder's working life in which funds are saved or accumulated until retirement age, followed by a decumulation period that is deferred to coincide with retirement age. This type of insurance product, therefore, includes an initial period during which premiums are accumulated, followed by a second period during which a life annuity is paid. To give a more concrete example, let us consider a person at the age of $x = 25$ who starts working and pays into pension insurance at the beginning of each year for $s = 40$ years. A life annuity, deferred by s years, is paid when the individual reaches the retirement age of $x + s = 65$ at the beginning of each year. The timeline for this product is illustrated in figure 6.14.

The accumulated premiums (due, non-deferred, over s years, see figure 6.3) can be expressed as follows:

$$
\ddot{a}_{x:\overline{s}|} = \sum_{t=0}^{s-1} v^t \cdot {}_tp_x.
$$

The payments for a life annuity due deferred by s years are:

$$
{}_{s|}\ddot{a}_x = \sum_{t=s}^{(\omega-1)-x} v^t \cdot {}_tp_x.
$$

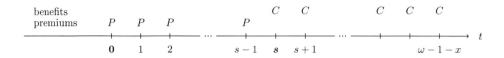

The premium payments P and the annuity payments C depend on the survival of the policy-holder (probability $_tp_x$ at time t).

Figure 6.14: Timeline for a deferred life annuity with level premiums P and annuity C.

Financial equilibrium gives the relationship between the level premiums P and an annuity of C:

$$P \cdot \ddot{a}_{x:\overline{s}|} = C \cdot {}_{s|}\ddot{a}_x,$$

which makes it possible to determine what premiums must be paid in order to receive a predetermined annuity; or, conversely, to determine what annuity will be received based on a known amount of premiums. The latter relationship can be made more explicit:

$$P \cdot \left(1 + v \cdot {}_1p_x + v^2 \cdot {}_2p_x + \ldots + v^{s-1} \cdot {}_{s-1}p_x\right)$$
$$= C \cdot \left(v^s \cdot {}_sp_x + v^{s+1} \cdot {}_{s+1}p_x + \ldots + v^{(\omega-1)-x} \cdot {}_{(\omega-1)-x}p_x\right),$$

which, after multiplying both sides by l_x, can be written as

$$P \cdot \left(l_x + v \cdot l_{x+1} + v^2 \cdot l_{x+2} + \ldots + v^{s-1} \cdot l_{x+s-1}\right)$$
$$= C \cdot \left(v^s \cdot l_{x+s} + v^{s+1} \cdot l_{s+1} + \ldots + v^{(\omega-1)-x} \cdot l_{\omega-1}\right).$$

With $x = 25$ and $s = 40$ we get

$$P \cdot \left(1 + v \cdot {}_1p_{25} + v^2 \cdot {}_2p_{25} + \ldots + v^{39} \cdot {}_{39}p_{25}\right)$$
$$= C \cdot \left(v^{40} \cdot {}_{40}p_{25} + v^{41} \cdot {}_{41}p_{25} + \ldots + v^{\omega-26} \cdot {}_{\omega-26}p_{25}\right),$$

or

$$P \cdot \left(l_{25} + v \cdot l_{26} + v^2 \cdot l_{27} + \ldots + v^{39} \cdot l_{64}\right)$$
$$= C \cdot \left(v^{40} \cdot l_{65} + v^{41} \cdot l_{66} + \ldots + v^{\omega-26} \cdot l_{\omega-1}\right).$$

The latter relationship shows how this type of insurance works in concrete terms. The values of the various actuarial parameters $_tp_x$ can be found in mortality tables, and the discount rate v is determined by estimating the interest rate i.

6.4   Mathematical reserves

The principle of actuarial equivalence—see definition 6.1—requires that the present value of premiums and the present value of benefits be equal. This principle is satisfied at the time the contract is issued ($t = 0$). However, this initial equality does not hold throughout the life of the contract and must be adjusted for several reasons in order for the equivalence principle to continue to hold. First, the probabilities of death and survival change from one year to the next. In particular, the probability of death increases, and the probability of survival decreases. Second, if the contract includes a savings component, it is generally not constant. The funds earmarked for the payment of future benefits (death benefit or annuity) do not belong to the insurer but are future obligations of the insurer. In order to ensure that these commitments are honored at all times, the insurer must set aside reserves on its balance sheet. This is where the concept of a mathematical reserve comes in. From an actuarial perspective, this mathematical reserve is the excess of the present value of future benefits over the present value of (current and) future premiums. If we write $_tL$ as the random variable corresponding to the difference between the present value of future benefits and the present value of premiums, the mathematical reserve is the expected value of that difference, i.e., $\mathbb{E}(_tL)$. The value of $_tL$ depends on the policyholder's age x, hence the typical notation $_tL_x$.

Definition 6.5 (*Mathematical reserve*)

> *The **mathematical reserve** at time t, noted $_tV_x$, is the expected excess of the present value of future benefits over the present value of future premiums for an individual aged x at the beginning of the contract. If the random variable $_tL_x$ refers to this excess, then:*
> $$_tV_x = \mathbb{E}(_tL_x).$$

The mathematical reserve can be thought of as a fund whose value changes as a function of premium payments, interest, and benefits paid so that they form a balanced whole over the life of the contract. As mentioned above, at the beginning of the contract, the present value of the benefits is exactly equal to the present value of the premiums. Thus, the mathematical reserve at time $t = 0$ is zero, i.e., for any age x, we always have:
$$_0V_x = 0.$$

There are three methods for calculating the mathematical reserves: the recursive approach and the prospective and retrospective methods.

Recursive method In a recursive approach, we proceed period by period, updating the mathematical reserve in each period. Here, we consider the concept of the terminal reserve, calculated at the end of the year, i.e., after the payment of the year's benefits but before the collection of the next year's premiums. Let us consider the example of a term life insurance policy with level premiums P and death benefit C. With annual premiums due, i.e., at the beginning of the year, we derive the value of the reserve $_tV_x$ for the current year $t > 0$ using the following formula:
$$l_{x+t} \cdot {_tV_x} = l_{x+t-1} \cdot (_{t-1}V_x + P) \cdot (1 + i) - C \cdot d_{x+t-1}.$$

The left-hand side of the equation, namely $l_{x+t} \cdot {}_tV_x$, is the aggregate value of the individual reserves at time t. This is the collective value of all policy-holders, corresponding to the reserve for each policyholder ${}_tV_x$ at time t multi-plied by the number of living policyholders at time t. The right-hand side, that is $l_{x+t-1} \cdot ({}_{t-1}V_x + P) \cdot (1 + i) - C \cdot d_{x+t-1}$, corresponds to the value of the fund at the end of the year. It consists of the previous year's reserve ${}_{t-1}V_x$ plus the current year's premiums P, aggregated over all l_{x+t-1} policyholders in year $t - 1$. The fund is credited with the interest rate i, and the benefits paid at the end of the year, $C \cdot d_{x+t-1}$, are subtracted from the fund.

The equation above, which applies to term life insurance, must be adapted to the characteristics of each contract. Thus, a different equation is used in the case of an annuity, survival benefit, or premiums immediate. Equations must be constructed for each specific case, taking into account the premiums collected, the benefits paid, and the applicable interest rate.

If, with the term life insurance above, the premiums are immediate, the relation-ship is

$$l_{x+t} \cdot {}_tV_x = l_{x+t-1} \cdot {}_{t-1}V_x \cdot (1 + i) + l_{x+t-1} \cdot P - C \cdot d_{x+t-1}.$$

In this equation, note that the interest i does not apply to the premiums because they are paid at the end of the year.

Finally, if there are no premiums to pay in a given year t, the premiums P no longer appear, and we have the following recurrence relation:

$$l_{x+t} \cdot {}_tV_x = l_{x+t-1} \cdot {}_{t-1}V_x \cdot (1 + i) - C \cdot d_{x+t-1}.$$

This is the case, for example, for years $t > 1$ for single-premium policies payable at inception.

Calculation of reserves for a contract with level premiums

Consider the example of a term insurance policy for $n = 3$ years with a death benefit of $C = 100{,}000$ francs offered to $l_x = 1{,}000$ policyholders aged x. The contract involves the payment of non-deferred level premiums paid at the beginning of the year. The death benefit is paid at the end of the year of death. The technical bases with $i = 3\%$ are those of table 6.1. We propose to determine the annual premium P for this contract and the individual mathematical reserve after 1, 2, and 3 years.

The annual premium is calculated according to the principle of actuarial equiv-alence:

$$P \cdot \ddot{a}_{x:\overline{3|}} = C \cdot A^1_{x:\overline{3|}},$$

i.e., the premium P must satisfy the equation:

$$P \cdot \left(l_x + v \cdot l_{x+1} + v^2 \cdot l_{x+2}\right) = C \cdot \left(v \cdot d_x + v^2 \cdot d_{x+1} + v^3 \cdot d_{x+2}\right)$$
$$\Leftrightarrow \quad P = C \cdot \frac{v \cdot d_x + v^2 \cdot d_{x+1} + v^2 \cdot d_{x+2}}{l_x + v \cdot l_{x+1} + v^3 \cdot l_{x+2}}$$

Introducing the numerical values, we have

$$P = C \cdot \frac{0.9709 \cdot 3 + 0.9426 \cdot 4 + 0.9151 \cdot 6}{1{,}000 + 0.9709 \cdot 997 + 0.9426 \cdot 993} = 419.2.$$

The annual premium for this policy is, therefore, 419.2 francs.

The prospective mathematical reserve satisfies the following recurrence formula for $t = 0, 1, 2$:

$$l_{x+t+1} \cdot {}_{t+1}V_x = l_{x+t} \cdot \left({}_t V_x + P\right) \cdot (1 + i) - C \cdot d_{x+t}.$$

At the end of the first year, the reserve ${}_1 V_x$ is such that

$$l_{x+1} \cdot {}_1 V_x = l_x \cdot \left({}_0 V_x + P\right) \cdot (1 + i) - C \cdot d_x.$$

Introducing the numerical values and knowing that ${}_0 V_x = 0$, we have

$$_1 V_x = \frac{1{,}000 \cdot (0 + 419.2) \cdot (1 + 0.03) - 300{,}000}{997} = 132.2.$$

By applying the recurrence formula, we obtain the results shown in table 6.4, which can be reconstructed step by step. We find ${}_2 V_x = 167.4$ and ${}_3 V_x = 0$.

The individual reserve ${}_t V_x$ is obtained by dividing the value of the fund at the end of the previous year by the number of survivors l_{x+t}. The level premium is calculated so that the present values of premiums and benefits are equal. Thus, the premiums and interest are exactly enough to pay the benefits. At the end of the contract, i.e., at the end of the nth year, the fund has a balance of zero. The same applies to the mathematical reserve. Note that in our example, the fund and the mathematical reserve increase in the first two years to build up the provision needed to pay the higher benefits in the third year (6 deaths, as opposed to 3 and 4 in the first and second years, respectively).

Year t	Age	l_{x+t}	$_tV_x$	P	$l_{x+t} \cdot (_tV_x + P)$	Interest	d_{x+t}	Benefits	Fund
0	x	1,000	0.0	419.2	419,200	12,600	3	300,000	131,800
1	$x+1$	997	132.2	419.2	549,700	16,500	4	400,000	166,200
2	$x+2$	993	167.4	419.2	582,500	17,500	6	600,000	0
3	$x+3$	987	0.0						

Interest, benefit, and fund values are based on a single premium of 419.2 francs and are reported rounded to the nearest hundred (retaining the unrounded value for calculations).

Table 6.4: Illustration of mathematical reserves in term insurance with level premiums.

Calculation of reserves for a contract with a single premium

Now consider the example of a term insurance policy for $n = 5$ years with a death benefit of $C = 10,000$ francs offered to $l_x = 1,000$ policyholders aged x. The insurer applies the technical bases of table 6.1. We have seen above that the single premium paid at the start of the contract is $A = 322.5$ francs. What is the individual mathematical reserve at the end of each year?

In the case of a single premium, there is no series of constant premiums P, but rather a series in which the first premium is the single premium A, and all others are zero. At the end of the first year, the reserve $_1V_x$ is such that

$$l_{x+1} \cdot {_1V_x} = l_x \cdot (_0V_x + A) \cdot (1 + i) - C \cdot d_x,$$

where $_0V_x = 0$. Introducing the numerical values, we find $_1V_x = 303.1$.

For the following years, with no premiums paid, the recurrence formula for $t = 1, 2, 3, 4$ is:

$$l_{x+t+1} \cdot {_{t+1}V_x} = l_{x+t} \cdot {_tV_x} \cdot (1 + i) - C \cdot d_{x+t}.$$

We report the values we found for $_2V_x$, $_3V_x$, $_4V_x$, and $_5V_x$ in table 6.5, where we find the same values for the fund reported above in table 6.3 for the same policy. Note that the single premium is held as a mathematical reserve over the life of the policy to pay the benefits.

Prospective and retrospective methods To know the mathematical reserve at time t, the prospective method uses the discounting of cash flows that will occur between t and the end of the contract (see Bowers et al., 1997; Promislow, 2015). This makes it possible to calculate the mathematical reserve reference to past payments. In this case, the formula for the mathematical reserve $_tV_x$ is

$$_tV_x = \mathbb{E}(_tL_x | T(x) > t),$$

Year t	Age	l_x	$_tV_x$	P	$l_{x+t} \cdot (_tV_x + P)$	Interest	d_x	Benefits	Fund
0	x	1,000	0.0	322.5	322,500	9,700	3	30,000	302,200
1	$x+1$	997	303.1	0.0	302,200	9,100	4	40,000	271,200
2	$x+2$	993	273.1	0.0	271,200	8,100	6	60,000	219,400
3	$x+3$	987	222.3	0.0	219,400	6,600	9	90,000	136,000
4	$x+4$	978	139.1	0.0	136,000	4,100	14	140,000	0
5	$x+5$	964	0.0						

Interest, benefit, and fund values are based on a single premium of 322.5 francs and are reported rounded to the nearest hundred (retaining the unrounded value for calculations).

Table 6.5: Illustration of mathematical reserves in term insurance with a single premium.

where $_tL_x$ is the random variable representing the difference between the present value of future benefits and the present value of future premiums. The random variable $T(x)$ represents the future life expectancy of policyholders at age x.

We illustrate the idea behind this formula by using the case of a term life insurance policy covering n years and paying a death benefit of C, with non-deferred level premiums P paid at the beginning of the year, for policyholders aged x when the policy is purchased. The expression for the mathematical reserve at time t, using the prospective method and actuarial notation, is

$$_tV_x = C \cdot A^{1}_{x+t:\overline{n-t|}} - P \cdot \ddot{a}_{x+t:\overline{n-t|}}.$$

This shows how easily this type of insurance can be expressed using actuarial notation. The expression at time t typically includes the stream of benefits paid by term insurance to a policyholder aged $x + t$ over $n - t$ years and the stream of annual premiums paid by a policyholder aged $x + t$ over $n - t$ years. This formulation must be adapted for each specific situation.

Actuarial formulas for prospective mathematical reserves

We present here the actuarial formulas for prospective mathematical reserves for selected contract examples. We use C to represent lump sum benefits, A a single premium, and P periodic (annual) premiums. In the following formulas, we always assume that $t > 0$.

- Whole life insurance with single premium:

$$_tV_x = \begin{cases} C \cdot A_{x+t} - A & \text{if } t = \text{year of premium payment} \\ C \cdot A_{x+t} & \text{if } t \neq \text{year of premium payment} \end{cases}$$

- Whole life insurance due with annual premiums over n years:

$$_tV_x = \begin{cases} C \cdot A_{x+t} - P \cdot \ddot{a}_{x+t:\overline{n-t}|} & \text{if } t < n \\ C \cdot A_{x+t} & \text{if } t = n \end{cases}$$

- Whole life insurance due with annual premiums over n years, deferred by s years:

$$_tV_x = \begin{cases} C \cdot A_{x+t} & \text{if } t < s \\ C \cdot A_{x+t} - P \cdot {}_{s|}\ddot{a}_{x+t-s:\overline{n-(t-s)}|} & \text{if } s \le t < n \\ C \cdot A_{x+t} & \text{if } t \ge n \end{cases}$$

- Whole life insurance immediate with annual premiums over n years:

$$_tV_x = \begin{cases} C \cdot A_{x+t} - P \cdot a_{x+t:\overline{n-t}|} & \text{if } t \le n \\ C \cdot A_{x+t} & \text{if } t > n \end{cases}$$

- Term life insurance due with annual premiums over n years:

$$_tV_x = \begin{cases} C \cdot A^{1}_{x+t:\overline{n-t}|} - P \cdot \ddot{a}_{x+t:\overline{n-t}|} & \text{if } t < n \\ 0 & \text{if } t = n \end{cases}$$

- Pure endowment insurance due with annual premiums over n years:

$$_tV_x = \begin{cases} C \cdot {}_{n-t}E_{x+t} & \text{if } t < n \\ C & \text{if } t = n \end{cases}$$

- Endowment insurance due with annual premiums over n years:

$$_tV_x = \begin{cases} C \cdot A_{x+t:\overline{n-t}|} - P \cdot \ddot{a}_{x+t:\overline{n-t}|} & \text{if } t < n \\ C & \text{if } t = n \end{cases}$$

- Non-deferred life annuity due with annual premiums over n years:

$$_tV_x = \begin{cases} C \cdot a_{x+t} - P \cdot \ddot{a}_{x+t:\overline{n-t}|} & \text{if } t \le n \\ C \cdot a_{x+t} & \text{if } t = n \end{cases}$$

- Non-deferred temporary annuity with single premium:

$$_tV_x = \begin{cases} C \cdot a_{x+t:\overline{n-t}|} - A & \text{if } t = \text{year of premium payment} \\ C \cdot a_{x+t:\overline{n-t}|} & \text{if } t \ne \text{year of premium payment} \end{cases}$$

The mathematical reserve at time t can also be determined using the retrospective method. Here, the goal is to determine the reserve at t on the basis of payments already made. As explained by Dellinger (2006), the retrospective reserve expresses the mathematical reserve in terms of past premiums and benefits. Thus, the formulas used express the reserve as the excess value of all premiums collected over all benefits paid. An equivalent view is to understand that the value of premiums at any time t must equal the value of benefits paid and benefits to be paid. For example, in calculating the reserve for a whole life insurance policy with annual premiums due for a policyholder aged x when the policy is purchased, the reserve at time t using the retrospective method is

$$_tV_x = P \cdot \ddot{s}_{x:\overline{t|}} - \frac{(1+i)^t}{_tp_x} \cdot A^1_{x:\overline{t|}},$$

where $\ddot{s}_{x:\overline{t|}} = \ddot{a}_{x:\overline{t|}} \, / \, _tE_x$ corresponds to the future value (the opposite operation to discounting), at time t, of the premiums already paid. The equation shows that only past information is used to calculate the present value of the reserve at time t.

In figure 6.15, we illustrate the view that must be taken in order to calculate prospective and retrospective reserves at time t. It should be noted that in the examples given, we only consider the discrete formulation of reserves. It is theoretically possible to calculate the value of mathematical reserves at any non-integer time t using continuous formulas.

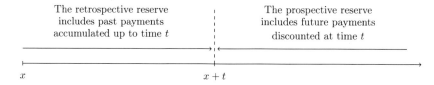

Figure 6.15: Illustration of the perspectives adopted for the calculation of mathematical reserves at time t using the prospective and retrospective methods.

6.5 Non-life insurance

In this chapter, we study the pricing of non-life insurance products. As we saw in section 5.4, there is a wide variety of insurance products (see figure 5.7), and non-life insurance products differ from life insurance products in several important ways. First, the amount of compensation paid out by a non-life insurance policy depends on the severity of the loss, while the benefits of a life insurance product are, in principle, well-defined and often fixed in advance. For example, a comprehensive motor vehicle, fire, or water damage policy covers actual losses incurred by the policyholder, while a life insurance policy pays a predetermined benefit when the insured dies. Second, non-life insurance policies are more often of shorter duration, generally covering one year or at least renewable each year. Life insurance policies generally cover a longer period of time. A life insurance policy often covers more than ten years, and if it includes savings and an old-age annuity, it may cover more than fifty years. Finally, the level of risk in non-life insurance means that more factors need to be taken into account, often more than in life insurance.

Client segmentation In a competitive market, it is necessary to take into account risk factors and determine an appropriate premium for each type of policyholder. To illustrate this, consider a non-life insurance product for which the insurer charges the same premium, CHF 150, to all policyholders. Suppose it sells this product to n policyholders who are divided into two groups, A and B, of equal size $n/2$. After analyzing the factors that influence risk, the insurer determines that the expected cost of a policyholder in group A is 100 francs, while the expected cost of a policyholder in group B is 200 francs. The average cost per policyholder is

$$\frac{\frac{n}{2} \cdot 100 + \frac{n}{2} \cdot 200}{n} = 150.$$

Thus, the average cost per policyholder is equal to the premium collected. Overall, the insurer's portfolio is balanced because the total cost is equal to the sum of the premiums collected.

Suppose, however, that a competitor notices the difference between groups A and B and offers the same coverage to people in group A (and only to them) for a premium of CHF 125 instead of CHF 150. The policyholders in group A can then benefit from an arbitrage gain by switching insurance companies. So they leave their current insurer. In this new situation, the competitor makes a profit of 25 francs per policyholder, while the first insurer keeps only the policyholders in group B and loses 50 francs per policyholder. This example shows that it is essential to charge an appropriate premium for each type of policyholder.

In this context, the term *segmentation* refers to the division of policyholders into subgroups with common risk characteristics and, therefore, the same level of costs. To perform this segmentation, the criteria used must satisfy several conditions in order for the categories to be relevant. In particular, the criteria must:

- Be observable and simple,
- Have a causal link with the level of risk,
- Not be unfairly discriminatory,
- Be statistically and financially significant.

Non-life insurance companies use a variety of factors to price their products. Here are a few examples for illustrative purposes:

- Age and sex of the policyholder and others covered by the policy,
- Policyholder's marital status, place of residence, and country of citizenship,
- Policyholder's level of education, occupation, and type of the activities performed,
- Value of the insured object.

Depending on the type of product, about twenty factors are used to determine the premium. It should be noted, however, that there are very strict regulations on which classification factors can and cannot be used. For example, the "unisex" pricing system in place in the European Union since 2012 requires not to use gender as a classification criterion. The main problem with segmentation is that many criteria that are easy to identify and observe from an insurer's perspective, especially demographic and socio-demographic criteria, turn out to be of little relevance in determining purchasing and risk behavior. These criteria are becoming less and less representative of actual behavior. Dimensions relevant to customer value are often difficult to assess and cannot be observed by the insurer.

Pricing factors   The pricing of non-life insurance follows a top-down approach. First, the insurer predicts the total cost of an insurance portfolio, which is then distributed among policyholders according to their level of risk. The total cost is given by the following relationship:

$$\text{total cost} = (\text{total number of claims}) \cdot (\text{average cost of a claim}),$$

where the total number of claims is calculated as follows:

$$\text{total number of claims} = (\text{number of policyholders}) \cdot \text{frequency}.$$

Frequency is defined as the expected number of claims per policyholder. It can be modeled using statistical techniques such as regression. The same is true for the average cost of a claim. This process must be performed at regular intervals because frequency changes over time for a policyholder. The average cost of a claim also changes over time, particularly as a result of inflation, technological developments, and changes in legislation.

The next step is to allocate costs among policyholders; thus, premiums vary based on policyholder classification criteria. We start by defining a *baseline policyholder* as one who pays the baseline premium. The characteristics of the baseline policyholder correspond to the most common category for each criterion. For example, if there are more men than women in a portfolio, the baseline policyholder is a man. Then, we define relativities r. Relativity r_i is the relative value of class i compared to the baseline value for a given classification criterion. For two criteria, we define as r_{ij} the relativity that combines the values for criterion A, i.e., $r_i^{\text{criterion A}}$, and B, i.e., $r_j^{\text{criterion B}}$. The symbols i and j represent the possible values for criteria A and B, respectively. Assuming that the effects of the criteria are multiplicative, the relativity r_{ij} is determined by

$$r_{ij} = r_i^{\text{criterion A}} \cdot r_j^{\text{criterion B}},$$

where $i \in \{1, \dots, I\}$ with I the number of categories for criterion A and $j \in \{1, \dots, J\}$ with J the number of categories for criterion B. In general, we will refer to the relativity r_{ij} as the relativity corresponding to the *cell* (i, j). The term "cell" is used because relativities can be represented as a table showing the intersections of different categories i and j for criteria A and B. Note that relativities can also be computed in more than two dimensions: r_{ijkl} represents a four-dimensional relativity, that is, it combines the effects of four criteria. Still assuming that the effects of the criteria are multiplicative, the reasoning is the same as with two criteria.

Relativities in the presence of two classification criteria

Consider the example of a motor insurance policy for which two classification criteria have shown statistically significant: the sex of the policyholder and the region of the policyholder's primary residence. We write $i = 1$ and $i = 2$ for male and female, respectively, and assume that there are more men than women in the portfolio. We observe that, on average, a woman ($i = 2$) generates 0.8 times as many costs as a man ($i = 1$). For the second criterion, we consider four regions of residence: Romandy ($j = 1$), Italian-speaking Switzerland ($j = 2$), urban German-speaking Switzerland ($j = 3$), and non-urban German-speaking Switzerland ($j = 4$). Of these regions, urban German-speaking Switzerland has the highest number of policyholders. Finally, we note that the costs in Romandy and Italian-speaking Switzerland are 1.1 and 1.3 times higher, respectively, than in urban German-speaking Switzerland. The costs in non-urban German-speaking Switzerland are 20% lower than in urban German-speaking Switzerland. What are the combined relativities, assuming that the effects of the criteria are multiplicative?

The relativities related to sex are the following:

$$r_1^{\text{sex}} = 1,$$
$$r_2^{\text{sex}} = 0.8.$$

For the regions of residence, we have the following relativities:

$$r_1^{\text{region}} = 1.1,$$
$$r_2^{\text{region}} = 1.3,$$
$$r_3^{\text{region}} = 1,$$
$$r_4^{\text{region}} = 0.8.$$

We compute the combined relativities, assuming multiplicativity:

$$r_{ij} = r_i^{\text{sex}} \cdot r_j^{\text{region}}, \qquad i = 1, 2, \quad j = 1, 2, 3, 4.$$

The baseline policyholder is a man ($i = 1$) living in urban German-speaking Switzerland ($j = 3$). Cell $(1,3)$ is called the baseline cell. In this case, we have

$$r_{13} = r_1^{\text{sex}} \cdot r_2^{\text{region}} = 1.0 \cdot 1.0 = 1.$$

For a female policyholder living in Italian-speaking Switzerland, we find that she generates 1.04 times the cost of the baseline policyholder. Indeed,

$$r_{22} = r_2^{\text{sex}} \cdot r_2^{\text{region}} = 0.8 \cdot 1.3 = 1.04.$$

The other relativities can be calculated following the same approach. We summarize these relativities in table 6.6.

Sex (i)	Region (j)			
	1	2	3	4
1	1.10	1.30	1.00	0.80
2	0.88	1.04	0.80	0.64

Table 6.6: Illustration of relativities in the presence of two classification criteria.

To calculate the baseline premium, we use the principle of actuarial equivalence (see definition 6.1) introduced in the context of life insurance in section 6.1: the sum of premiums must be equal to the total expected cost. These total costs can be calculated using the following formula:

$$\text{total expected cost} = \text{sum of premiums} = n \cdot (\text{average premium}) = \sum_i \sum_j n_{ij} \cdot P_{ij},$$

where n is the total number of policyholders, n_{ij} is the number of policyholders in cell (i, j), and P_{ij} is the premium paid by a policyholder in cell (i, j). This premium, P_{ij}, is calculated from the baseline premium as follows:

$$P_{ij} = r_{ij} \cdot k,$$

where k is the baseline premium and r_{ij} is the relativity for cell (i, j).

Note that the sum of premiums for cell (i, j) must be proportional to the number of policyholders in that cell and the level of costs incurred by those policyholders relative to the baseline policyholder. Formally, several expressions can be used to partition the total cost, depending on the data available:

$$\sum_i \sum_j n_{ij} \cdot P_{ij} = \sum_i \sum_j n_{ij} \cdot r_{ij} \cdot k = n \cdot (\text{average premium}) = \text{total cost.}$$

The baseline premium k can be expressed in several ways:

$$k = \frac{n \cdot (\text{average premium})}{\sum_i \sum_j n_{ij} \cdot r_{ij}} = \frac{\text{average premium}}{\sum_i \sum_j r_{ij} \cdot \frac{n_{ij}}{n}} = \frac{\text{total cost}}{\sum_i \sum_j n_{ij} \cdot r_{ij}}.$$

Evolution of pricing models   We have mentioned above that the cost and frequency of claims can be modeled using regressions. Generalizing the concept of relativities, regression models calibrated using historical claims data can establish relationships between the cost or frequency of claims and the characteristics of the policyholder or the object covered by the policy. This type of regression model is increasingly used by insurance companies today. These analyses use traditional econometric tools and are most often based on linear regression or generalized linear models (GLM).

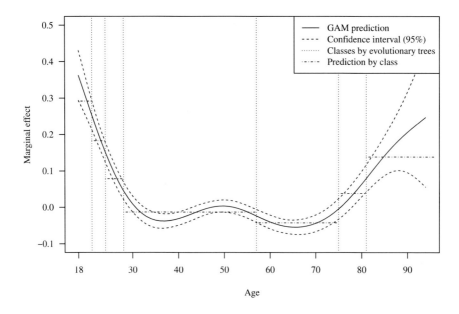

Note: GAM stands for generalized additive model. The marginal effect on the vertical axis corresponds to the prediction made using a smoothing function in the effect of age.

Figure 6.16: Modeling the effects of age on losses in comprehensive motor insurance (adapted from Staudt and Wagner, 2021, figure 2a).

More recently, when the explanatory factors are continuous variables, actuaries have used generalized additive models. In these models, continuous variables affect the response through smoothing functions (see, for example, Henckaerts et al., 2018, and Denuit et al. 2019a; 2019b; 2020). This type of approach, combined with a classification method, also allows actuaries to optimize the categories to use if they wish to return to categorical variables for pricing. For example, an interesting application is the use of evolutionary trees to determine age groups for comprehensive motor insurance coverage. We illustrate this concept in figure 6.16. The illustration shows the effect of the age of the primary driver on the severity of claims in the case of a comprehensive motor insurance policy based on data from a Swiss insurer (Staudt and Wagner, 2021). To model the effects, a generalized additive model (GAM) is used, which allows to define a functional relationship between age and the amount of losses. The use of evolutionary trees allows the separation of ages into several categories. Figure 6.16 illustrates the eight groups (vertical lines) that this type of algorithm can derive from the GAM. For each group, the horizontal lines show the predicted average effect.

A similar application can be developed in two dimensions. We illustrate this by extending the previous example to include the zip codes of the policyholders' residences. We represent the corresponding regions by their geographic coordinates: longitude and latitude.

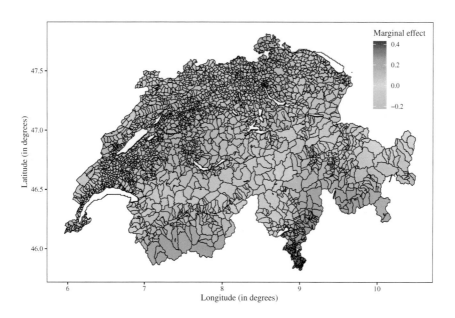

(a) Marginal effect of place of residence taken by zip code region.

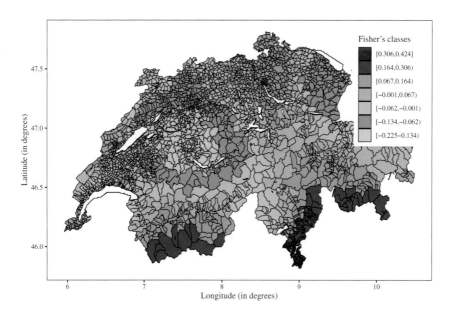

(b) Fisher's classes derived from figure 6.17(a).

Figure 6.17: Modeling the effects of place of residence on losses in comprehensive motor insurance (adapted from Staudt and Wagner, 2021, figures 3 and 5).

The effect of residence on claims is illustrated by the graph in figure 6.17(a). We can see that the effect varies greatly by zip code region. By applying Fisher's natural break classification algorithm, regions whose effect on claims is similar are obtained. These regions are shown in figure 6.17(b). Note that the regions determined in this way are very different from the cantons of the country, which are typically used by insurers to define groups.

With the advent of more sophisticated methods and machine learning, new ways of classifying policyholders are becoming possible. Some of these methods are still difficult to implement in practice because the statistical relevance of risk factors must be proven, the results are often difficult to interpret, and many algorithms operate like black boxes.

It should be noted that innovation in insurance products may also require the development of new pricing models. In motor insurance, for example, new types of "pay as you drive" contracts offer usage-based pricing. Vehicle usage is tracked using a GPS device, and the vehicle's position and speed data are sent to the insurer. Premiums are then calculated based on the information collected (Verbelen et al., 2018; Geyer et al., 2020; Guillen et al., 2021).

Mathematical reserves In section 6.4, we defined the concept and presented the relevant calculations for mathematical reserves in the context of life insurance policies. Non-life insurance is more diverse, and different types of reserves may be determined. We present here only an overview of the methods used to calculate reserves intended to cover future claims. While there are various calculation methods, the choice of method depends on, among other things, the branch of insurance, the data or information available, and the degree of accuracy required. In general, when a large amount of data is available—as is typically the case with the claims history of an insurance portfolio—one of the following methods can be used.

Deterministic methods can provide a simple estimate of the reserve requirement, assuming that the claims experience is stable. Stochastic methods, which are more complex than deterministic methods, can then be used to define a confidence interval around the calculated estimate. If many characteristics of the policyholders in the portfolio are known, it is sometimes advisable to use regression or machine learning models, which can provide more accurate results. Finally, in situations with low numbers of claims but high loss amounts, methods based on extreme value theory can be used. The book by Denuit and Charpentier (2005) provides a complete overview of the mathematics of non-life insurance.

Bibliography

Abdel-Khalik, A. R., 2013, *Accounting for Risk, Hedging and Complex Contracts*. Routledge, New York. ☑ www.routledge.com/p/book/9780415808934

Arnold, S., A. Jijiie, E. Jondeau, and M. Rockinger, 2019, Periodic or generational actuarial tables: which one to choose?, *European Actuarial Journal*, 9(2):519–554. ☑ https://doi.org/10.1007/s13385-019-00198-x

Arrow, K. J., 1963, Uncertainty and the Welfare Economics of Medical Care, *The American Economic Review*, 53(5):941–973. ☑ www.jstor.org/stable/1812044

Aven, T., 2011, On the new ISO guide on risk management terminology, *Reliability Engineering and System Safety*, 96(7):719–726. ☑ https://doi.org/10.1016/j.ress.2010.12.020

Aven, T., 2012, Foundational Issues in Risk Assessment and Risk Management, *Risk Analysis*, 32(10):1647–1656. ☑ https://doi.org/10.1111/j.1539-6924.2012.01798.x

Bakker, J. A., J. Kruk, A. E. Lanting, and S. Milisauskas, 1999, The earliest evidence of wheeled vehicles in Europe and the Near East, *Antiquity*, 73(282):778–790. ☑ https://doi.org/10.1017/S0003598X00065522

Baranoff, E., P. L. Brockett, Y. Kahane, and D. Baranoff, 2019, *Enterprise and Individual Risk Management*. ☑ https://catalog.flatworldknowledge.com/catalog/editions/baranoff_2-risk-management-enterprises-individuals-2-0

Basel Committee on Banking Supervision, 2006, *International Convergence of Capital Measurement and Capital Standards*. June. ☑ www.bis.org/publ/bcbs128.pdf

Berliner, B., 1982, *Limits of Insurability of Risks*. Prentice-Hall, Englewood Cliffs.

Bernoulli, D., 1954, Exposition of a New Theory on the Measurement of Risk, *Econometrica*, 22(1):23–36. ☑ www.jstor.org/stable/1909829

Biener, C., M. Eling, A. Matt, and J. H. Wirfs, 2015a, *Cyber Risk: Risikomanagement und Versicherbarkeit*. Institut für Versicherungswirtschaft, Universität St. Gallen, St. Gallen. ☑ www.kessler.ch/fileadmin/09_PDFs/Cyber_Risk_Risikomanagement_und_Versicherbarkeit_de.pdf

Biener, C., M. Eling, and J. H. Wirfs, 2015b, Insurability of Cyber Risk: An Empirical Analysis, *The Geneva Papers on Risk and Insurance - Issues and Practice*, 40(1):131–158. ☑ http://doi.org/10.1057/gpp.2014.19

237

Blum, V., P. E. Thérond, D. Alexander, E. Laffort, and S. Jancevska, 2019, New developments in language issues in accounting regulation: likekihood terms and the certainty of uncertainty, *HAL Working Papers*, 01991845. ☑ https://hal.archives-ouvertes. fr/hal-01991845https://hal.archives-ouvertes.fr/hal-02387303

Blundell-Wignall, A., 2008, The Subprime Crisis: Size, Deleveraging and Some Policy Options, *Financial Market Trends*, 94. ☑ www.oecd.org/finance/financial-markets/ 40451721.pdf

Borghesi, A. and B. Gaudenzi, 2013, *Risk Management*. Perspectives in Business Culture. Springer, Milan. ☑ https://doi.org/10.1007/978-88-470-2531-8

Bowers, N. L., H. U. Gerber, J. C. Hickman, D. A. Jones, and C. J. Nesbitt, 1997, *Actuarial Mathematics*. The Society of Actuaries.

Boyer, M., 2008, Une brève histoire des assurances au Moyen Âge, *Assurances et gestion des risques*, 76(3):83–97. ☑ www.revueassurances.ca/wp-content/uploads/2016/01/2008_ 76_no3_Boyer.pdf

Brulhart, V., 2010, Petite histoire de l'assurance: du commerce maritime à la protection du consommateur, In S. Fuhrer, editor, *Schweizerische Gesellschaft für Haftpflicht- und Versicherungsrecht: Festschrift zum fünfzigjährigen Bestehen*, pages 59–69. Schulthess. ☑ https://stephan-fuhrer.ch/assets/files/AufsaetzeDritter/ 2010FSSGHVR-BRULHART-VersGeschichte.pdf

Brulhart, V., 2017, *Droit des assurances privées*. Stämpfli, Bern.

Cambridge, 2023, Cambridge Advanced Learner's Dictionary & Thesaurus: risk. ☑ https: //dictionary.cambridge.org/dictionary/english/risk

Cebula, J. J. and L. R. Young, 2010, A Taxonomy of Operational yber Security Risks, Technical report, Carnegie Mellon University, Pittsburgh. ☑ www.sei.cmu.edu/reports/ 10tn028.pdf

Crockford, G. N., 1982, The Bibliography and History of Risk Management: Some Preliminary Observations, *The Geneva Papers on Risk and Insurance - Issues and Practice*, 7(2):169–179. ☑ https://doi.org/10.1057/gpp.1982.10

Darsa, J.-D., 2016, *La gestion des risques en entreprise: identifier, comprendre, maîtriser*. GERESO, Angers. ☑ www.la-librairie-rh.com/livre-entreprise/ la-gestion-des-risques-en-entreprise-gese4.html

Dellinger, J. K., 2006, *The Handbook of Variable Income Annuities*. Wiley. ☑ https:// www.wiley.com/en-us/The+Handbook+of+Variable+Income+Annuities-p-9780471773764

Denuit, M. and A. Charpentier, 2004, *Mathématiques de l'Assurance Non-Vie. Tome I: Principes Fondamentaux de Théorie du Risque*. Collection Économie et Statistiques Avancées. Economica, Paris.

Denuit, M. and A. Charpentier, 2005, *Mathématiques de l'Assurance Non-Vie. Tome II: Tarification et Provisionnement*. Collection Économie et Statistiques Avancées. Economica, Paris.

Denuit, M., D. Hainaut, and J. Trufin, 2019a, *Effective Statistical Learning Methods for Actuaries I*. Springer Actuarial. Springer International Publishing, Cham. ☑ https: //doi.org/10.1007/978-3-030-25820-7

Denuit, M., D. Hainaut, and J. Trufin, 2019b, *Effective Statistical Learning Methods for Actuaries III*. Springer Actuarial. Springer International Publishing, Cham. ☑ https: //doi.org/10.1007/978-3-030-25827-6

Denuit, M., D. Hainaut, and J. Trufin, 2020, *Effective Statistical Learning Methods for Actuaries II*. Springer Actuarial. Springer International Publishing, Cham. ☑ https://doi.org/10.1007/978-3-030-57556-4

Diez, F. C., 1853, *Etymologisches Wörterbuch der romanischen Sprachen*. Bonn. ☑ https://archive.org/stream/etymologischesw00diezuoft

Dionne, G., 2013, Risk Management: History, Definition, and Critique, *Risk Management and Insurance Review*, 16(2):147–166. ☑ https://doi.org/10.1111/rmir.12016

Doherty, N., 2000, *Integrated Risk Management: Techniques and Strategies for Managing Corporate Risk*. McGraw-Hill, New York.

Dorfman, M. S. and D. A. Cather, 2012, *Introduction to Risk Management and Insurance*. Pearson, New York. ☑ www.pearson.ch/EAN/9780131394124

Durst, S. and M. Zieba, 2019, Mapping knowledge risks: towards a better understanding of knowledge management, *Knowledge Management Research & Practice*, 17(1):1–13. ☑ https://doi.org/10.1080/14778238.2018.1538603

Eccles, R. G., S. C. Newquist, and R. Schatz, 2007, Reputation and Its Risks, *Harvard Business Review*, Février. ☑ https://hbr.org/2007/02/reputation-and-its-risks

Ehrlich, I. and G. S. Becker, 1972, Market Insurance, Self-Insurance, and Self-Protection, *Journal of Political Economy*, 80(4):623–648. ☑ https://doi.org/10.1086/259916

Établissement d'assurance contre l'incendie et les éléments naturels du Canton de Vaud, 2020, Missions et principes. ☑ www.eca-vaud.ch/a-propos-de-l-eca/au-service-de-la-communaute/missions-et-principes

Federal Council, 2011, Receuil systématique du droit interne : Loi fédérale sur le contrat d'assurance. ☑ www.admin.ch/opc/fr/classified-compilation/19080008/index.html

Federal Council, 2020, Classified compilation of internal law: Social insurance. ☑ www.fedlex.admin.ch/en/cc/internal-law/83

Federal Office of Public Health, 2020, Assurances. ☑ www.bag.admin.ch/bag/fr/home/versicherungen.html

Federal Social Insurance Office, 2014, History of Social Security. ☑ www.historyofsocialsecurity.ch

Federal Social Insurance Office, 2020a, Aperçu de la sécurité sociale. ☑ www.bsv.admin.ch/bsv/fr/home/assurances-sociales/ueberblick.html

Federal Social Insurance Office, 2020b, Assurances sociales. ☑ www.bsv.admin.ch/bsv/fr/home.html

Federal Social Insurance Office, 2020c, Statistique des assurances sociales suisses 2020, Technical report. ☑ https://www.bsv.admin.ch/dam/bsv/fr/dokumente/themenuebergreifend/statistiken/SVS_DE_2020.pdf.download.pdf/Statistique%20des%20assurances%20sociales%20suisses%202020.pdf

Federal Social Insurance Office, 2021, Cotisations aux assurances sociales. ☑ www.bsv.admin.ch/bsv/fr/home/assurances-sociales/ueberblick/beitraege.html

Federal Statistical Office, 2020a, Accidents de la circulation routière: causes présumées. ☑ www.bfs.admin.ch/asset/fr/px-x-1106010100_106

Federal Statistical Office, 2020b, Assurance-vieillesse et survivants (AVS) : finances de l'AVS. ☑ www.bfs.admin.ch/asset/fr/je-f-13.04.01.01

Federal Statistical Office, 2020c, Enquête sur le budget des ménages : Dépenses détaillées de l'ensemble des ménages selon l'année. ☞ www.bfs.admin.ch/asset/fr/je-f-20.02.01.02.01

Federal Statistical Office, 2020d, Sécurité sociale. ☞ www.bfs.admin.ch/bfs/fr/home/statistiques/securite-sociale.html

Fracheboud, V., 2015, *Introduction de l'assurance invalidité en Suisse (1944-1960).* Antipodes. ☞ www.antipodes.ch/librairie/introduction-de-l-assurance-invalidite-en-suisse-1944-1960-detail

France, 1715, *Ordonnance de la marine du mois d'août 1681.* Charles Osmont, Paris. ☞ https://gallica.bnf.fr/ark:/12148/bpt6k95955s

Fraser, J. and B. J. Simkins, 2011, *Enterprise Risk Management.* John Wiley & Sons, Inc., Hoboken. ☞ https://doi.org/10.1002/9781118267080

Frenkel, M., U. Hommel, and M. Rudolf, 2005, *Risk Management: Challenge and Opportunity.* Springer, Berlin. ☞ https://doi.org/10.1007/b138437

Gaultier-Gaillard, S. and J.-P. Louisot, 2014, *Diagnostic des risques: identifier, analyser et cartographier les vulnérabilités.* AFNOR, Saint-Denis. ☞ www.boutique.afnor.org/livre/-/article/818170/fa092751

Geyer, A., D. Kremslehner, and A. Muermann, 2020, Asymmetric Information in Automobile Insurance: Evidence From Driving Behavior, *Journal of Risk and Insurance,* 87(4):969–995. ☞ https://doi.org/10.1111/jori.12279

Grey, H. M., 1893, *Lloyd's: Yesterday and to-day.* John Haddon. ☞ https://books.google.ch/books?id=sjUpAAAAYAAJ

Guichet cartographique du Canton de Vaud, 2020, Carte des dangers naturels. ☞ www.geo.vd.ch/?&mapresources=GEOVD_DANGER_NATUREL

Guillen, M., J. P. Nielsen, and A. M. Pérez-Marín, 2021, Near-miss telematics in motor insurance, *Journal of Risk and Insurance,* 88(3):569–589. ☞ https://doi.org/10.1111/jori.12340

Harrington, S. E. and G. Niehaus, 2003, *Risk Management & Insurance.* McGraw-Hill, New York.

Hauser, W., 2011, *Stadt in Flammen: Der Brand von Glarus im Jahre 1861.* Limmat, Glarus. ☞ www.limmatverlag.ch/programm/titel/138-stadt-in-flammen.html

Head, G. L. and S. Horn, 1997, *Essentials of Risk Management.* Insurance Institute of America, New York.

Hebrard, P., 2004, La détresse des Pays-Bas : De Witt, Hudde et les rentes viagères d'Amsterdam (1671-1673), *Mathématiques et sciences humaines,* 166:47–63. ☞ https://doi.org/10.4000/msh.2891

Henckaerts, R., K. Antonio, M. Clijsters, and R. Verbelen, 2018, A data driven binning strategy for the construction of insurance tariff classes, *Scandinavian Actuarial Journal,* 2018(8):681–705. ☞ https://doi.org/10.1080/03461238.2018.1429300

Heon, S. and D. Parsoire, 2017, La couverture du cyber-risque, *Revue d'Économie Financière,* 126:169–182. ☞ www.aef.asso.fr/publications/revue-d-economie-financiere/126-l-industrie-de-l-assurance-et-ses-mutations/3520-la-couverture-du-cyber-risque

Hull, J. C., 2018, *Risk Management and Financial Institutions.* Wiley, Paris. ☞ www.wiley.com/en-us/Risk+Management+and+Financial+Institutions%2C+6th+Edition-p-9781119932499

International Organization for Standardization, 2009, *ISO Guide 73:2009: Risk management - Vocabulary*. International Organization for Standardization, Geneva. ☑ www.iso.org/standard/44651.html

International Organization for Standardization, 2018, *ISO 31000:2018: Risk management - Guidelines*. International Organization for Standardization, Geneva. ☑ www.iso.org/standard/65694.html

Kaplan, R. S. and A. Mikes, 2012, Managing Risks: A New Framework, *Harvard Business Review*, Juin. ☑ https://hbr.org/2012/06/managing-risks-a-new-framework#comment-section

Kessler, 2009, *Gestion du Risque Ressources Humaines: Connaître les Risques et les Minimiser*. Zurich. ☑ www.kessler.ch/fileadmin/09_PDFs/KS_Factsheet_HRRM_fr.pdf

Koch, P., 2012, *Geschichte der Versicherungswirtschaft in Deutschland*. Verlag Versicherungswirtschaft, Karlsruhe.

Körner, M. and B. Degen, 2014, Assurances, In *Dictionnaire historique de la Suisse*. Académie suisse des sciences humaines et sociales. ☑ https://hls-dhs-dss.ch/fr/articles/014066

Kreager, P., 1993, Histories of Demography: A Review Article, *Population Studies*, 47(3):519–539. ☑ https://doi.org/10.1080/0032472031000147286

Kshetri, N., 2010, Diffusion and effects of cyber-crime in developing economies, *Third World Quarterly*, 31(7):1057–1079. ☑ https://doi.org/10.1080/01436597.2010.518752

Lam, J., 2014, *Enterprise Risk Management: From Incentives to Controls*. Wiley, New York. ☑ https://doi.org/10.1002/9781118836477

Louisot, J.-P., 2014, *Gestion des risques*. AFNOR, Saint-Denis. ☑ www.boutique.afnor.org/book/-/article/818882/ouv001059

Maquet, A., 1991, *Des primes d'assurance au financement des risques*. Bruylant, Bruxelles.

Mckeever, K., 2009, A Short History of Tontines, *Fordham Journal of Corporate & Financial Law*, 15(2). ☑ https://ir.lawnet.fordham.edu/jcfl/vol15/iss2/

McNeil, A. J., R. Frey, and P. Embrechts, 2015, *Quantitative Risk Management: Concepts, Techniques and Tools*. Princeton University Press, New Jersey. ☑ https://press.princeton.edu/books/hardcover/9780691166278/quantitative-risk-management

Mehr, R. I. and B. A. Hedges, 1963, *Risk Management in the Business Enterprise*. Homewood.

Métayer, Y. and L. Hirsch, 2007, *Premiers pas dans le management des risques*. AFNOR, Saint-Denis. ☑ www.boutique.afnor.org/livre/-/article/644896/fa092664

Meyer, K., A. Mikes, and R. S. Kaplan, 2021, When Every Employee Is a Risk Manager, *Harvard Business Review*. ☑ https://hbr.org/2021/01/when-every-employee-is-a-risk-manager

Molin, M., 2006, *Les Régulations sociales dans l'Antiquité*. Presses universitaires de Rennes. ☑ https://doi.org/10.4000/books.pur.20318

Müller, R., M.-N. Zen-Ruffinen, and J. Monnier, 2019, *Guide pratique du conseil d'administration*. Schulthess, Zurich. ☑ www.schulthess.com/verlag/detail/ISBN-9783725586448/

National Commission on Terrorist Attacks Upon the United States, 2004, *The 9/11 Commission Report*. ☑ https://9-11commission.gov/report

National Cyber Security Centre, 2020, National Cyber Security Centre. ☑ www.ncsc. admin.ch/ncsc/en/home.html

Nelli, H. O., 1972, The Earliest Insurance Contract: A New Discovery, *The Journal of Risk and Insurance*, 39(2):215–220. ☑ https://doi.org/10.2307/251881

OECD, 2013, Integrity Risk Management, In *OECD Integrity Review of Italy: Reinforcing Public Sector Integrity, Restoring Trust for Sustainable Growth*, Chapter 7, pages 105–151. OECD Publishing, Paris. ☑ https://doi.org/10.1787/9789264193819-en

Ofek, E. and M. Richardson, 2003, DotCom Mania: The Rise and Fall of Internet Stock Prices, *The Journal of Finance*, 58(3):1113–1137. ☑ https://doi.org/10.1111/1540-6261. 00560

Perrott, B. E., 2007, A strategic risk approach to knowledge management, *Business Horizons*, 50(6):523–533. ☑ https://doi.org/10.1016/j.bushor.2007.08.002

Piron, S., 2004, L'apparition du resicum en Méditerrannée occidentale, XIIe-XIIIe siècles, In E. Collas-Heddeland, M. Coudry, O. Kammerer, A. J. Lemaître, and B. Martin, editors, *Pour une histoire culturelle du risque : Genèse, évolution, actualité du concept dans les sociétés occidentales*, pages 59–76. Histoire et Anthropologie, Strasbourg. ☑ https://halshs.archives-ouvertes.fr/halshs-00004835

Pradier, P.-C., 2006, *La notion de risque en économie*. La Découverte, Paris. ☑ www. cairn.info/la-notion-de-risque-en-economie--9782707139085.htm

Pratt, J. W., 1964, Risk Aversion in the Small and in the Large, *Econometrica*, 32(1):122–136. ☑ www.jstor.org/stable/1913738

Promislow, S. D., 2015, *Fundamentals of Actuarial Mathematics*. Wiley, Chichester, UK. ☑ https://www.wiley.com/en-us/Fundamentals+of+Actuarial+Mathematics% 2C+3rd+Edition-p-9781118782460

Rejda, G. E. and M. J. McNamara, 2017, *Principles of Risk Management and Insurance*. Pearson, New Jersey. ☑ www.pearson.ch/EAN/9781292151038

Rockinger, M., 2012, Academic View: Underestimating Risk, *The Economist*. ☑ www. economist.com/whichmba/academic-view-underestimating-risk-0

Schein, E. H., 2016, *Organizational Culture and Leadership: A Dynamic View*. Wiley. ☑ https://www.wiley.com/en-us/Organizational+Culture+and+Leadership%2C+5th+ Edition-p-9781119212041

Shackelford, S. J., 2012, Should your firm invest in cyber risk insurance?, *Business Horizons*, 55(4):349–356. ☑ http://dx.doi.org/10.1016/j.bushor.2012.02.004

Shkolnikov, V., M. Barbieri, and J. Wilmoth, 2021, The Human Mortality Database. ☑ www.mortality.org

Statistique Vaud, 2019, Assurances des bâtiments et mobilière contre l'incendie 1985-2018. ☑ www.stat.vd.ch/ass_privees

Staudt, Y. and J. Wagner, 2021, Assessing the Performance of Random Forests for Modeling Claim Severity in Collision Car Insurance, *Risks*, 9(53). ☑ https://doi.org/10. 3390/risks9030053

Suva, 2020, Le modèle Suva. ☑ www.suva.ch/fr-ch/la-suva/autoportrait/la-suva

Swiss Confederation, 2023, Federal Act on the Amendment of the Swiss Civil Code: The Code of Obligations. ☑ www.fedlex.admin.ch/eli/cc/27/317_321_377/en

Swiss Financial Market Supervisory Authority, 2020, Insurance market report 2019, Technical report. ☑ https://www.finma.ch/en/documentation/finma-publications/reports/insurance-reports/

Swiss Insurance Association, 2018, «Emerging risks», évaluation sous l'angle de la responsabilité civile. ☑ www.svv.ch/fr/secteur/assurance-de-la-responsabilite-civile/emerging-risks-evaluation-sous-langle-de-la

Swiss Insurance Association, 2019, Value creation by the Swiss insurance industry. ☑ www.svv.ch/en/sia/sia-publications/facts-and-figures/facts-and-figures/economic-performance

Swiss Insurance Association, 2020, Statistique du personnel, Technical report, Zurich. ☑ www.svv.ch/sites/default/files/2020-10/ASA_Statistiquedupersonnel_2019_FR_01.pdf

Swiss Re, 1999, Le transfert alternatif des risques (ART) pour les entreprises : phénomène de mode ou formule idéale pour gérer les risques au IIIe millénaire ?, Technical report, Zurich.

Swiss Re, 2003, Transfert alternatif des risques (ART) : état des lieux, Technical report, Zurich.

Swiss Re, 2005, Innover pour assurer l'inassurable, Technical report, Zurich.

Swiss Re, 2009, The role of indices in transferring insurance risks to the capital markets, Technical report, Zurich. ☑ www.swissre.com/institute/research/sigma-research/sigma-2009-04.html

Swiss Re, 2012, Insuring ever-evolving commercial risks, Technical report.

Swiss Re, 2013, Kaleidoscope of Insurance History. ☑ https://history.swissre.com

Swiss Re, 2014, *A History of Insurance.* Zurich. ☑ www.swissre.com/dam/jcr:638f00a0-71b9-4d8e-a960-dddaf9ba57cb/150_history_of_insurance.pdf

Swiss Re, 2017, *Histoire de l'Assurance en Suisse.* Zurich. ☑ www.swissre.com/dam/jcr:c4313ff1-60fc-43af-b33e-a0dbd8819189/150Y_Markt_Broschuere_Schweiz_FR_Inhalt.pdf

Swiss Re, 2019a, *Natural catastrophes and man-made disasters in 2018: "secondary" perils on the frontline.* Zurich. ☑ www.swissre.com/institute/research/sigma-research/sigma-2019-02

Swiss Re, 2019b, World insurance: the great pivot east continues, Technical report, Zurich. ☑ www.swissre.com/institute/research/sigma-research/sigma-2019-03.html

Swiss Re, 2020a, Sigma-explorer: World insurance premiums. ☑ www.sigma-explorer.com

Swiss Re, 2020b, World insurance: riding out the 2020 pandemic storm, Technical report, Zurich. ☑ www.swissre.com/institute/research/sigma-research/sigma-2020-04.html

Tanzi, T. J. and P. D'Argenlieu, 2013, *Gestion des risques et création de valeur.* Hermes Science / Lavoisier, Paris.

The Geneva Association, 2002, *Insurance and September 11 – One Year After: Impact, Lessons and Unresolved Issues.* Geneva. ☑ www.genevaassociation.org/publications/books/insurance-and-september-11-one-year-after

The Museum of the City of San Francisco, 2020, The Great 1906 Earthquake And Fire. ☑ www.sfmuseum.org/1906/06.html

Trieschmann, J. S., S. G. Gustavon, and R. E. Hoyt, 2004, *Risk Management and Insurance*. Cengage, Cincinnati.

Vaughan, E. J. and T. Vaughan, 2013, *Fundamentals of Risk and Insurance*. Wiley, New York. ☐ www.wiley.com/en-us/Fundamentals+of+Risk+and+Insurance,+11th+Edition-p-9781118534007

Verbelen, R., K. Antonio, and G. Claeskens, 2018, Unravelling the predictive power of telematics data in car insurance pricing, *Journal of the Royal Statistical Society: Series C (Applied Statistics)*, 67(5):1275–1304. ☐ https://doi.org/10.1111/rssc.12283

Webster, 2010, Webster's New World College Dictionary: risk. ☐ www.collinsdictionary.com/dictionary/english/risk

Willett, A. H., 1901, *The Economic Theory of Risk and Insurance*, volume XIV, no. 2. Columbia University Press, Pennsylvanie. ☐ https://doi.org/10.7312/will93384

World Economic Forum, 2019, *The Global Risks Report 2019*. Geneva. ☐ www.weforum.org/reports/the-global-risks-report-2019

World Health Organization, 2012, *The Great East Japan earthquake: a story of a devastating natural disaster, a tale of human compassion*. Manila, WHO Regional Office for the Western Pacific. ☐ http://apps.who.int/iris/handle/10665/207516

Zeier Roeschmann, A., 2014, Risk Culture: What It Is and How It Affects an Insurer's Risk Management, *Risk Management and Insurance Review*, 17(2):277–296. ☐ https://doi.org/10.1111/rmir.12025

Zweifel, P. and R. Eisen, 2012, *Insurance Economics*. Springer, Berlin. ☐ https://doi.org/10.1007/978-3-642-20548-4

List of figures

List of tables

List of definitions and theorems

List of boxes

Authors' bibliographies

Joël Wagner is a Professor of Actuarial Science at HEC Lausanne, a member of the Swiss Finance Institute and the Enterprise for Society Center at the University of Lausanne, an invited lecturer at the Swiss Federal Institute of Technology Lausanne (EPFL), and a Privatdozent at the University of St. Gallen (HSG). He is a non-executive board member of Retraites Populaires, a non-executive board member of La Luxembourgeoise, and a former Swiss Occupational Pension Supervisory Commission member. Before joining the Faculty of Business and Economics, he was a Professor at the HSG and a member of the executive board of the Institute of Insurance Economics. His industry experience includes work as a consultant with the Boston Consulting Group. He holds a venia legendi in business administration, with special emphasis on risk management. He has a PhD in mathematics and an engineering degree in physics from EPFL.

With a PhD and a Master's degree in Actuarial Science from HEC Lausanne, **Michel Fuino** is an actuary specializing in 3rd pillar insurance at Retraites Populaires. He started his career as an actuary at Swiss Re in Zurich. Then, he obtained his PhD from the Department of Actuarial Science at the University of Lausanne under the supervision of Professor Joël Wagner. He later worked as a senior SNSF researcher and project leader in the same department. His research focuses on issues such as population aging and loss of autonomy in health, life insurance, and risk management. He is a member of the Swiss Association of Actuaries editorial board.